THE ROAD TO COLLEGE

THE HIGH SCHOOL STUDENT'S GUIDE TO DISCOVERING YOUR PASSION, GETTING INVOLVED, AND GETTING ADMITTED

By Joyce Suber
and the Staff of The Princeton Review

PrincetonReview.com

THE ROAD TO COLLEGE

THE HIGH SCHOOL STUDENT'S GUIDE TO DISCOVERING YOUR PASSION, GETTING INVOLVED, AND GETTING ADMITTED

By Joyce Suber
and the Staff of The Princeton Review

Random House, Inc.
New York

The Princeton Review, Inc.

2315 Broadway

New York, NY 10024

E-mail: bookeditor@review.com

© 2007 by The Princeton Review, Inc.

ISBN 978-0-375-76617-6

Publisher: Robert Franek

Editor: Michael V. Palumbo and Adam O. Davis

Designer and Production Manager: Scott Harris

Production Editor: Christine LaRubio

Printed in the United States of America.

9 8 7 6 5 4 3 2 1

2008 Edition

ACKNOWLEDGMENTS

Many thanks are in order:

To my wonderful family and many great friends, thank you for your support and patience during the interesting journey that led me to be in the right place at the right time. I love you all so very much.

To my sons, Eric and Rich, who, no matter what, always believe in me. Thank you for the love and the laughter you provide and for being my best friends.

To my "daughter," Shelice—thank you for loving me so much, never complaining about the mounds of paper, books, and other book-related stuff that overtook your space for months. Thanks also for your input and editorial suggestions along the way.

To my colleagues, former students, my nieces and nephews, and the young people across the nation who let me pick their brains and print their stories and statements without hesitation, a resounding "Thank you!"

Very special thanks to Nancy Beane, Wade Boggs, Missy Sanchez, Andre Phillips, Kimberly Teegarden, Dan Walls, Jean Jordan, Calvin King, Audley Bridges, T.J. Vassar, and Dr. Sharon Jones for your professional input and ideas that helped me complete *The Road to College*.

Special thanks to my editors at The Princeton Review, Michael Palumbo, Adam Davis, and Christine LaRubio, for their hard work, assistance, and patience in helping me get things right. Also, thanks to The Princeton Review and Random House for the opportunity to write something that could make a difference in the lives of young people.

And above all, I offer a heartfelt thank you to God—my source of inspiration and energy. You are awesome!

Sincerely,

Joyce E. Suber

I'd like to thank Rob Franek for pitching this book and Tom Russell at Random House for liking Rob's pitch. Many thanks also go to Adam Davis, the best co-editor anyone could ask for, and Adrinda Kelly, Senior Editor, who provided crucial help in the final days of the editorial process.

Our production pros, Christine LaRubio and Scott Harris, deserve thanks for agreeing, time after time, to 'make it work.' This book also benefited from the contributions of Lisa Marie Rovito, Andrea Kornstein, and Erica Ciccarone, freelancers extraordinaire.

Extra-special thanks go to the friends and family I've neglected the last couple of months in order to finish this book.

Finally, I'd like to thank Joyce.

Michael V. Palumbo

January 2007

CONTENTS

Introduction 1

Chapter 1: Who Are You?.......................................7

Chapter 2: Your Roadmap to College.............................37

Chapter 3: After School and in the Community 77

Chapter 4: Summer Experiences 113

Chapter 5: Do It Yourself!...................................153

Chapter 6: Tools of Engagement......................................191

Chapter 7: Getting Admitted (and Financial Aid)......................229

Appendix A: My Personal Profile................................261

Appendix B: My College Planning Profile.......................273

Appendix C: College Planning Checklist...........................283

Appendix D: Additional Resources 291

Bibliography...295

About the Author...311

INTRODUCTION

When Jessica was 5 years old, she spent part of each day teaching her "kids." Her "kids" were dolls and stuffed animals who listened attentively as she expounded the virtues of learning one's lessons well

> "I'm an idealist; I don't know where I'm going, but I'm on my way."
> —Carl Sandburg
> (American Poet and Biographer)[1]

and preparing for college. Using college guidebooks provided by her aunt, a college admissions officer, she showed them colorful fall scenes of a Northeastern college campus. She described various pictures: Science students wearing goggles in a lab, student athletes playing soccer and basketball, drama students amusing a delighted audience with their onstage antics. Then Jessica gave her students a test on what it would take for them to get into college, where they could do the things they saw in the photos she had shared with them.

Jessica's classroom was a sight to behold! When asked about her goals as a five-year-old teacher, she explains, "They learn to read and write and count at school . . . I was trying to see if they [could learn] how to think too. I wanted them to go to college. There's a lot more to do there than just book stuff. They needed to learn to do other things. [I wanted] the pictures in those books to help them see some other things they could learn to do before they grew up. I wanted them to know that they could do anything!"

Today Jessica is an early-childhood education major and a student-teacher in a 1st grade classroom. She laughs as her aunt reminds her of her first teaching role, but she makes it clear that, as a teacher today, her basic message to students is the same as it was with her original classroom of "kids."

While it is unlikely any students in Jessica's original classroom have matriculated at a college or university, given their nonhuman limitations, she was on to something. There's "a lot more" to college than "just book stuff." This is why college admissions officers like to admit people who do more than what is required of them. Yes, they value initiative in and of itself, but they are not simply testing prospective students to see if they are willing to do things *just to gain admission*. Rather, admissions officers want to admit people who look for opportunities to do things that *make a positive difference*—in their own lives, in the community, in society, and in the lives of others. They value the characteristics these positive actions instill in the doers. After all, these characteristics have a tendency to carry over to all sorts of good places: lasting relationships, schoolwork, successful careers, productive citizenship. Meaningful experiences can offer greater perspective on life and make one a more interesting person. It's why college admissions officers like to discover these experiences in their applicants. It's why you should want to have these experiences too.

In high school, you are on the road to becoming who you are and discovering what you will make of your life. There are many experiences ahead of you, and each one will be important in shaping the person you become. Though much in life happens regardless of what we do or do not do, it is up to you to be proactive and find ways to become involved in experiences that will enrich your future.

As you head toward the college selection process, you may be wondering just what, specifically, will have a positive effect on your admission to college. Be aware that the rigor of the courses you take, your grades, and your college entrance exam scores—where applicable—are only basic criteria for admission at many colleges and universities.

Your involvement in interesting, meaningful activities and challenges is significant in the admission process. You should also give attention to behavior and social choices, as good character counts. College recommendations, interviews, and, ultimately, your admission to college will be based, in part, on whom you are as a person and not just as a classroom student.

Beginning with the activities offered by your school and community—the academic, artistic, athletic, and other endeavors probably most accessible to you—you can develop skills and gain valuable knowledge that you will be able to use for the rest of your life. Even more importantly, trying new things and putting your ideas to work in creating new experiences for yourself and others will help you to grow intellectually, increase your self-awareness, and make new friends and contacts. In this way, meaningful precollege experiences not only make you a more attractive candidate for college admission, they also increase your options for your future.

How to Use This Book

The Road to College: The High School Student's Guide to Discovering Your Passion, Getting Involved, and Getting Admitted is designed to make you aware of the wealth of opportunities available to you during your high school years and in the years that follow.

This isn't to say we want you to sign up for a laundry list of activities and keep yourself so busy that you don't have time to rest, study, enjoy the company of family and friends, or just have fun. Rather, we want to spark various interests and talents by urging you to find and participate in activities well suited to you as an individual.

As you read this book, we encourage you to focus not only on the descriptions of experiences you expect to find appealing but to open yourself to new things. Starting with self-assessment tools to help you identify your interests and strengths, you'll find much food for thought in the pages that follow. You'll find information on specific extra- and co-curricular programs, academic enrichment opportunities, volunteer options, shadow experiences, internships, summer programs, and travel opportunities. You'll also find information on how to search for additional experiences, start your own activity or business, find professional and financial support for your experiences, and develop a resume or portfolio to help you to present yourself in the best possible light. The role of mentors—people you can look to for wisdom and guidance—is discussed as well. Throughout the book, you will be able to read stories and testimonials of students who have participated in many of the experiences described. We also answer numerous common questions about the college search and selection process, offering you insider information and advice from the mouths of college admissions professionals and current college students.

More than a few of the experiences mentioned in the following pages will be appealing to you. We suggest you keep a journal as you read *The Road to College*, making note of what you learn and how to further explore these possibilities. Who knows what you will uncover? By trying new things, you may discover hidden talents or unearth undiscovered passions. We hope you enjoy the journey as you travel *The Road to College*. Let's see what happens along the way to your success!

ENDNOTES

1   Sandburg, Carl. Quotation.
    www.quotationspage.com/quotes/Carl_Sandburg.

CHAPTER 1
WHO ARE YOU?

Ashley, an 8th grader in Illinois, is an honor student and a talented athlete. She plays on her school's volleyball team and trains with her dad, a former track star, in the long jump and relay racing. In the near future, she hopes to join her school's track team.

Describing herself as a "former klutz," Ashley has changed since elementary school. "When I was in 3rd grade," she explains, "I decided that I wanted to go to Harvard and become a lawyer. I am still thinking Ivy League, but now I am not focused on just one college. And I want to get a master's degree in business now, instead of studying law. I love fashion and beauty and want to be my own boss someday by owning a chain of full-service beauty salons and boutiques."

Further down the road is Michael, a third-year college student who recently transferred to University of California—Berkeley. He currently works for "a national political organization in the Bay Area" and plans to earn a law degree.

Michael's plans were very different when he started college. "I started college on a football scholarship at a moderately-sized liberal arts college in the Northwest," he says. "After a few months as a college student, I realized that football, my passion in high school, was just not fun anymore." He also admits that he did not feel "connected to the campus environment," so he "transferred to a small college near home"—for him, the Bay Area—to complete basic courses and to "decide what my real interests and strengths were." While there, he interned for a couple of years and learned about the business world.

"Somewhere along the way, I got more interested in social justice and politics," Michael reports. "I began to notice that many talented, motivated individuals never reach their full potential. I realized that often this was not because of lack of drive or ability, but because of circumstances and lack of opportunity." He continues, "I began to see the responsibility we all have to look out for those less fortunate than we are. I also began to recognize the power of government and the responsibility we have to protect our civil liberties. This led me to my present job."

As you can see from what they shared, Ashley and Michael found new interests and new challenges as they grew up. They both have passions that—far from being immutable facts—are relatively recent developments.

WHO ARE YOU, REALLY?

This sounds simple enough. You *are* who you are, right? Well, yes, to some extent. Some aspects of who you are at present have come naturally. You had no control over when or where you were born, who your parents are, or how many siblings you have. Yet all of these factors have influenced who you are right now.

At this point in your life, you've developed quite a few distinct tastes, habits, and abilities. Certain foods appeal to you, while others make you queasy. You like particular styles, but would never wear certain clothes. Perhaps you are terrific in math, but you struggle with grammar. Or you might be a budding visual artist who always sings off key, no matter how hard you try. All of these traits are an indication of who you are today. Each of these traits, however, could change as you mature or gain experience that gives you a different perspective or teaches you new ways to approach these things.

Like Ashley and Michael, who you are today is not exactly who you were yesterday, who you will be when you finish high school, and certainly not who you will be 10 years from now. Each event in each day of your life influences the you of tomorrow. Your life is *your* personal journey, *your* passage from one stage of life to the next. Each experience along the way—even those not to your liking—is an opportunity to learn and to become a stronger, more complete person.

"Who are you?" said the Caterpillar . . . . Alice replied, rather shyly, "I—I hardly know, sir, just at present—at least I know who I was when I got up this morning, but I think I must have been changed several times since then."

—Lewis Carroll from *Alice's Adventures in Wonderland* [2]

Your Journal: A Tool for Reflection

Keeping a journal—an informal record of your day-to-day experiences—is an important way to learn more about yourself. You may have kept a journal in the past, either for yourself or as a school assignment. You may currently keep a journal—if so, that's great!

> "We delight in the beauty of the butterfly, but rarely admit the changes it has gone through to achieve that beauty."
>
> —Maya Angelou[3]

The potential benefits of keeping a journal, however, are not dependent on your previous experience with one. You should purchase a journal or notebook with lots of empty pages and dedicate it to keeping a record of your life as you read

> "Allow regular time for silent reflection.
> "Turn inward and digest what has happened. Let the senses rest and grow still."
>
> —John Heider[4]

this book. Or, if you prefer, use a computer. More important than the medium you write in or on is that you write about your experiences soon after they occur and explore your internal and external reactions to those experiences.

Journaling should be a consistent and frequent activity. According to 42eXplore.com, a website that provides starting points for research on various themes, a journal involves "*regularly* writ[ing] down your thoughts and experiences . . . . [It] is a *continued* series of writings made by a person in response to [his or her] life experiences and events" (emphasis added).[5] Journaling in this way—consistently and frequently—will help you learn about yourself and give perspective on your day-to-day life. It will also help you to decide what steps to take toward personal goals.

You should use your journal as a tool to help you think seriously about your interests, abilities, talents, and dreams. When you read about all the activities and experiences available to you (in Chapters 3 through 5 of this book), be sure to use your journal to list those that inter-est you. At the end of each chapter, you will be asked to jot down ideas and feelings about what you have discovered. You can use your journal to help you:

- Reflect on who you are
- Think about how you and the activities in question would be enriched by your involvement
- Brainstorm ways to get involved
- Focus on solutions to any obstacles
- Develop an action plan
- Utilize your resources fully
- Take the next step (apply, sign up, or volunteer)
- Record your actions and feelings, as well the outcomes of your efforts throughout the process

You may also find that recording your thoughts can help you remem-ber the things you've learned or experienced. Writing down your feel-ings and ideas can help you explore them fully and give you insights that mere passing thoughts usually won't provide.

In her article, "Reflect on Where You're Going," Alison Strickland writes that "by sitting down to record your thoughts, you can help clear the clutter from the mind." She suggests setting aside about 20 minutes of quiet time for your journaling and offers the following four-step approach:

1 Quiet your mind
2. Capture your experience
3. Reflect, learn, and discover
4. Set your intentions[6]

You can read the full article by visiting WritersDigest.com/articles/pj_mag/stickland_reflect_where_going.asp.

Journaling Activity

Why not take a few moments right now to reflect on what you have learned so far and practice your journaling skills? For the next 15 to 20 minutes, follow the steps above and see what happens. Though you may be anxious to move on, carving out time for this process on a regular basis will actually help you to accomplish more, as it will help you focus on the things that are most meaningful to you.

Did you take the time to journal? How did it go? Keep in mind that journaling is one of those things that, for most of us, gets easier with practice. Be patient with yourself as you learn to journal effectively. At first, you may be unable to find the words to get started. That's fine. Just keep at it until words, symbols, or pictures allow you to record your thoughts in your own way.

Stay organized by keeping all of your journal entries in the same place. At the end of a journaling session, always read what you have written and make an additional comment or two (in words or pictures) about what you wrote. The next time you open your journal, read your last entry and reflect on what you've learned since then. It might also be helpful to write comments in the margins such as "idea," "discovery," or "to do" to categorize your entries.

Whether you choose to write by hand in a notebook or type your thoughts on a computer, keeping a journal can be a lot of fun. It has the potential to be a lifelong experience and a great tool for navigating the maze of opportunities life will offer you.

Now, let's continue to discover who you are!

FINDING CORE VALUES (CHARACTER COUNTS)

To some people, **character** is simply doing the right thing when no one is looking. A more formal definition, offered in 1913 by *Webster's Revised Unabridged Dictionary*, is:

"The peculiar quality, or sum of qualities, by which a person or thing is distinguished from others; the stamp impressed by nature, education, or habit; that which a person or thing really is . . . ."[7]

A more modern definition, offered online by *Hyperdictionary*, defines character as:

". . . the inherent complex of attributes that determine a person's moral and ethical actions or reactions . . . ."[8]

All these definitions share the idea that character is an essential aspect of who you are. It's believed that your character is shaped by your experiences up to the present and reflects the core values you hold.

Values are defined by *Webster's Online Dictionary* as:

"Beliefs of a person or social group in which they have emotional investment (either for or against something) . . . ."[9]

When we speak of "core values," we're talking about the guiding principles of our lives—the principles that govern our beliefs and are reflected in our actions and personality. We demonstrate these principles through our character traits. People you interact with during your high schools years—and, for that matter, the rest of your life—will look for evidence of admirable character traits. The individuals who seek out your company, the activities you find yourself involved in, and even your admission to college will be influenced by the character traits you exhibit. Identifying what you believe in and the code by which you want to live is, therefore, an important milestone on the road to figuring out who you are.

> "Be more concerned with your character than your reputation, because your character is what you really are, while your reputation is merely what others think you are."
>
> —John Wooden[10]

Positive Character Traits

What is meant by the term "good character"? Most would describe it as a exhibiting behaviors and attitudes that agree with standards generally regarded as appropriate by the culture in which he or she lives. The agreement of a person's traits with what is viewed as appropriate typically makes for a healthy person and a productive citizen. The chart below is a partial list of behaviors and attitudes viewed as positive character traits in American society.

JOURNALING ACTIVITY

As you read about the character traits defined below, list them in your journal. Ask yourself how you feel about each one. Place a plus sign (+) next to the traits you believe are clearly evident in your day-to-day behavior. Place an asterisk (*) next to the traits you believe you need to work on.

TRAIT

Respect—willingness to show consideration or appreciation for someone or something; the polite expression of consideration or appreciation.

CONTEXT

This principle includes respect for the person, rights, and property of others as well as self-respect. When you respect others, you treat them the way you would want to be treated. When you respect yourself, you do not engage in behavior that would lower your self-esteem (opinion of yourself) or allow anyone to persuade you to do things that would conflict with your values.

INSIGHT

"Respect for ourselves guides our morals; respect for others guides our manners."

—Laurence Sterne[11]

Responsibility—the quality, state, or fact of being dependable and accountable for one's actions, duties, or obligations.

CONTEXT

Can you be counted on to: complete tasks on time, feed and care for your pets or younger siblings, do your part on a team, and take good care of your belongings and those of others? Each of these acts is an indication that you are a responsible person who can be trusted to meet your obligations.

INSIGHT

"The price of greatness is responsibility."

—Winston Churchill[12]

TRAIT

Commitment—the state of being impelled to fulfill responsibilities, obligations, or promises.

CONTEXT

When you are committed to something or someone, you not only do what you have promised, but demonstrate an internal motivation to do what is necessary fulfill that promise.

INSIGHT

"The difference between involvement and commitment is like ham and eggs. The chicken is involved; the pig is committed."

—Anonymous

TRAIT

Perseverance—persistence in a purpose or task despite obstacles; patience in continuing to pursue a goal.

CONTEXT

This trait is sometimes called "stick-to-it-iveness" because it means not giving up until you are certain that you have done all that you can do to reach your desired outcome.

"Perseverance is the hard work you do after you get tired of doing the hard work you already did."

—Newt Gingrich[13]

TRAIT

Integrity—honesty to oneself; strict adherence to a standard of conduct or values.

CONTEXT

This trait is evident in actions that demonstrate your personal principles of right and wrong.

INSIGHT

"Real integrity is doing the right thing, knowing that nobody's going to know whether you did it or not."

—Oprah Winfrey[14]

TRAIT

Discipline—training to adhere to internal or external standards of behavior.

CONTEXT

Discipline involves elements of self-motivation and self-control. It can mean following through on a task or responsibility even when you don't feel like doing so. Practicing piano, engaging in fitness activities on a regular basis, pursuing a healthy diet, and doing your homework when you'd rather be watching TV are all actions that involve discipline.

INSIGHT

"No life ever grows great until it is focused, dedicated, and disciplined."

—Harry Emerson Fosdick[15]

TRAIT

Trustworthiness—reliability; the state of being worthy of the faith of others.

CONTEXT

Another way to define trustworthy is "deserving of confidence." Others are not hesitant to share secrets or count on the word of a trustworthy person.

INSIGHT

"To be trusted is a greater compliment than to be loved."

—George MacDonald[16]

TRAIT

Patience—the ability to persevere calmly when faced with obstacles, complications, or delays.

CONTEXT

Have you ever been stuck in traffic or forced to wait in a slow-moving line when you were in a hurry? If you're patient, you accept such delays as unavoidable obstacles and find ways to get through the experience without losing control of yourself.

INSIGHT

"A handful of patience is worth more than a bushel of brains."

—Dutch Proverb[17]

TRAIT

Compassion—sympathy or concern for the feelings or suffering of others; mercy.

CONTEXT

A compassionate person not only feels the hardship or pain of another, but he or she also takes action to mitigate the hardship or pain.

"The dew of compassion is a tear."

—Lord Byron[18]

TRAIT

Fairness—justice; impartiality; accordance with rules and standards.

CONTEXT

Fair-minded may be a more accurate way to describe this principle as a character trait; it implies a lack of favoritism, stereotyping, or prejudice.

INSIGHT

"Fairness is an across-the-board requirement for all our interactions with each other."

—Barbara Jordan[19]

TRAIT

Cooperation—willingness to work amiably with others toward a common goal.

CONTEXT

A cooperative person is usually a good team player—someone who, in a group effort, can work to find agreeable solutions and produce outcomes that reflect the contribution of all parties concerned.

INSIGHT

"Great discoveries and improvements invariably involve the cooperation of many minds. I may be given credit for having blazed the trail but when I look at the subsequent developments I feel the credit is due to others rather than to myself."

—Alexander Graham Bell[20]

Courage—the ability to face new experiences (including dangerous ones) without fear; fortitude.

Courage is, in many ways, the self-confidence or strength to do what is right in the face of challenges to one's beliefs or values. It often takes courage to be an individual when your peers are encouraging you to think or to act like the group.

"It takes courage to grow up and turn out to be who you really are."

—e. e. cummings[21]

Character and Your College Application

Andre Phillips, a seasoned admissions professional who serves as Associate Director of Undergraduate Admissions at the University of Chicago, underscores the importance of character in the college application process:

Central to the application is, of course, evidence whether or not students have the foundation to do the work required at the university. However, we increasingly recognize that the ability to do the work is not enough. Because citizenship is an integral part of membership in a collegiate community, more and more we rely on evidence that informs us regarding the applicant's character in the application review process. This information is conveyed not just through the essay topics but through the depth of involvement in meaningful experiences and what difference that involvement has made in the development of the applicant as an individual. We want to see not only that students have been involved but also the reasons for their involvement—their deliberate decisions to sign onto a specific experience . . . . Internal discussion during the review process involves such questions as: "Will this applicant pass the roommate test?"; "Can this applicant be expected to contribute to the campus environment in a constructive way?"; and "What dynamics will this applicant bring to the classroom and the living environment?" . . . . Good character is, after all, an extension of the personality. If it is not a part of your true makeup, it shows. How? As an inherent part of the personality it will be reflected by passion and grand energy. If it is not inherent, there will be evidence that the student is just going through the motions to make an impression in the admission office . . . .

Dan Walls, Associate Vice President for Enrollment Management at Emory University, concurs with Mr. Phillips' viewpoint and adds:

Letters of recommendation and what others have to say about an applicant go a long way in indicating character, as well. There is a great deal of gamesmanship going on in the admission process. We rely on experienced counselors and faculty to provide the context for . . . perspective on students' true character.

> "The best indices to a person's character are (a) how he treats people who can't do him any good, and (b) how he treats people who can't fight back."
>
> —Abigail Van Buren[22]

Beyond the Looking Glass

The "looking-glass self" is a concept first introduced in 1902 by sociologist Charles Horton Cooley in his work, *Human Nature and the Social Order*. "Looking glass" is another term for mirror, and this concept suggests that the way you view yourself is influenced by the way others respond to or see you. As part of a family, school, community, or society, the views of the larger group help you determine what behavior is acceptable and what is not. This is an important aspect to the development of your personality and your growth as a productive citizen. However, as you mature, you should become more able to maintain your self-concept despite the opinions of other people.[23]

For example, you may make a decision to engage in a certain activity or apply to a certain college—a decision which suits you personally. Your friends may disagree with or not understand this decision. Learning to see yourself beyond "the looking glass" will help you resist peer pressure and live by the principles and values you believe in. Finding and participating in activities and opportunities that influence your life in positive ways often means overcoming the pressure to follow the crowd. It may mean ignoring the opinions of others who do not share your particular interests or passions. Other people may share some of your interests or appear to be like you in some ways, but they are not you. They will never have the exact same set of characteristics, abilities, interests, and needs that are present in you. They cannot achieve anything for you or take care of your responsibilities. You are a unique person. As you explore your options and look for opportunities that suit your needs, interests, and abilities, you should do so, first of all, as an individual. This does not mean that you should live your life with a selfish "Me, first!" attitude. Throughout your life it will be necessary to work in teams and partnerships, cooperating and sharing responsibilities. However, you should recognize that, at the end of the day, you're accountable to make the best choices for your own life.

HOW TO FIND ACTIVITIES THAT ARE RIGHT FOR YOU

Focus on Solutions

Earlier in the chapter you began taking a serious look at yourself. Because of this, you are ready to start exploring the many opportunities available to you to gain meaningful experiences during your high school years. It should be noted that, while such experiences can potentially open doors when it's time to apply to college, "getting admitted" to a particular college should not be your primary objective as you approach these experiences; they're for you—for your growth as a student and as a person. It's important to keep this in mind: The activities most beneficial to you tend to impress admissions officers at the colleges and universities at which you're most likely to thrive.

An essential part of finding the activities that will benefit you most is careful planning. For each activity you consider, reflect on whether it is suited to your needs, interests, and abilities. Also note the eligibility requirements and cost, as well as the amount of travel it requires. Depending on these and additional factors, some options will be a better fit than others. Even with careful planning, involvement in some activities will present real challenges. Don't let these challenges discourage you. Take stock of your blessings—your interests, talents, knowledge, and the opportunities readily available to you. Think of the obstacles you face as temporary roadblocks. Focus your attention on appropriate ways to get around them. By focusing on solutions, you will increase your understanding of such situations and learn how to bypass similar barriers in the future. The keys to overcoming these challenges are creative thinking and initiative.

> "Cheshire Puss . . . [w]ould you tell me, please, which way I ought to go from here?"
>
> "That depends a good deal on where you want to get to," said the Cat.
>
> "I don't much care where—" said Alice.
>
> "Then it doesn't matter which way you go," said the Cat.
>
> "—so long as I get *somewhere*," Alice added as an explanation.
>
> "Oh, you're sure to do that," said the Cat, "if you only walk long enough."
>
> —Lewis Carroll from *Alice's Adventure in Wonderland* [24]

Below are some suggestions to help you get started in your search and, later on, staying focused on solutions. Though these suggestions will reappear in subsequent chapters, now is a good time to record them in your journal as steps to ensure that you are proceeding in the right way toward the activities—and the colleges—that are right for you.

1. **Do research**

   Use the Internet, school and public libraries, and other resources at your disposal to find out how to get involved in the programs and activities that interest you. Don't hesitate to ask older siblings, parents, teachers, counselors, college students, family friends, community leaders, or others for help in finding ideas or solutions to your concerns. This is necessary research and is essential to finding the right activities and interests for you.

2. **Be on time**

   Checking into this information early is important; the earlier you start, the greater your edge.

3. **Sweat the details**

   Record and write yourself reminders about program requirements and deadlines.

4. **Get connected**

   Get the address, phone number, or e-mail address of a person who can answer your questions and give you sound advice about the program or experience that interests you.

Financing Your Experience

Many meaningful activities won't cost you a cent. But, if you're wondering how you can afford to participate in an experience that comes with a price tag, know that there are numerous funding resources for teens who show an interest in doing something that makes a difference.

First, let's discuss those activities available at little or no cost to you. Extra- and co-curricular activities at your school are such opportunities. There may be a minimal activity or registration fee, but your counselor or the activity sponsor can help you to find ways to cover this cost if you cannot afford it yourself. Programs through your church, synagogue, or mosque are similar in this respect.

Volunteer or community service in your neighborhood is something else you can do that involves minimal out-of-pocket costs. Most communities have youth programs or agencies that can assist you in identifying activities that will not require any payment on your part.

If a program you're interested in requires money in order for you to participate, there are numerous ways to approach the issue. You can ask your parents, grandparents, other relatives, or, perhaps, a close family friend to help pay for the activity. Or you may speak with someone at your school, church, synagogue, or mosque to find out what funds might be available to assist young people who wish to take part in meaningful programs (outside of those they offer themselves). Local banks, the Chamber of Commerce, the United Way, Kiwanis, Rotary Club, Lions Club, and other community organizations may also be sources of funding. When looking for funding, you should not only seek money from those you speak with—you should also ask for help in finding other leads for potential assistance. And, of course, you can use your creativity to find ways to earn, save, or raise money to pay for your experience. Babysitting, lawn care, bake sales, and car washes are common fundraising activities. Book and candy sales are also popular. Search the Internet for ideas (keywords: fundraising, activities, teens). You will find information on recycling programs, "Scratch & Help" fundraising cards, sales (pizza, popcorn, candles, etc.), and many other ideas that may spark your interest.

There are also various funding sources at the national level throughout the United States and Canada that may offer you assistance depending on your interests and the nature of the proposed experience. Idealist.org lists a number of these sources including the following:

- **The Edward W. Hazen Foundation** supports young people and youth organizing groups with a particular interest in assisting minorities and the disadvantaged to reach their potential.

- **National 4-H Council** gives grants to support young people in the proposal, design, implementation, and evaluation of funded projects.

- **W.K. Kellogg Youth Innovation Fund** "supports diverse groups of young people" in projects and experiences that bring or promote "lasting change in their communities."[25]

- **Youth As Resources** assists young people ages 5 to 21 in finding funding sources and adult support for their projects.

- **Youth Venture** provides start-up funds—up to $1,000—and support to implement your own community-focused business or organization.

Transportation (From A to B and Back Again)

If public transportation is unavailable, you do not drive a car, and you are unable to find a ride, school or church programs—which frequently provide transportation for participants—are good options. Other types of programs do on occasion provide transportation; if you need a ride, it's always a good idea to ask. It would also be wise to investigate opportunities close enough for you to walk or ride a bike to get to.

But traveling to participate in an interesting experience may not be necessary. There are many interesting opportunities for you to start something new in your community through virtual (online) volunteerism. Randy Tyler, Virtual Volunteering Program Developer for MacDonald Youth Services in Winnepeg, Canada, defines this phenomenon the following way:

> At MacDonald Youth Services, we've learned that volunteering via the Internet is . . . an all-inclusive concept that eliminates barriers and borders to bring people of varying religions, races, ethnicities, and/or abilities together, whether from around the corner or around the world, to help nonprofit organizations fulfill their missions . . . . [V]irtual volunteering gives the Internet a pulse—a heartbeat.[26]

Visit MacDonald Youth Services at Mys.ca/media.

There are scores of virtual volunteer programs on the Internet. Nickelodeon has a program called The Big Help for youth of all ages. (You can read more about The Big Help at http://origin.nick.com/all_nick/specials/bighelp/how.jhtml.) At DoSomething.org, you will find an idea swap, information on grants and awards, and many other things that may inspire you to start something new right out of your own house or garage.

Don't let any transportation challenges get in the way of your chance to make a difference. Look for ways around that obstacle and start changing your world!

STARTING YOUR PERSONAL PROFILE

In Chapter 6 you will find detailed information on creating a resume or portfolio. Development of a personal profile over the following chapters will lay the groundwork for the creation of these documents, which you can use in the application processes for various activities, programs, and experiences (and, later, colleges). In Chapter 6, you'll also find ideas on how to package yourself when applying for programs or seeking funding. This information, along with assistance from your parents, counselors, mentors, and other key resources, will allow you to put your best foot forward in your search for the experiences that are right for you.

To start a personal profile, collect the following in a large folder:

- A record of your past achievements
- Completed surveys
- Notes you make as you read *The Road to College*
- Photos and other memorabilia related to current or past experiences
- A list of individuals willing to serve as personal references
- Letters of commendation or recommendation
- Anything else that might help paint a picture of you as a unique individual

By doing this, you won't have to go searching for things when you are ready to put together your resume or portfolio. (Appendix A can provide you with additional help in building a quality personal profile.)

REWARDS OF PRECOLLEGE EXPERIENCES

You cannot anticipate all of the wonderful things that will come out of service to others or creating something new and meaningful. There are, however, some intrinsic rewards of meaningful activities.

Learning something new is one reward. The feelings of self-confidence and self-worth that follow achievement are other positive results of such experiences. In addition, you will build new relationships and establish a network of important contacts who can open new doors for you. You will develop skills and talents that may spark your creativity and give birth to passionate interests or future endeavors. You may even gain public recognition through awards, honors, or even media coverage. And, unquestionably, you will make yourself a more interesting and informed person who will a more attractive applicant in the college admission process.

Are you ready for the next step? Complete the self-assessment surveys below. When you finish, take some time to jot down your reactions to what you have discovered about yourself in your journal.

SELF-ASSESSMENT SURVEYS

Survey 1 (Who Am I?)

1. What do I like to do for fun?

_____

_____

_____

2. Who are my closest friends?

_____

_____

_____

3. What do I like most about each one?

_____

_____

_____

4. What do I like least about each one?

_____

_____

_____

5. Why do they like me?

_____

_____

_____

6. What do I like most about myself?

_____

_____

_____

7. What do I like least about myself?

_____

_____

_____

8. Is this something I can change? If so, how?

_____

_____

_____

9. What are my strengths?

_____

_____

_____

10. What are my weaknesses?

_____

_____

_____

11. Do I like school? Why or why not?

_____

_____

_____

12. What two subjects do I enjoy most?

_____

_____

_____

Do I do well in these subjects?

_____ Yes _____ No

13. Do I see myself as talented in some area?

    ____ Yes   ____ No

If yes, what area?

_____

_____

_____

14. Have I had lessons or special training in this area?

    ____ Yes   ____ No

If not, would I like to have lessons or special training in this area?

    ____ Yes   ____ No

15. Do I have an interest in something that I'd like to learn more about or take lessons in?

    ____ Yes   ____ No

If yes, name the area or describe the interest.

_____

_____

_____

17. Do I work best alone or as part of a group?

_____

17. Do I see myself as a leader?

    ____ Yes   ____ No

18. Which best describes me?

    ____ Caring person

    ____ Intellectual

    ____ Artist

    ____ Athlete

    ____ None of the above

(Write your own one- or two-word description.)

_____

19. Which would I enjoy most?

____ Community service/helping others

____ Making a lot of money

____ Inventing something useful to others/society

____ Finding a cure for a serious illness

____ Starting a business

____ Creating a work of art

____ Performing for the enjoyment of others

____ Traveling to new or exotic places

____ Solving a societal problem

____ Research (social or scientific)

____ Tackling an intellectual challenge

20. What do I see myself doing in 10 years?

_____

_____

_____

21. Do I enjoy playing or working with little children?

____ Yes ____ No

22. Do I enjoy being around adults?

____ Yes ____ No

23. Do I enjoy being around elderly people?

____ Yes ____ No

24. Do I have an interest in environmental issues?

____ Yes ____ No

25. Do I have an interest in health issues?

____ Yes ____ No

26. What would I like to learn more about (computers, literature, the arts, social science, starting a business, community service, etc.)?

_____

_____

_____

27. Which extracurricular and co-curricular activities am I involved in at my school?

_____ Athletics

_____ Cheerleading

_____ Theater

_____ Band/Orchestra

_____ Academic competition

_____ Community service

_____ Debate/Forensics

_____ Others (Be specific)

_____

_____

_____

28. Of the activities above, which ones do I enjoy most and least?

I most enjoy _____ because

_____

_____

_____

I least enjoy _____ because

_____

_____

_____

Survey 2: My Current Activities

List the character traits you believe are important to succeed in the activities you are currently involved in. Place a check mark above the character traits you believe you exhibit.

In School

Activity	Character traits required

Outside of School

Activity	Character traits required

What did you learn about yourself in listing these things? Are you content with your answers? Do you need to improve in any way? If so, how can you approach this improvement?

_____

_____

_____

ENDNOTES

1   Gross, Jennifer. "Surviving Your College Search: The Adventure Begins."
    Steps to College Newsletter. September/October 2000.
    www.nacacnet.org/MemberPortal/News/StepsNewsletter/Surviving+Your+
    College+Search.htm.

2   Carroll, Lewis. *Alice's Adventures in Wonderland.* The Millennium Fulcrum
    Edition 3.0. Chapter 5. http://www.cs.cmu.edu/~rgs/alice-table.html.

3   Angelou, Maya. Quotation. www.quotationspage.com/quote/34697.html.

4   Heider, John. "A Time for Reflection." Tao of Leadership: Lao Tzu's Te
    Ching Adapted for a New Age. Atlanta: Humanics New Age, 1985. 23.

5   Lamb, Annette. "The Topic: Journal Writing." 4 2 eXplore. http://annette-
    lamb.com/42explore/journl.htm.

6   Strickland, Alison. "Reflect On Where You Are Going." Writer's Digest.
    www.writersdigest.com/articles/pj_mag/stickland_reflect_where_going.asp.

7   Webster's Revised Unabridged Dictionary. Definition of "character."
    Springfield, Massachusetts: G&C Merriam, 1913.Webster's Online
    Dictionary. www.webster-dictionary.org/definition/character.

8   HyperDictionary. "Meaning of Character."
    www.hyperdictionary.com/search.aspx?define=character.

9   Parker, Philip M. ed. "Values." Webster's Online Dictionary. www.websters-
    online-dictionary.org/definition/values.

10 Wooden, John. Quotation. www.utpb.edu/JBS/quotes2.htm.

11 Sterne, Laurence. Quotation.
    www.quotationspage.com/quotes/Lawrence_Sterne.

12 Churchill, Winston. Quotation.
    www.quotationspage.com/quotes/Sir_Winston_Churchill.

13 Gingrich, Newt. Quotation.
    www.pbs.org/wgbh/pages/frontline/newt/newtquotes.html _gingrich.html.

14 Winfrey, Oprah. Quotation.
    http://quotationspage.com/quotes/Oprah_Winfrey.

15 Fosdick, Harry Emerson. Quotation.
    http://en.wikiquote.org/wiki/Dedication.

16 MacDonald, George. Quotation.
    http://faculty.tcu.edu/rmillsap/PowerWords/Contents.htm.

17 Dutch Proverb. Quotation. www.quotationspage.com/quote/1502.html.

18 Lord Byron. Quotation.
    www.websters-online-dictionary.org/definition/dew.

19 Jordan, Barbara. Quotation.
    www.utexas.edu/lbj/barbarajordanforum/aboutbj_quotes.htm.

20 Bell, Alexander Graham.
    Quotation.www.bcm.edu/solutions/v2i2/traber.html.

21 cummings, e.e. Quotation.
    www.quotationspage.com/quotes/e_e_cummings.

22 Van Buren, Abigail. Quotation.
    www.quotationspage.com/quotes/Abigail_van_Buren.

23 Cooley, Charles Horton. Human Nature and the Social Order. New York:
    Scribner's, 1902. 179–185.

24 Carroll, Lewis. Alice's Adventures in Wonderland. The Millennium Fulcrum
    Edition 3.0. Chapter 6. www.cs.cmu.edu/~rgs/alice-table.html.

25 Idealist.org. "Take the Lead in Your Community." Idealist.org.
    www.idealist.org/kt/activism.html#SEC2.

26 Tyler, Randy. "Our Definition of Online Volunteering." MacDonald Youth
    Services. Click "our definition." www.mys.ca/media.

CHAPTER 2
YOUR ROADMAP TO COLLEGE

Destination: College

In the previous chapter, you contemplated the value of self-reflection and the role the character traits we exhibit play in our day-to-day lives. It was an important first step in the process of finding experiences that can enhance your life and your college application.

While getting into college should not be the main reason you engage in interesting and enriching activities, everything you do over the next few years will impact the profile that you present in the college admissions process. You should begin thinking about your college applications and the way your strengths, talents, and activities will affect them.

At this point, you may be wondering why going to college is important; or which courses you should take in preparation for your college studies. Regardless of your questions, you should be armed with facts and not be left to wander the maze that is often created by common myths.

> "The college admission process seems to be a breeding ground for inaccurate perceptions and faulty statements. Students and families often hear comments that are made with the best intentions, but . . . are not based in fact."
>
> —Missy Sanchez,
> Woodward Academy

Debunking College Admission Myths

You've probably already heard several myths about college admission. Dispelling these myths is an important first step in your college selection process. Missy Sanchez, Director of College Counseling at Woodward Academy in Atlanta, GA, offers a list of 10 common myths and her responses to them.

- **Myth #1:** "Cost is really important in determining where I can go to college, so I will likely have to attend a local school."

  Not necessarily. Millions of dollars are given to students and families annually to help defray the costs of—or, in some cases, completely pay for—a college education. The federal government, states, individual colleges, and thousands of public and private organizations make funds available to college students. Research is important. Investigate financial aid at each college on your search list carefully. Talk with the financial aid office and meet its deadlines for applying for merit scholarships and need-based money.

- **Myth #2:** "There is only one perfect college for me."

  Perfect colleges do not exist. Your goal is to find several colleges that best meet your needs.

- **Myth #3:** "Colleges X, Y, and Z are good colleges. Colleges A, B, and C are not so good."

  The academic quality of an institution is not easily determined and, while some colleges are recognized as outstanding in particular areas, it is not necessarily true that those colleges are "good" and the rest are poor by comparison. The key question is not whether College X is good or bad, but whether it is the right school for you to attend.

- **Myth #4** "If none of my family or friends have ever gone to or heard about a college, it probably does not have a good reputation."

  This is a very subjective way to look at college choices. Though your Aunt Helen went to Stony Bay University and loved it, it does not follow that you would love it too, or that it is a "very good school." Colleges also change over time and Stony Bay may be a very different place now than when Aunt Helen went there 20 years ago, or when your family or friends heard about it. Rely on your own research and make decisions based on your needs as a student.

- **Myth #5:** "Colleges don't look at senior year grades."

  The vast majority of colleges will consider not only first-semester senior-year grades, but also the degree of difficulty of the entire senior-year course of study when deciding whether to offer or to deny you admission. As for second semester grades, if there is a significant drop-off in academic performance, colleges that have accepted you may require you to attend summer school, put you on probation for your first semester of college, or withdraw your acceptance on the grounds that you do not appear to be the same student as the one they originally admitted.

- **Myth #6:** "To impress college admissions officers, it's important to have as many different extracurricular activities as possible."

  Colleges are looking for quality of involvement, not quantity. They want a diverse student body composed of students who are vitally interested in activities for which they are suited or have a passion, rather than students who have spread themselves so thin that they demonstrate no commitment to anything. Colleges prefer, for example, the student who was totally engaged in the yearbook all 4 years of high school, serving various roles before becoming a skilled editor her senior year, over the student who sampled a dozen activities, never making a difference in any of them.

- **Myth #7:** "A big university will have more to offer me than a small college will."

  Equating size with quality is particularly risky when it comes to choosing a college. A large university may be ideal for many students, depending on their needs, interests, and personality. Other students, however, will have much greater success in a smaller, more personal environment. It is important to know yourself and to understand what it will take to make your college experience a good one.

- **Myth #8:** "Colleges receive too many essays to have time to read all of them."

  If they require them, they read them. In fact, most private and many public college admissions officers read personal essays with great care. An essay that demonstrates depth of insight, skill in written communication, or strength of character is one significant way to counteract lackluster test scores or a less-than-impressive academic record. Don't wait until the deadline looms and then dash off anything that comes to mind. A well-written essay can tip the scales in your favor.

- **Myth #9:** "If I decide to attend the wrong college, my life will be ruined."

  Your college choice is a significant decision. You should take it seriously and spend time on all stages of the admissions process. But if you find that, despite your efforts to make an informed choice, you are not well suited to the college you chose, you can always transfer. Be conscientious about the selection process, but don't cast yourself as a character in a Greek tragedy. Bad decisions happen to all of us—we can recover from most of them without having our lives "ruined."

- **Myth #10:** "Relying solely on guidebooks, magazines, and newspapers for a list of the 'Best Colleges' is the best way to find the college that is right for me."

  Guidebooks, magazines, and newspapers are great resources for information during your college search. However, students at times rely too heavily on subjective college rankings found in such publications. Colleges are multi-faceted enterprises—one size does *not* fit all. Qualities that would make a college right for you might not be the same qualities measured by a magazine or newspaper. Rankings cannot convey what the classroom or campus atmosphere will feel like to you, nor can they tell you what relationships you will build with your professors and other students. They cannot measure *your* suitability for a given academic field as it is taught on a particular campus nor can they measure your engagement as a student inside and outside of the classroom. In particular, they cannot tell you where *you* will discover *your* passion. Read the guidebooks, magazines, and newspaper articles carefully, and learn all you can from them. But gather additional information through campus visits, meetings with college representatives, and other college search activities. In short, take time to do your own research and draw your own conclusions during the college selection process. After you have learned all you can about the colleges on your list, decide what will work best for you.*

* The statements and responses above were edited for clarity and grammar.

These and other misconceptions about the college admissions process circulate among students and parents in every community. You should share the things you've heard on this topic with your college counselor and the college admissions officers you come into contact with. They will be happy to offer their perspectives and to help you separate the myths from the realities.

I Just Want to Know . . .
(14 Questions Answered)

The students interviewed for this book—young people from Atlanta, Chicago, Minneapolis, New York, and San Francisco, as well as smaller towns in the Carolinas, Indiana, Michigan, New Jersey, and Wisconsin—didn't just share their insights and experiences, they asked a good number of questions as well. Some of their questions on the college admissions process are included below, along with a relatively brief answer (more information on this topic is given in Chapter 7). Many students were surprised by these answers and, upon hearing them, came to view college admissions as a more friendly process than they had imagined.

Q: "Why should I even go to college?"

A: Think of it as a major investment in your future. While college is not for everyone, and you can certainly make a good life for yourself and your family without it, in his or her lifetime the average college graduate earns significantly more than the person who ends his or her formal education with a high school diploma. Many of the occupations projected to grow in availability over the next 10 years will require an associate's or a bachelor's degree. On a more personal level, many college graduates cite intellectual and emotional growth— gained through the development of critical thinking skills and a greater understanding of the world—as an invaluable reward of a college education.

Q: "What if my family can't afford to pay for my college education?"

A: This is a common question. The quick answer is your family may qualify for some form of financial aid to help lessen college costs, so you shouldn't immediately rule out a school because of its price tag. You should submit the Free Application for Federal Student Aid (FAFSA), available online at Fafsa.ed.gov, early in the second half of your senior year (it must be submitted *after* January 1). The FAFSA determines eligibility for federal financial aid. In addition, your parents should complete the CSS/Financial Aid PROFILE, which is administered by The College Board and available online at ProfileOnline.collegeboard.com/index.jsp. The PROFILE is required by many private colleges and universities to determine your eligibility for non-government financial aid, such as the institution's own grants, loans, and scholarships. This form can be submitted in the fall of your senior year and will give you some early information about your eligibility for financial aid.

Q: "What types of colleges are there?"

A: Colleges* may be described in many ways. Below is a list of some variables to consider when exploring colleges.

- **Is it public or private?** Public institutions are supported largely by a state or local government; private institutions are funded mainly by tuition and fees paid by students, private gifts, and various endowments (large sums of money earning interest that can be spent for specific purposes). Public schools generally charge lower tuition and fees to—and feature student bodies composed mainly of—state or local residents.

- **Is it affiliated with a particular religion?** The extent to which religious affiliation affects day-to-day life varies considerably from one school to the next. Some schools

---

* Please note that in the United States, "college" is a generally accepted term for a postsecondary, or post–high school, institution. For example, one can answer the question, "Where do you want to go to college?" with the name of a university. In this book, the term "college" does not only refer to institutions with "college" in their name.

feature mandatory religious services and lengthy rules of conduct for students. Other schools give nod to a religious affiliation in the curriculum only.

- **Is it a Historically Black College or University (HBCU), or a Hispanic Serving Institute (HSI)?** HBCUs refer to colleges formed before 1964 to serve African American students. HSIs feature undergraduate enrollments that are 25-percent-or-more Hispanic.

- **Is it coed or single-sex?** There are more than 100 institutions at which the enrollment is predominantly or exclusively female or male.

Colleges may also be categorized by their focus.

- **Liberal arts colleges** focus on intellectual development in the humanities, social sciences, sciences, and fine arts rather than the development of vocational skills. They are largely private undergraduate institutions with small classes where students generally receive a lot of individual attention and access to their professors and advisors.

- **Universities** offer liberal arts programs as well. They're typically composed of several smaller colleges or schools. Depending on their size and enrollment, they can provide a broader range of majors and research facilities than a liberal arts college. They may also have larger classes, a sizable percentage of which may be taught by graduate students. In most cases, they offer not only undergraduate (bachelor's) degrees, but graduate (master's and doctoral) degrees as well. They may be public or private.

- **Community and junior colleges** are 2-year institutions. They may offer technical training that leads to work in a particular field or grant an associate's degree upon completion of 2 years of full-time study. Students who earn an associate's degree at a community or junior college may transfer to a 4-year liberal arts college or university if the subject matter they've studied is taught at the 4-year institution.

- **Agricultural, technical, and specialized colleges** offer training that prepares students for specific careers.

Examples of specialized colleges are: art schools, Bible colleges, business colleges, music schools, nursing schools, and seminaries.

Q: "How can I find colleges that are right for my needs, interests, and abilities?"

A: First know that there is no *one* college that is right for you. There are more than 3,500 colleges and universities in the United States, plus thousands more abroad. Many colleges would serve your needs, interests, and abilities well. You should be prepared to do the research necessary to find colleges and universities that appear to be a good match for you. Various resources are at your disposal. Your school's guidance or college counseling office is a good place to start. Internet resources, such as PrincetonReview.com and college websites, are also great sources of information. Whenever possible, you should visit colleges in person and get a firsthand look. Take an official tour of the campus and talk to college personnel and current students—only by getting information from multiple sources will you get a complete picture of what the institution has to offer.

COLLEGE VISITS

Your first few visits to a college campus can be casual—pulling off the highway to check out a school highlighted on a road sign, or riding your bike through the grounds of a local college. Over time, your visits should become more deliberate. You may wish to attend a college's weekend program for prospective students, or to visit a friend or relative at her college. You should plan to visit several schools during spring break of your junior year (if considerable travel is involved, this may require the company of a parent or trusted adult). Once you have narrowed your search list, a second or third visit is often wise. For each school you're seriously interested in, you should make every effort to take an official tour of the campus. Other options during your visit may include: Spending the night in a dormitory (with a student host, if possible), attending a day of classes, eating in the dining hall, and getting a taste of the social life—all of which can be arranged through the college's admissions office. By gaining firsthand experience, you will have a greater sense of your comfort level in that environment. And an in-person visit scheduled through the admission office indicates a serious interest in attending the school and can positively affect your admissions decision. When you're ready to start planning your trip, The Princeton Review publishes a book called *Guide to College Visits,* that has lots of useful ideas and how to's for visiting colleges.

Q: "What if I have no idea about what major to choose?"

A: If you have an interest, talent, or "calling" that you're sure you want to pursue, go right ahead. If not, relax—you have company. "Undecided" is one of the most popular college majors in the United States. Most colleges and universities won't require you to declare a major until your sophomore or junior year. This allows you time to explore your interests, strengths, and options—often through a series of required courses called a core curriculum. In fact, choosing a school based on the strength of a particular program, unless you are 100 percent sure "what you want to do," is a bad idea. And it is not unusual for high school seniors—or college students, or, for that matter, adults—to be uncertain about career goals. You should not feel pressured to choose a particular field of study until you have had the opportunity to learn more about yourself and all the possibilities open to you.

Q: What are "name" or "top" schools?

A: The terms "name" and "top" often say more about a particular person's knowledge and experience with today's institutions of higher learning than about the colleges or universities to which these tags are applied. Quite often, such a branding is based on information that is outdated or reflects a regional or local opinion of the school's quality. For example, a school considered to be a "name" or "top" school in the Southeast may not be thought of as a "name" or "top" school in the Northwest. While the names of institutions in well-known athletic conferences, such as the Ivy League and the Big Ten, are known by most people, there are many outstanding American colleges and universities that even extremely well-read individuals know little about. Do not believe that a school's quality is dependent on what you and the people you know have heard about it.

Q: "What is a 'selective' college?"

A: There are various ways to assess selectivity in college admissions. A fairly simple response is that, in a given year, the percentage of students a college admits from its applicant pool is a good barometer of its selectivity.

Colleges and universities utilizing an open admission policy admit students based, primarily, on space availability. Colleges considered to be **selective** admit 50–75 percent of applicants; those considered to be **very selective** admit 26–50 percent of applicants; those considered to be **highly selective** admit less than 25 percent of applicants. (Only a small number of the nation's 3,500-plus colleges admit less than 25 percent of applicants.[1])

There are a couple of good resources for more information on selectivity in college admissions. The College Board offers a very helpful overview of selectivity in college admissions at CollegeBoard.com/parents/csearch/know-the-options/21348.html. The Princeton Review produces an Admission Selectivity Rating for each college it provides data for on its website. An explanation of this rating is located at PrincetonReview.com/college/research/articles/find/ratings.asp#selectivity.

Q: "What do selective colleges look for in applicants?"

A: Below are the general criteria college admissions officers use to select applicants suited to attend their institutions. In general, applications for admission are evaluated in two fundamental areas.

1. Academic record
   - Grades
   - Quality of course of study
   - College entrance exam scores
   - Academic awards and distinctions

2. Personal characteristics

   - Degree and quality of extra-/co-curricular involvement
   - Community service
   - Overall quality of written expression (including essays)
   - Recommendations from teachers and counselors
   - Admissions interview
   - Special considerations—i.e., legacy status (awarded if someone in the applicant's family had previously attended the institution); talent (in the arts, athletics, forensics, leadership, etc.); demonstration of initiative or character; or other criteria, sometimes including a demonstrated interest in attending the institution

For the information above that can be quantified—that is, expressed as a number—you should seek out median information for recently admitted classes at the colleges you're interested in applying to. This will help you determine what your chances of admission may be.

It's worth noting that some colleges and universities have recently eliminated the consideration of college entrance exam scores from their admissions decisions. It's not, however, safe to disregard this particular hurdle. Depending on which schools you want to apply to (and you probably don't have a solid idea just yet), your college entrance exam scores may be a very important part of your application. Large public universities often use mathematical formulae in their admissions decisions and still rely heavily on college entrance exam scores.

Q: "Should I go to the most selective college that I am admitted to?"

A: To equate selectivity with quality of instruction or to use it as your sole criterion for determining which colleges will be suitable matches for you is an unwise strategy. Many factors contribute to a particular student's compatibility with a college, and they're all important. These factors can include, but are not limited to, the institution's:

- Location
- Size
- Student-faculty ratio and average class size
- Academic environment
- Campus environment and social life
- Extra- and co-curricular offerings
- Housing options
- Career planning and job-placement resources
- Tuition, fees, and room and board

Chances are, many selective colleges would suit you well. To truly determine whether or not a given institution is a good match for you, however, you will need to take the all of the factors that are important to you—academic, social, financial, environmental, etc.—into consideration. Choosing a school based solely on its selectivity would be like choosing an apartment because it's a certain number of flights from the ground. Arlene Cash, Vice President for Enrollment Management at Spelman College in Atlanta, GA, puts it this way:

> Retention and students' persistence [to] graduation begins with the college selection process. Neither the student nor the college should be so greedy as to ignore match. Who's happy at a given school and who's not is largely dependent on . . . both the students' enrollment choices and the choices that colleges make regarding who is admitted. Students should not allow their perceptions of a school's prestige or the offer of a scholarship to draw them into a situation that will not provide a healthy environment for them. When that happens, students often spend valuable time away from campus, trying to escape to a more nurturing environment . . . . [They leave] on weekends, looking for a place where they can be who they really are, . . . dress like they want to dress, listen to the music they enjoy, eat "comfort food"—trying to find that place where they "fit in."

Q: "What do I need to do to be admitted to the school of my choice?"

A: Being well prepared, academically, is the first thing you need to do. Throughout high school, you should focus your attention on selecting courses that will prepare you for the rigors of college work. You should also engage in activities that demonstrate your character, abilities, and interests. You shouldn't, however, engage in an activity simply because you think it'll impress a certain college. As stated earlier, the extra- and co-curricular activities most beneficial to you as a person will impress the admissions officers at colleges and universities at which you're most likely to thrive. Wade Boggs, College Counselor at The Westminster School in Atlanta, GA, says:

> Be sure that the college of your choice is the right school for you. No college is perfect, and a great deal depends on the "fit" between you and the institution . . . . Students should approach both the application process and the decision to attend a particular college with the right attitude and the desire to seek opportunities available to them wherever they are admitted and decide to enroll . . . . Remember that you, as an individual, can get an outstanding education at hundreds of colleges across the country . . . . So-called prestige schools should not be stricken from the list by students who are qualified to attend them, but [a good] match is the key. By creating a final list of realistic choices, you will increase your chances of being admitted to schools that are right for you.

As you progress through your high school years, periodically take a realistic look at what you will have to offer a college community upon the completion of high school. At each juncture, create a list of the colleges you're interested in and divide it into three sections regarding your admissions chances—"reach," "good match," and "safety." When we revisit the college admission process in Chapter 7, we will discuss this topic in more detail.

Q: "What does it mean to be 'well-rounded'?"

A: "Well-rounded," as it pertains to college applicants, defies concrete definition. As such, it's not productive to be hung up on it. Andre Phillips, Senior Associate Director of Undergraduate Admissions at the University of Chicago, has the following to say on this topic:

> In my opinion, there is no such thing! Colleges are in the business of building a diverse community of learners and contributors. "Roundedness" has nothing to do with it . . . . . A fine record of achievement and impressive experiences or accomplishments that demonstrate talent and character are what college admission is all about.

Q: "How can my skills, talents, and experiences be utilized to create the best possible impression of myself through my college application?"

A: Choosing schools for which you are qualified is the first step. Next is making sure that you follow the directions and meet the deadlines set forth in the application materials. With regards to application content, make sure the materials are neatly and orderly presented. Demonstrate your personality and ability to communicate ideas effectively through a well-written essay. Let those who read your application know that are serious about wanting to attend their institution and that you will bring something of value to the campus community, both inside and outside of the classroom. Finally, be sure you and your parents put your best foot forward when communicating with the various admissions offices you're working with. Be patient and trust that admissions personnel know what they are doing. They want to do right by you. Taking an adversarial position or checking constantly on their every move will not help your application's standing.

Q: "I am homeschooled. How do I handle extracurricular activities, testing, recommendations, and applying for college?"

A: Community activities and those offered by religious organizations are often good options. (Chapter 3 offers a good selection of such activities.) In some cases, you can also take part in certain activities offered through your local school district. Show initiative and find ways to engage yourself as much as possible in things that will broaden your horizons in interesting ways and offer you a chance to grow outside of your homeschool environment.

Some colleges and universities publish guidelines for home-schooled students. The most important issue is producing an authentic and accurate transcript of your courses that is accompanied by course descriptions and grading information. College entrance and Advanced Placement (AP) testing will take place at public and private schools in your area. Recommendations and verification of activities may be written by persons who supervise your activities.

Many families seek independent college counseling for their homeschooled students. You may find reputable independent counselors through a state or regional Association for College Admission Counseling (ACAC) in your area. (State and regional ACAC information can be found at NACACnet.org.) There are also organizations, such as College Options Foundation (CollegeOptionsFoundation.net), which offer software and seminars that may be helpful to you in your college search and application process.

Q: "What can I do to avoid common mistakes in the college application process?"

A: *The Road to College* is full of helpful college admissions advice. While information on this topic can be found throughout the book, the following is a quick overview of eleven steps you can take to ensure that the application process runs as smoothly as possible for you:

1. **Build a solid record of achievement and behavior during high school.**

   The key word is "build." A successful college application presents a record of consistent accomplishment through the high school years. If you've persistently demonstrated low academic achievement, a lack of involvement in meaningful activities, or behavioral problems, you won't be able to make up for it in a single semester, no matter how you try. Colleges much prefer a sustained level of high achievement to sporadic successes interspersed with periods of poor performance.

2. **Don't take the easy road.**

   As you travel through your high school years, regularly challenge yourself. Demonstrate initiative through your academic choices and activities outside of the classroom. A little extra effort will make this trip a rewarding one when it's time to apply to college.

3. **Start the college selection process early.**

   Though the bulk of this process will take place over your junior and senior years, you should begin thinking about your options and conducting informal research as early as possible. Talk to teachers and counselors about your ideas and interests—they may know of schools that would be a good fit for you. Visit the guidance department or, if your school has one, the college resource room for information about college and other postsecondary options.

4. **Become knowledgeable about the college admissions process and the colleges that interest you.**

   Understand what colleges generally look for in applicants and, more importantly, what the colleges on your personal list are looking for. Learn all you can about these colleges and the recent demographics of the classes they've admitted—it will help you determine which ones would be best suited to your abilities, needs, and interests.

5. **Use all the resources at your disposal.**

   You don't know what you don't know. Listen to the advice of those who have experience in the area of college admissions. Attend college fairs and college nights offered at your school or in your area. When admissions representatives visit your school, try to meet with them. (Ask questions about things you don't fully understand!) Avoid reliance on myths and the advice of people who may be as unfamiliar as you are with the process. If at all possible, visit the colleges you're interested in. Read college guidebooks, catalogues, and other printed materials carefully. Frequent college websites and other Internet resources—e.g., CollegeBoard.com, NACACnet.org,

PrincetonReview.com—for timely information about colleges and college admissions issues.

6. **Avoid focusing on admission to a particular school at the expense of others.**

   There are no guarantees in the admissions process. Apply to several schools at which you believe you can get a quality education, achieve your goals, and have a fulfilling social life. You should have satisfactory options should you be denied admission to your first-choice school.

7. **On your college application, don't declare an intended major for which you are unsuited or about which you are uncertain.**

   Most colleges do not require you declare a major until you have completed at least 1 year of academic work. Some even offer a freshman seminar in which you are able to become acquainted with the academic expectations of the institution and work with an advisor to identify strengths, interests, and potential career directions. If you are not certain about which field you want to enter, relax. You can explore the possibilities once you begin college.

8. **Don't make price the top priority in considering a college.**

   Don't rule out an appealing college based on cost alone. You may be eligible for a scholarship provided by the college or some other source. Talk to admissions officers at each college you're interested in about the cost of attending their institution and what their financial aid policies and practices are. Prepare for these conversations by doing independent research on scholarships, grants, loans, work-study, and other options for financing your college education. CollegeBoard.com, Fastweb.com, NACACnet.org, PrincetonReview.com, and your state's student aid website are all good places to start this research.

9. **Follow admission timelines and directions to the letter.**

   Do all you can to submit timely neat, well-organized, and complete applications. You should make a good impression with the material you present as an applicant. Take time to type or carefully handwrite or type everything. Proofread each finished application several times to ensure that the information you include is accurate and that there are no misspelled words, then have someone else proofread it. Be sure to meet every deadline and allow time for each application and any accompanying documents to be processed by your counselor.

10. **Hone your writing skills now and devote serious time to each application essay.**

    Many colleges require applicants to compose an essay (or several essays). Do not wait until you are in the middle of the application process to hone your writing skills. No matter how good a writer you currently are, you can always improve. Writing in your journal is excellent practice in putting your thoughts on paper. You can also talk with your English teacher about what you can do to increase your written communication skills. If possible, equip yourself with an unabridged dictionary and a good composition and grammar handbook. (*English Composition and Grammar* by John Warriner, *The Element of Style* by William Strunk Jr. and E. B. White, and *The Little, Brown Handbook* by H. Ramsey Fowler and Jane Aaron are great resources.) Developing good reading habits will enhance both your vocabulary and your ease in using the English language. In addition to novels, short stories, and periodicals, you may enjoy biographies of famous people or even college essays that have impressed admission officers in the past (an excellent source for real college admissions essays is The Princeton Review's *College Essays that Made a Difference*)—the last two can give you ideas of ways to write about yourself when it's time to compose your own essay.

11. **Prepare for your college interviews.**

CollegeBoard.com offers a list of typical interview questions at http://collegeboard.com/student/apply/the-application/138.html. Using this list as a rough guide, ask a parent, counselor, or friend to play the role of a college admission officer and engage you in a mock interview. Be sure to ask him or her some questions you'd want to ask of a school you applied to. When you're done, have the mock interviewer critique your performance.

YOUR CRITERIA FOR CHOOSING A COLLEGE

The college search is an important decision-making process and keeping the proper perspective sometimes may be difficult. The sheer number of choices may feel overwhelming. Friends and family may be questioning you about college and career on a regular basis. Remember that the desired outcome of a careful college search is a list of postsecondary options that are excellent matches for *your* needs, interests, and abilities. While your parents' concerns and expectations should be taken into consideration, you are the key person in this picture. Your future will unfold one day at a time and you do not have to know what you want to do at the end of your college years. Don't take someone else's experience as an indication of what college or career is right for you.

> "Think of your college essay as an interview in your absence."
>
> —Andre Phillips,
> University of Chicago

Of course, when you consider a college, there are some basic factors to be examined. Several of these factors have already been mentioned in this chapter. They include the institution's academic and social profile, location, size, extracurricular offerings, cost, financial aid offerings, and overall feel, based on research and campus visits. But what are the ideal expressions of these factors for you? (For example, what size institution will you most thrive in?) And what additional factors—factors important to you but perhaps not important to every prospective college student—should you be looking at? An approach to answers to these questions can be found below.

A College Planning Curriculum

By following the suggestions offered in the College Planning Curriculum (CPC) outlined below, you should begin your senior year with a sense of your personal criteria for choosing where the next stage of your life—your years as an undergraduate student—will take place. The CPC provides activities and programs designed to assist students in making wise and deliberate decisions about postsecondary school choices. As you will surely change as you move through your high school years, the CPC is progressive, utilizing a philosophy of student development to help students build on their strengths, interests, and experiences as they move toward adulthood. It supplements formal college counseling in four stages—awareness, exploration, growth, and decision making. You can use the CPC in conjunction with PrincetonReview.com to prepare a list of possible colleges that truly reflects all of the factors related to your needs, interests, and abilities.

Awareness (Grades 8–9)

As you finish 8th grade and prepare to enter 9th grade, you begin the awareness phase. Key to this period is an understanding of how current and future performance, activities, and behavior will affect postsecondary options. Counselors or advisors should assist students in choosing their 9th grade courses wisely. You should, for example, become aware of the standards for honors courses and what will qualify you for taking AP courses later in your high school years. This is extremely important if you are interested in attending a college or university noted for its selectivity in admissions. Through 9th-grade orientation activities designed to acquaint you with life as a high school student, or informational meetings with your advisor, you may be made aware of general criteria for college admission. There also may be some discussion of the meaning of "significant" involvement in school activities, the need for responsibility in academic performance and social behavior, and preparation for ACT's PLAN Assessment (PLAN). PLAN is a test designed to help students prepare for the ACT exam, a college entrance exam favored by many schools, particularly those in the mid-western and western U.S. While PLAN is most frequently administered to 10th grade students, some schools allow their students to take it in 9th grade as practice.

If you have not had the opportunity to obtain information on the above topics, you should meet with a counselor or advisor. You may also want to complete learning style and career exploration inventories, and gain exposure to a variety of career choices to assist you in thinking in general way about your future. If your school does not provide these services, youth organizations, religiously affiliated youth groups, and independent counselors and educational consultants can be excellent resources.

What Is a Learning Style?

Learning styles—the conditions under which a student is most able to or prefers to learn—differ among individuals. A learning style inventory is a tool to assess your learning preferences and aid your teachers and your parents in optimizing your instructional experience and achievement. The results also can help you to recognize how you learn best and help you to develop effective study skills.

Career Exploration Inventories

A career exploration inventory is a tool that can help identify individual interests, strengths, aptitudes, and goals as they relate to a particular career or field of study leading to a career. The results of such an assessment can help you to plan experiences that will allow you to build on these characteristics and to engage in meaningful career exploration opportunities.

Two 9th Grade Inventories

The Index of Learning Styles, an instrument developed by Richard Felder and Barbara Soloman at North Carolina State University, is designed to provide information about "possible strengths and possible tendencies or habits that might lead to difficulty in academic settings." Results of this inventory help students recognize the way in which they learn and assist them in balancing academics and extracurricular activities.[2]

IDEAS is an introductory interest and career exploration inventory authored by Charles B. Johansson, PhD and offered by Pearson Assessments, a testing company. It was created for use in guidance counseling and career exploration programs, providing help to those with little or no work experience.[3]

Exploration (Grade 10)

As a sophomore, you should begin to explore your postsecondary options and, whenever possible, engage in personal assessment. In addition to journaling, you should periodically review your academic progress and the general criteria for college admission with a parent, guardian, counselor, advisor, or teacher. With a college counselor you should discuss taking PLAN and preparing for College Board's Preliminary SAT/National Merit Scholarship Qualifying Test (PSAT/NMSQT), a test designed to help students prepare for the SAT Reasoning Test (a college entrance exam favored by many schools, particularly those in the eastern U.S.) as well as determine their eligibility for a National Merit Scholarship. The PSAT/NMSQT is generally administered to 11th grade students, but some schools allow their students to take it in 10th grade as practice. Ask your counselor whether your school offers PLAN and whether you can be allowed to take the PSAT/NMSQT as a sophomore.

You should also find out if your school provides the opportunity to complete the Myers-Briggs Type Indicator or the Campbell Interest and Skill Survey during your sophomore year. If you are able to take these surveys or participate in other personality or career exploration activities, you should review with a counselor the information gathered from these experiences and assess your strengths, interests, and future options. Find out if there are opportunities for you to engage in activities such as career shadowing that will allow you greater insight into various career options.

MYERS-BRIGGS TYPE INDICATOR (MBTI)

Sometimes informally referred to as the Myers-Briggs *personality* type indicator, the MBTI "continues to be the most trusted and widely used assessment in the world for understanding individual differences and uncovering new ways to work and interact with others." It must be administered by someone who has been certified to do so. Popular with colleges and universities as a career planning tool, it is also offered by some high schools to aid students in self-discovery and college and career planning.[4] Your school counselor may be qualified to administer the MBTI. If not, you may be able to take this inventory on your own through a career planning office at a 2- or 4-year college in your area.

CAMPBELL INTEREST AND SKILL SURVEY (CISS)

Authored by David Campbell, PhD, CISS "measures self-reported vocational interests and skills . . . . [It] focuses on careers that require postsecondary education and is most appropriate for use with individuals who are college bound or college educated." It must be administered by a Pearson Assessments-certified individual.[5] Find out if your school is able to offer the CISS. If not, you can take the inventory online at PearsonAssessments.com/tests/ciss.htm.

In your sophomore year you should also consider taking the first standardized exams that will actually factor into your admissions decisions—SAT Subject Tests. Formerly called SAT IIs, these tests are, according to the College Board website, one-hour multiple-choice exams "designed to measure your knowledge and skills in particular subject areas, as well as your ability to apply that knowledge." They're divided into five general subject areas—"English, history, mathematics, science, and language[s]." (A complete list of SAT Subject Tests can be found at CollegeBoard.com/student/testing/sat/about/SATII.html.) While test content is compatible with current curricular trends, "the tests are independent of any particular textbook or method of instruction . . . . [M]any colleges use the Subject Tests for admission, for course placement, and to advise students about course selection."[6]

Not all colleges require SAT Subject Tests, but it is common for the most selective schools to ask for three, often with some specific requirements (some schools, for example, ask that an SAT Subject Test in mathematics to be among the three). If in your sophomore year you are studying a subject covered by an SAT Subject Test and are doing well in the course, it may be wise to get an SAT Subject Test out of the way at this juncture. However, tests that draw on several years of knowledge—e.g., languages, mathematics, literature—may yield better results in your junior or senior year when your knowledge of the subject is more advanced. It's wise to speak with a counselor before registering for an SAT Subject Test.

Growth (Grade 11)

Following the awareness and exploration phases, your growth as a high school student will be clear. As an 11th grader, you will be ready to focus in a more specific way on college choices. Early in the year, you should take the PSAT/NMSQT. In the spring semester, you should take the SAT Reasoning Test (SAT) or the ACT. As colleges generally take your best scores, you may take either test more than once; you can even take both tests.

Armed with your test scores, your inventory results (e.g., Index of Learning Styles, MBTI), and a record of five semesters in high school, you—and your parents, if possible—should formally meet with your counselor or a college consultant to look seriously at college admission criteria and to set goals for you. A list of 15 to 30 colleges that match your abilities, needs, and interests should emerge from this meeting.

The remainder of the school year and the summer before your senior year will be very busy. In addition to your school work and activities, you should research and visit colleges. You should also take stock of your personal profile and figure out whether there's anything "missing" that you'd like to add. In addition, you should work with your English teacher on the techniques involved in writing an effective college admission essay and write a sample essay or two. CollegeBoard.org offers information on three types of admission essay prompts—the "you" prompt, the "why us" prompt, and the "creative" prompt—at CollegeBoard.com/student/apply/essay-skills/108.html. It also provides a list of actual prompts used by colleges in recent years.

If SAT Subject Tests are required by any of the colleges you're looking at, you should take them in May or June.

Decision Making (Grade 12)

Your school may schedule one-on-one sessions, advisory groups, or class meetings to provide seniors with information about the college application process. Through these events, seniors can receive assistance in making decisions about which schools to apply to. If such events are not available to you, it will be up to you to keep your college application process on track. You should find a teacher or some other adult who can help.

In the fall, you should meet frequently with the person who is assisting you to review your progress and narrow down your list of college options. At this juncture, you can take the ACT or SAT one last time; you can also take SAT Subject Tests. College visits and research should continue until a final list of three to six (eight is the recommended maximum) colleges to which you will apply has emerged. As the year progresses, you should apply to the schools on your final list and await their admissions decisions. Those seeking admission via Early Decision, Early Action, or Early Notification plans will have to get started sooner than others. If you're in this boat, you should begin work on your applications by late September, as many of them will be due between November 1 and December 15.

Once you have heard from all of the colleges to which they you applied, you and your family will have to decide which of the schools appears to be the best option for your undergraduate studies. If you have been placed on a wait list, you may need assistance in determining the wisdom of remaining on the list and of making the college aware of your degree of interest in attending that institution. If help is not available through your school, an employer or a mentor (see Chapter 6) may be a good resource for assistance in this area.

Testing Options for High School Students

Grade 9

Test A: Index of Learning Styles

When is it?
Fall

What's the Deal?
This test is usually taken online; it "is an on-line instrument used to assess preferences on four dimensions (active/reflective, sensing/intuitive, visual/verbal, and sequential/global) of a learning style model formulated by Richard M. Felder and Linda K. Silverman."[7]

Test B: Ideas

When is it?
Spring

What's the deal?
If tests A and B are not available through your school, you may be able to take them through a private career, college, or educational consultant.

Test C: PLAN

When is it?
Fall

What's the deal?
This test is designed for 10th graders. Ask your guidance counselor if you can take it for practice in the 9th grade.

Grade 10

TEST A: PLAN

WHEN IS IT?
Fall

WHAT'S THE DEAL?
This test is suggested for all 10th graders.

TEST B: PSAT/NMSQT

WHEN IS IT?
October

WHAT'S THE DEAL?
This test is designed for 11th graders. Ask your guidance counselor if you can take it for practice in the 10th grade.

TEST C: CAMPBELL SKILLS AND INTEREST SURVEY AND D: MYERS-BRIGGS TYPE INVENTORY

WHEN IS IT?
Spring

WHAT'S THE DEAL?
Tests C and D are best administered in the spring of 10th grade so that the results may be used in 11th grade college-planning activities. If these tests are not available through your school, you may be able to take them through a private career, college, or educational consultant.

TEST E: SAT SUBJECT TESTS

WHEN IS IT?
May and June

WHAT'S THE DEAL?
Tenth grade students who have done well in course work covered by SAT Subject Tests are encouraged to take such tests at the end of the school year.

Grade 11

Test A: PSAT/NMSQT

When is it?
October

What's the deal?
This test is suggested for all 11th graders.

Test B: SAT Reasoning Test

When is it?
March, May, and June

Test C: SAT Subject Tests

When is it?
May and June

Test D: ACT

When is it?
April and June

What's the deal?
Tests B, C, and D are exams used by many colleges in their admissions processes.

Grade 12

TEST A: SAT REASONING TEST

WHEN IS IT?
October, November, and December

TEST B: SAT SUBJECT TESTS

WHEN IS IT?
October, November, and December

TEST C: ACT

WHEN IS IT?
October and December

WHAT'S THE DEAL?
Tests A, B, and C are exams used by many colleges in their admissions processes.

COLLEGE ENTRANCE EXAMS

Because these tests—ACT, PLAN, PSAT/NMSQT, SAT, and SAT Subjects Tests—cause many students a fair amount of anxiety, they warrant their own section. It's important to remember that, while these exams do play an important role in the college admissions process, they're just one facet of the process (and they're certainly less important than your high school record). More information about each test should make them, as a group, a little less scary.

College Board Exams

- **PSAT/NMSQT (Grades 10 and 11)**
  The first College Board test in the college admissions process is the PSAT/NMSQT. It tests your critical reading skills, math problem-solving skills, and writing skills.[8] It does so in two 25-minute Critical Reading sections (48 questions), two 25-minute Math

sections (38 questions), and one 30-minute Writing section (39 questions).[9] Prior to the administration of the PSAT/NMSQT, you should review information your school gives you about the exam. You should also complete sample questions at CollegeBoard.com/student/testing/psat/prep.html.

When your scores are returned in early December, you will receive "Score Report Plus" information that will help you understand you performance. Scores are reported for each section on a scale of 20–80. On each section, the average score for juniors is about 49. By adding the scores for the Critical Reading, Math, and Writing sections, a selection index (maximum 240) is generated. The average selection index for juniors is about 147.[10]

One of the main purposes of the PSAT/NMSQT is to give you practice in taking the SAT. (The SAT, however, will be longer and somewhat more difficult.) A second purpose is to allow you to estimate your SAT scores. By adding a zero to your score on each section, you can get some idea of how you might fare on the sections of the SAT. You can use these estimates to see how your scores compare with the profile of students admitted to colleges in which you are interested. If you do this, however, you should bear in mind you're only working with estimates and that test scores, in general, are only one of several factors in admission decisions.

It's important to note that PSAT/NMSQT scores are *not* used by colleges for admission purposes. The most important purpose of the test is to determine who is eligible to become a National Merit Scholarship semifinalist. In early September of your senior year, semifinalists, who usually receive scores well above 200, are announced. This group—about 16,000 students nationwide—must meet additional requirements to become finalists who will compete for about 8,000 National Merit Scholarships. A second, larger group of students— approximately 34,000, nationwide—receive letters of commendation later in the month. The latter group is not eligible to compete for National Merit Scholarships.[11]

- **SAT (Grades 11 and 12)**

  The SAT is neither an intelligence test to measure your innate capacity for learning nor an achievement test to indicate how much you have learned in an academic setting. Rather, according to CollegeBoard.org, "The SAT Reasoning Test is a measure of the critical-thinking skills you'll need for academic success in college. The SAT assesses how well you analyze and solve problems—skills you learned in school that you'll need in college." The nearly 4-hour SAT consists of the same sections as the PSAT/NMSQT. Each of the three sections has a score range of 200—800, allowing for a maximum total score of 2400.[12] The national mean scores for college-bound seniors in 2006 were 503 for Critical Reading, 518 for Mathematics, and 497 for Writing (1518 total).[13]

  If you take the SAT, it is recommended that you take it at least once in the spring of your junior year and then in the fall of your senior year. There is normally a score increase from junior to senior year. Though some students receive a lower total score when they repeat the test, colleges usually take the highest score in each category when making admissions decisions. To see a list of frequently asked questions about the SAT and answers to those questions, go to CollegeBoard.com/student/testing/sat/about/sat/FAQ.html

- **SAT Subject Tests (Grades 10–12)**

  Many selective colleges require SAT Subject Test scores. If a college does not require but strongly recommends that you take these exams, it would be wise to do so. As early as possible, check the catalogues of the institutions you are considering to make sure that you will meet their SAT Subject Test requirements by the application deadline. If you think you might apply Early Action or Early Decision (see Chapter 7) to one or more colleges, you should take three SAT Subject Tests by the end of your junior year; if you wait until fall of your senior year to take these exams, your scores may not be received by the schools in time. Even if you do not apply Early Action or Early Decision, however, you will need to take all of your SAT Subject Tests in the fall of your senior year to meet admissions deadlines for selective colleges, which tend to be the following spring.

Always discuss the decision to take an SAT Subject Test with your teacher for the subject *and* your counselor or advisor. If you can, take SAT Subject Tests in May or June, when you have just completed course work in areas covered by the exams you will take. If you have not studied a particular subject recently, you will need to review the subject before taking the test. You can repeat an SAT Subject Test, but you should do so only if you are certain that you are more prepared to take it the second time.

Registering for the SAT and SAT Subject Tests

While your school will register you for the PSAT/NMSQT (if it offers the test), it will be up to you to register for the SAT and SAT Subject Tests. Fortunately, registration for these tests is rather straightforward, and it is explained in detail in the SAT registration materials available at your school's guidance office. During the 11th grade, you should receive these registration forms along with student bulletins providing instructions for their completion. You may also register for the SAT and SAT Subject Tests online at CollegeBoard.org.

The following is good advice for the registration process:

- Use your full name and spell it the same way when you register for each test. Different spellings can create different records with College Board.

- Learn your high school's CEEB code. (This is an identification number issued to each high school by College Board.) Your CEEB code will be available in your school's guidance or counseling office.

- Carefully complete your SAT Questionnaire. The answers you provide will, according to College Board, give your counselors "information to use in assisting you with making future plans."[14]

- Check "yes" to the Student Search Service (SSS) when you register for the first SAT or SAT Subject Test of your junior year. When you do so, you will provide colleges, scholarship programs, and nonprofit educational organizations information from your SAT Questionnaire. Those seeking students like you will contact you with further information.[15]

ACT Exams

- **PLAN (Grades 9 and 10)**

  PLAN measures proficiency in four curriculum-based subject areas: English, math, reading, and science. According to ACT, "Your skills in these subjects will make a big difference—in school and, eventually, in your career . . . . [Y]our PLAN test results can show you where you're strong or weak." In addition, PLAN collects data to assess needs, explore career interests, and, later, provide college and scholarship information.[16]

  A couple of months following the exam, you will be provided a Student Score Report explaining your results and containing, according to ACT, "information about your skills, interests, plans, and goals . . . . You can use this information to make sure your remaining high school courses are the best ones possible to prepare you for college [and to] help you consider your options for after high school."[17] Details about PLAN, the report, and tips for taking this exam are available at ACTStudent.org/plan.

- **ACT (Grades 11 and 12)**

  According to information on ACT.org, the ACT is used to measure students' capacity for college-level work. In this way, it is very much like the SAT. The ACT, however, assesses a greater number of subject areas—English, math, reading, and science—and its writing test is optional.[18] Some believe that the ACT, which is scored on a scale of 1 to 36 for each of its four areas (these four scores are then averaged to create a composite score), enables you to score relatively higher than the SAT does.

  The ACT is widely accepted among colleges and universities. Nearly all colleges will accept the ACT in lieu of the SAT. In fact, many colleges prefer it. It's always a good idea to consult the catalogues or contact the admissions offices of colleges you are interested in to find out which test they prefer.

Reviewing Your Test Scores

Except for your PSAT/NMSQT and PLAN results, which will be given to you by your counselor in mid-December, your test scores will be sent directly to your home 4 to 7 weeks after the test date. Your school's guidance or counseling office will also receive your scores, and someone from this office should be available to discuss your scores with you. Along with your results, you will receive information that will help you interpret your scores. In particular, you will learn how you scored in comparison to students who have been accepted by the colleges for which you indicated interest during the test registration processes.

To "Prep" or Not to "Prep"

Test preparation can take many forms, from the review of vocabulary, grammar, and math, to instruction in test taking and problem solving. It can be intense or relaxed, formal or informal.

> "At a minimum, test preparation helps a student become familiar with the types of questions on a test. In many cases, test preparation is essentially concentrated study. I believe many large test-preparation companies are successful for many students simply because they impose rigor and discipline. If one is able to provide [his or her] own rigor and discipline, then a good test preparation guide may prove helpful."
>
> —Lawrence Rudner, PhD[19]

Opinions differ on the extent to which scores can be raised via preparation. College Board has historically argued that only small increases on the SAT can be gained through coaching. In 2002, however, a professor in the Mathematics Department at Quinnipiac College reported that he was able to raise the SAT math section scores of students in his own SAT-prep program by an average of 67 points.[20]

While the extent of their usefulness is debated, the fact is there are many online, print, and classroom-based resources available to high school students who want to "prep" for college entrance exams. Some high schools offer such resources as a part of their curriculum. (Even College Board, though it does not believe coaching can substantially raise scores, advertises an online course and print resources on its website.) However, for students in schools that do not offer such resources, or students looking to get an extra edge, there are numerous third-party programs that have a long history of effectiveness in preparing students for the SAT, ACT, and other college entrance exams.

The Princeton Review offers written test preparation resources, such as its *Cracking the SAT* guidebook, as well as private tutoring, small group tutoring, classroom courses,

> "Test preparation seminars vary, but it is clear that preparation for standardized tests is here to stay."
>
> —Thomas Seaton[21]

and online programs. It also offers free online practice tools for the PSAT/NMSQT, SAT, and ACT. Information about these resources is available through PrincetonReview.com/college/testprep.

In addition, The Princeton Review teams up with school districts serving ethnically and economically diverse students. Examples of such partnerships may be found via The Princeton Review website, at PrincetonReview.com/educators/guidance/caseStudy.asp. If your school doesn't currently offer students much help in preparing for college entrance exams, you may want to bring these efforts to the attention of your guidance or college counselor.

A Final Note on Testing

You should read information provided in College Board and ACT registration materials carefully. Answers to many questions can be found there. CollegeBoard.org and ACTstudent.org also provide much detailed information and allow you to register online for the exams.

Remember, while these exams are necessary to the college admissions process, your scores are only one of the factors considered in your admissions decisions. In many instances, you can also retake them if you're unhappy with your scores. Don't let entrance-exam apprehension mar what can be one of the most enjoyable times of your life!

Now that you have a greater understanding of the college admissions process, return to your journal for a moment. Make note of the things you have learned about college admissions *and* yourself that will be useful as you begin your search for activities and colleges that will suit you. You should also write down any questions you have about college selection and college entrance exams. Use all this in discussions with your counselor, your parents, and your peers as you plan and develop strategies for "getting involved" and "getting in."

The final stage of your "roadmap to college," specifically the process of applying for admission and financial aid, is covered later in this book. Now, let's look at your possibilities for precollege experiences.

ENDNOTES

1   Fiske, Edward B. and Bruce G. Hammond *The Fiske Guide to Getting into the Right College*. 2nd Edition. Naperville, IL: Sourcebooks, Inc., 2004. 147–8. Quoted in Cate School, "College Selectivity." www.cate.org/public/index.php?id=243.

2   Felder, Richard M. "Index of Learning Styles." North Carolina State University. www.ncsu.edu/felder-public/ILSpage.html.

3   Johansson, Charles B. "IDEAS: Interest Determination, Exploration and Assessment System." Pearson Assessments. 2007. www.pearsonassessments.com/tests/ideas.htm.

4   CPP, Inc. (formerly Consulting Psychologists Press). "Myers-Briggs Type Inventory Assessment." 2006. www.cpp.com/products/mbti/index.asp.

5   Campbell, David. "Campbell Interest and Skills Survey (CISS)." Pearson Assessments. 2007. www.pearsonassessments.com/tests/ciss.htm.

6   College Board. "About the SAT Subject Tests." 2007. www.collegeboard.com/student/testing/sat/about/SATII.html.

7   Index of Learning Styles. www.ncsu.edu/felder-public/ILSpage.html.

8   College Board. "About PSAT/NMSQT." 2007. www.collegeboard.com/student/testing/psat/about.html.

9   College Board. "What's on the Test." 2007. www.collegeboard.com/student/testing/psat/about/ontest.html.

10 College Board. "Scores & Review." 2007. www.collegeboard.com/student/testing/psat/scores.html.

11 National Merit Scholarship Corporation. "National Merit Scholarship Program." 2007. www.nationalmerit.org/nmsp.php.

12 College Board. "SAT Reasoning Test" 2007. www.collegeboard.com/student/testing/sat/about/SATI.html.

13 College Board. "SAT Average (Mean) Scores." 2007. www.collegeboard.com/student/testing/sat/scores/understanding/average.html.

14 College Board. "SAT Questionnaire." 2007. www.collegeboard.com/student/testing/sat/reg/quest.html.

15 College Board. "Student Search Service." 2007. www.collegeboard.com/student/testing/sat/reg/sss.html.

16 ACT, Inc. "The PLAN Test." 2007. http://actstudent.org/plan/tests/index.html.

17 ACT, Inc. "What Your Score Report Tells You." 2007. http://actstudent.org/plan/score/index.html.

18 ACT, Inc. "ACT Assessment: An ACT Program for Educational Planning." 2007. www.act.org/aap.

19 Clearinghouse on Assessment and Evaluation/Ericae.net. "Finding Test Preparation Materials." Clearinghouse on Assessment and Evaluation/Ericae.net. 1999–2005. http://ericae.net/faqs/testprep.htm#Comment.

20 FairTest Examiner. "Study: SAT Coaching Raises Scores." http://fairtest.org/examarts/Spring%2002/SAT%20Coaching.html.

21 Seaton, Thomas. "The Effectiveness of Test Preparation Seminars on Performance on Standardized Achievement Tests." 1992. ERIC #ED356233. 1999–2005. 12. http://ericae.net/faqs/testprep.htm#ecites.

CHAPTER 3

AFTER SCHOOL
AND IN THE COMMUNITY

Believe it or not, occasional breaks from school work can play a huge part in a successful college experience. In fact, they can play a huge part in getting into college! Now that you've learned a little about self-assessment and the college admissions process, it's time to think about activities that can maximize your out-of-school time and provide you with life-enriching experiences.

> "What if becoming who and what we truly are happens not through striving and trying but by recognizing and receiving the people and places and practices that offer us the warmth of encouragement we need to unfold? "
>
> —Oriah Mountain Dreamer from *Your Heart's Prayer: Following the Thread of Desire into a Deeper Life*[1]

This chapter will address co- and extracurricular activities that are provided by schools and communities throughout the United States. Be sure to have your journal handy to record information about the various programs that interest you, as well as your ideas or plans for engaging in them. You should also use your journal entries and your responses to the Self-Assessment Surveys in Chapter 1 to help you decide which activities suit you best.

OUT-OF-SCHOOL TIME

The Forum for Youth Investment (the Forum) is a nonprofit organization that, according to its website, "help[s] communities and the nation make sure all young people are *Ready by 21—ready for college, work, and life*." In keeping with its mission, the organization "provides youth and adult leaders with the information, technical assistance, training, network support, and partnership opportunities needed to increase the quality and quantity of youth investment and youth involvement."[2] Data that the organization collected on the way teens spend their out-of-school time suggests that 60 percent of America's high school seniors work at paid jobs for seven or more hours a week during the school year. Of these students, 80 percent report involvement in at least one school-based co- or extracurricular activity, such as sports, performing arts, and academic clubs. Additionally, 67 percent of high school students say they are engaged in community service through their school, church, or another community-based organization. As you can gather from these statistics, a student's life doesn't quiet with the day's final bell. This is a good thing, as a healthy number of activities is strongly linked with overall success. Simply put: The more you do, the more you want to do.

To give you an idea of what to expect from afterschool programs, the January 2003 issue of the Forum's "Out-of-School Time Commentary Series," listed seven general categories of programs.

- Academic support/mentoring (afterschool programs that place an emphasis on academics)

- Service-learning (volunteer experience)

- Youth empowerment/organizing (programs that give students the opportunity to form organizations that employ valuable academic skills such as critical thinking and research)

- Employment/career development (mentor-driven internships in a variety of professions)

- Recreation (a wide array of sports and athletics)

- Prevention (a combination of afterschool programs, which serves to encourage students to support a healthy lifestyle)

- Culture, arts, and media (a series of programs that challenge students to use artistic mediums to express their ideas and perspectives)[3]

The above list should give you a picture of the various types of afterschool opportunities that exist, and perhaps even some ideas for new directions you and your school could take when it comes to co- and extracurricular activities. For further information, check out the Forum's website at ForumForYouthInvestment.org.

The Not-So-Secret Link Between Activities and College Admission

So how does making the most of the co- and extracurricular opportunities in your school and community relate to getting into the college of your dreams? The answer is simple: Colleges love a well-rounded student. This means that a few well-chosen activities—when combined with an impressive academic record—go a long way with admissions officers.

In the previous chapter, you learned that you should challenge yourself by taking harder classes (whenever possible, you should elect honors-level and Advanced Placement courses); don't fool yourself into thinking that the easy route is the safest! The decision to challenge yourself not only reflects your character and maturity, but also sends a message to college admissions officers that you're an ambitious and dedicated student—two qualities that add up to success when it comes to college-level work.

The same principle applies to co- and extracurricular activities. Provided in large part for students' benefit, these activities play an integral part in the mental, physical, and emotional development of young people. In fact, they have been proven to teach cooperation and teamwork, promote initiative and leadership, enhance critical thinking, and reinforce learning that takes place in the classroom. Selective colleges *expect* to admit students who have engaged purposefully in such activities and who show evidence of these experiences in their character and studies. Just as with academics, you should look for a challenge. What you give is what you get, and a complete commitment to an activity will pay off come graduation day.

The University of Chicago Laboratory Schools—a private high school associated with the university—posts on its website its philosophy regarding student activities: "Opportunity is the keynote of the Student Activities Program . . . in fact, the very existence of such groups is dependent upon student interest and initiative. Through opportunities for the pursuit of varied interests students are challenged to learn how to work together. They learn to originate, plan, and execute activities. Their success is measured in terms not only of tangible results, but also of the personal growth of participants as individuals and as contributing members of a larger society."[4]

If you took the Self-Assessment Surveys in Chapter 1, you have a record of your academic performance, interests, and talents to date, as well as a list of the activities that you're currently involved in. If you did not take these surveys, it is strongly suggested that you do so now. Armed with the self-awareness these surveys provide, you can stretch yourself a bit by expanding your interests and looking for ways to build on the experiences you have had up to this point.

You should make deliberate choices about your activities, and participate in those that appeal to you most, even if they represent unfamiliar territory. By doing so, you will both broaden your horizons and deepen your knowledge, thus increasing your appeal come college admissions time. Of course, signing up for activities that interest you is just the first step. Your approach to them is crucial. Even if you're already considering specific colleges, you shouldn't think of your activities as bargaining chips in the admissions process. If you do, you'll largely miss the personal benefits they can provide. Approach each one as a vehicle to assist you in gaining knowledge, building character, and developing new skills.

So Much to Do, So Little Time . . .

The following sections offer descriptions of school- and community-based activities widely available in the United States and Canada. Since many schools partner with a variety of organizations to offer students the opportunity to participate in a large selection of programs, the line between school- and community-based programs is frequently blurred. However, a strict dichotomy here isn't all that important—what's more important is the number and variety of opportunities that a school or town offers its students.

As you read the offerings below, jot down in your journal those that appeal to you. Which are available in your school or community? If you find an opportunity that interests you but is not available in your area, you might take the initiative to start it yourself—colleges love a self-starter! (For tips on how to start your own program, check out Chapter 5.)

All Things Academic

Academic Bowls

Many schools offer opportunities for bright students to put their knowledge to the test in academic bowls. Students generally compete in teams and demonstrate their academic savvy by answering questions on a variety of subjects, including mathematics, science, history, and the humanities. There are also academic bowls in specific fields.

Computer/Technology Training and Clubs

In addition to classes in computer technology, many high schools provide students with a variety of internships and student assistantships as options for further experience in the field. Many also have a computer or technology club where students can share ideas and interests while taking part in activities—both in and out of school—that will enrich their understanding and prepare them for future careers.

Honor Societies

They're called honor societies because it's an honor to be part of them. Well, that and they reward your academic efforts with a fun, social environment and opportunities for service, leadership, and scholarship. Below are a few of the more popular societies.

- **National Honor Society**

  Founded in 1921 by the National Association of Secondary School Principals, the National Honor Society (NHS) now includes more than a million members. Each year, NHS inducts outstanding high school students who have demonstrated excellence in the areas of scholarship, leadership, service, and character. Eligibility for membership in the organization is determined by national standards enforced by school or local chapters. Those who receive membership agree to abide by those standards and to continue to involve themselves in serving their school and community.[5]

- **National Beta Club**

  The National Beta Club was established in 1934 with just 15 members, a far cry from today's 417,000 members and 5.2 million alumni. The specific academic standards for membership in the organization are determined by the school or school district. In order to be considered for Beta Club, students must achieve at or above grade level and exhibit "moral and ethical character, good mentality, creditable achievement, and commendable attitude."[6] Beta Club's objectives include the recognition of excellence in achievement as well as the promotion of character, leadership development, and student involvement in school and community service. In addition, the organization encourages the use of modern technology and offers a variety of advantages in this area. And last but not least, members are presented with a number of scholarship opportunities.[7]

- **Cum Laude Society**

  "Areté, Diké, Timé (Excellence, Justice, Honor)." These are the principles that govern the members of the Cum Laude Society, a national academic honor society. (Note: Schools may have both a Cum Laude Society and a National Honor Society—if you're really ambitious, you could try joining both!) According to the organization's website, "The presence of a Cum Laude chapter at a secondary school is an indication that superior scholastic achievement is honored." The induction ceremony can range from a formal, stand-alone event to a presentation at an awards-day program. Individual Cum Laude chapters promote various activities, including service projects, scholarly writing, and other works appropriate for their campus. Activities are also designed to benefit the local community as well as the school community.[8]

- **Governor's Honors Programs/Governor's Schools**

  A number of states in the U.S. offer Governor's Honors programs or Governor's Schools each summer. These programs usually allow students to take part in an academically advanced program of study in the humanities, arts, and sciences with their peers at a nearby college. The program can last anywhere from one week to the entire summer. The availability of these programs in your state is entirely dependent on your state's governmental representatives, while eligibility for participation (if your state does indeed have such a program) is usually dependent on schools' nomination of students. After nomination, selected students compete for admission into their state's program. What if your state doesn't fund this type of program, you ask? Petition them to do so! With a little help from your fellow constituents—i.e., the residents of your state—you could have yet another opportunity on your proverbial doorstep.[9] For more information on these programs, visit the National Conference of Governor's Schools website, NCOGS.org.

- **Language Honor Societies**

  Phi Sigma Iota International Foreign Language Honor Society, a widely respected language organization in the academic community, "recognizes outstanding ability and high standards of students and faculty of foreign languages, literatures, and cultures (including classics, linguistics, philology, comparative literature, ESL, bilingual education, and second language acquisition)."[10] For more information on high school foreign language honor societies, check out the Phi Sigma Iota website (PhiSigmaIota.org) and the website of the American Council on Teaching Foreign Languages (ACTFL.org). You can also talk to your language teacher.

Junior Engineering Technical Society (JETS)

This organization's motto, "Opening the world of engineering to students, parents, and educators," illustrates its goal of providing "Real-World Engineering Insight and Challenges for High School Students . . . to increase interest and awareness of engineering and technology-based careers—with student competitions, assessment tools, career guidance resources, an e-newsletter, and more." The result of such a program, JETS says, is exciting students "about careers in engineering and related technical fields," and helping them "understand the critical role engineers play in the world around us."[11] If your school doesn't have a JETS Club, you can join the organization as a club leader and organize a group of your schoolmates and teachers to participate in it. Alternatively, a teacher or a parent can start up the club. For more information about JETS, visit JETS.org.

Language Clubs

These clubs complement schools' foreign language academics. Popular language clubs in the U.S. and Canada include French, German, Japanese, Latin, and Spanish. Going beyond language, these clubs connect students with foreign customs and culture, and may sponsor field trips or international travel experiences. But language comes first: Clubs often require that students only speak in the foreign language during club meetings and gatherings.

Literary Clubs

Think of literary club as a book club—only it's not Oprah's, it's your own. Students involved these clubs choose and read literary works for group discussion. Some clubs even select student work to read and review as a group.

Math Teams

Many high schools offer team-based competition in mathematics. Teams of outstanding math students compete with students from other schools or school districts in the hope of securing a chance to compete in regional and national competitions.

In recent years, schools have become involved in projects to bridge via cyberspace any physical distances between teams. An example of this is Drexel University's Virtual Math Teams (VMT) project. VMT provides grammar and high school students with opportunities to interact online with math students throughout the nation.[12]

Visual and Performing Arts

If you have an affinity for the visual or performing arts, taking part in co- or extracurricular activities in this area is a must. Besides offering you an environment where you can foster your creative vision, these activities provide a network—networks and networking are discussed in detail in Chapter 6—that can be a boon to both your art career *and* your social life. (Just keep in mind that some activities require auditions, so check beforehand and polish up on your skills.) According to the Devon Arts in Schools Initiative—a UK-based organization that supports the arts programs in schools—some additional benefits of arts programs and activities are an increase in art appreciation, growth of students' self-esteem, and the strengthening of ties between schools, families, and the community.[13]

Check out the below list of visual and performing arts activities to see what interests you.

VISUAL AND PERFORMING ARTS ACTIVITIES

Art Club/Art Guild	Glee Club
Art History Club	Jazz Club
Film Society	Orchestra
Photography Club	Dance Club
Band	Drama Club
Chorus	Thespian Society
Drill Team	Theater
Drum and Bugle Corps	Technical Theater
	(Sound, Stage, Lighting, Wardrobe, etc.)

ATHLETICS

Sports are a great way to get exercise, have fun, make friends, and impress colleges. So what are you waiting for? Play ball!

- **Intermural Sports (Varsity and Junior Varsity)**

The *varsity* team is the principal athletic team that represents an institution in a given sport in interschool competition. If there is a second tier, it's the *junior varsity* (JV) team. JV players are generally younger, less experienced athletes for whom participation at the JV level often serves as preparation for varsity-level sports. Think of them as top-seeded amateurs, while varsity encompasses the pros.

The most popular way for rival schools to compete against each other is on the playing field. You can probably join some of your school's teams simply by expressing an interest; others will require you to try out. Intermural sports are governed by state high school athletic associations that set policies and establish standards for student participation. Schools or school districts may also impose academic and behavioral standards for participation, meaning that you can't experience gridiron glory without an equal number of academic victories.

INTERMURAL SPORTS

The variety of intermural sports available is dependent on each school, though you can usually find at least some, if not all (or more), of the following:

Baseball	Lacrosse
Basketball	Soccer
Cheerleading	Softball
Crew	Swimming
Cross-country	Tennis
Football	Track & Field
Field Hockey	Volleyball
Equestrian	Water Polo
Golf	Wrestling
Ice Hockey	

Competitive sports can be a very rewarding. While not everyone can be a star athlete, building a healthy body and developing character through competition and teamwork are excellent reasons to participate. It's also a great way to meet and hang out with friends.

- **Intramural ("Club") Sports**

  Club sports are played largely for enjoyment and skill development, rather than for competitive purposes. These programs only involve students from a single school and are not regulated by high school athletic governing organizations.

They don't afford students formal recognition—no letterman's jackets here. What they do offer is a much more social and relaxed athletic environment for those who simply want to play. Many sports with varsity teams will also be offered at the club-sport level at a given school. At most high schools, however, there will be sports particular to the club-sport level.

COMMON INTRAMURAL SPORTS

Badminton	Olympiad
Biking	Paintball
Billiards/Pool	Racquetball
Bowling	Rifle Club/Riflery
Dance	Skateboarding
Fitness/Weight training	Ski Club
Flag football	Table Tennis
In-line skating/In-line hockey	Ultimate Frisbee

Participating in club sport is a great way to exercise, relieve stress, and make new friends. Why not find a club sport that interests you?

JUNIOR RESERVE OFFICERS TRAINING CORPS (JROTC) AND COLOR GUARD

JROTC is a program for high school students funded by the U.S. Army, Navy, Air Force, and Marines. The goal of JROTC is "to instill in students in United States secondary educational institutions the values of citizenship, service to the United States, and personal responsibility [as well as] a sense of accomplishment."[14] Offered as an elective at more than 3,000 American high schools, the program serves nearly 400,000 students across the nation.[15] If there is a JROTC unit at a given school, the Color guard—a group that performs with the marching band at athletic events (it's the group with the flags)—will be comprised of its officers, who will the carry flags in accordance with their chain of command. (In the absence of a JROTC unit at a school, the Color guard is composed of "civilian" students.) Typically these flags include the national flag, a unit flag, and a military departmental flag. The Color guard sometimes even includes two rifle bearers, though this is largely dependent on school district policy.[16]

LEADERSHIP AND CITIZENSHIP PROGRAMS

Numerous leadership development programs are offered throughout the school year as well as during the summer. In certain schools and states, leadership programs are even offered as a part of the curriculum. The Leadership Training Institute at John F. Kennedy Academy in Silver Spring, Maryland and Leadership for the 21st Century—a leadership training curriculum for the Virginia Public Schools—are two such programs. Programs of this type generally offer instruction in leadership theory as well as experiential learning, role-model study, and training in conflict management and group decision-making.

Other types of leadership development programs unite groups of students from different schools and communities through a learning experience that involves lectures, interaction with established leaders, and opportunities to practice their newfound skills in the real world. Below are a few examples of this type of program.

"We are not called to be popular,
we are not called to be safe,
we are not called to follow,
we are the ones called to take risks,
we are the ones called to change
    attitudes;
to risk displeasures,
we are the ones called to gamble
    our lives,
for a better world."

—Mary Lou Anderson
(from "Leadership")[17]

- **Close-Up Foundation**

  The Close Up Foundation offers a variety of civic programs endorsed by NASSP and the National Council for the Social Studies. Since 1970, the organization has held true to its mission to provide programs that foster the understanding of and active participation in the democratic process. In particular, students focus on the roles participation, education, communication, and citizenship play in successful democracies. As you'd expect of such a politically oriented program, the majority of opportunities are available in Washington, DC. That doesn't mean, however, that you can't find Close Up closer to home with a local or state government (or that you won't be able to participate in a Close Up student trip to the nation's capital). Check out the foundation's website, CloseUp.org, for more information.[18]

  Not surprisingly, participation in Close Up has a way of changing lives. Kimbrell Teegarden—a young woman who is now assistant chaplain and a member of the college counseling team at The Westminster Schools in Atlanta, Georgia (she was previously a student there)—attributes a good deal of her personal growth to her participation in Close Up:

  As a Westminster student, I went with a group of my schoolmates to Washington, DC for a week with the Close Up program as a sophomore. This experience opened my eyes to the excitement of politics and the energy of DC. I ended up applying and being selected to be a Congressional page during my junior year. Some kids stayed for the entire school year but I was only there for the semester-long program in the fall semester. In my program, we attended school in the Library of Congress in the early mornings and worked the rest of the day on Capitol Hill, usually on the house floor. It was really exciting!

  This experience led me to successfully apply to Georgetown University, a wonderful school—but not exactly what I ended up wanting from my college experience. I stayed there a year and utilized much of my time in DC by working as an intern for my Congressman. I then transferred to the University of Georgia where I graduated with a Political Science degree. I ended up interning during my junior year of college, as well—this time at the Georgia State Legislature. I was very happy with my college experience and with all the experiences that my different paths allowed me.

Kimbrell recently received her Master of Divinity. She notes that, while she had planned to study law and pursue a career in politics, she eventually realized she'd be happier utilizing her citizenship education and desire to serve society through her faith, rather than a background in law. She attributes the self-awareness that allowed her to change direction largely to the opportunities and experiences the Close Up Foundation made possible, as well as the wise counsel of her parents, mentors, and friends.

If you are interested in participating in a Close Up program, talk to your social studies teacher. If such an activity is not already available at your school, perhaps you can be instrumental in organizing it!

- **Hugh O'Brian Youth Leadership (HOBY)**

  HOBY is one of the most popular and prestigious leadership programs in America, with a long history of motivating and empowering "individuals to make a positive difference within our global society through understanding and action, based on effective and compassionate leadership."[19]

  Endorsed by the National Association of Secondary School Principals (NASSP), HOBY offers leadership seminars for high school sophomores every year. Participating students are chosen by their schools to take part in the program. The standards for selection are set by individual schools and districts and are based on HOBY guidelines. Students travel from all over the world to participate in HOBY seminars, each one dealing with a specific theme (e.g., the democratic system and entrepreneurship, education, leadership for service, media and communications, or the future of our society). All this is applied, in the organization's words, "to teach you how to think, not what to think."[20]

- **National 4-H Council**

  According to its website, the mission of the National 4-H Council is "to advance the 4-H youth development movement to build a world in which youth and adults learn, grow, and work together as catalysts for positive change." This well-known organization currently boasts some 538,000 volunteers and 60 million alumni who share a history of participation "in fun, hands-on learning activities supported by the latest research of land-grant universities"; these activities "are focused on three areas: healthy living, citizenship, and science, engineering and technology."[21]

Many of the foundation's initial projects were focused on enhancing the lives of rural young people, so it's no surprise that agriculture is the first thing that springs to mind when 4-H is mentioned. And while this is still a part of 4-H, the focus nowadays is much broader, encompassing science, engineering, and technology. All of these areas of study are explored within the framework of 4-H's objectives of developing leadership skills, personal responsibility, self-confidence, and a volunteer ethic.[22]

SCHOOL SERVICE AND LEADERSHIP OPPORTUUNITIES

Students looking to take a proactive role in their school's development can do so in a multitude of ways. Programs available to students provide opportunities for event planning, tutoring, conflict mediation, and other tasks crucial to the maintenance of a healthy school community. If you'd like to pitch in, talk to your school's administration to see what is available and what you need to do to apply.

FOUR OF A KIND

Ever wonder where the name "4-H" came from? It comes from the organization's pledge: "I pledge my head to clearer thinking, my heart to greater loyalty, my hands to larger service, and my health to better living—for my club, my community, my country, and my world."

—National 4-H Council[23]

Student Government

Through addressing your peers' ideas and concerns and by putting plans into action, you can help to provide your classmates with a rewarding high school experience. Class officers—such as president, vice president, and treasurer—play an integral role in shaping events and community service projects for their class year. Student council members work directly with their school's administration to encourage and support student involvement in administrative decisions that will affect them. Not sure if student government is for you? Get a taste of it by holding a leadership position in a club or activity.

Peer Helpers

In a number of schools, certain 10th and 11th grade students are selected and trained to serve as peer helpers to assist the school administration in meeting the needs of students. Peer helpers can mediate conflict and facilitate discussion between students. In some cases, these students are assigned as mentors to a particular group of students who remain under their wing until the peer helper graduates. Serving your school as a peer helper can be an extremely rewarding experience, challenging you to develop impressive interpersonal skills and problem-solving abilities that will pay off in your studies and life.

Lower/Middle School and Peer Tutoring

Elementary, middle, and high school students often need help in reading, math, the arts, and other subject areas. Increasingly, high schools are encouraging their students to share their spare time with the school community by tutoring younger students and classmates. Rebecca, a sophomore honor student at a public school in southwestern Michigan, has been tutoring other students since the 6th grade. She explains, "I love tutoring younger kids and my classmates in subjects that are easy for me—like math, science, and Spanish . . . . Nothing is more fun than seeing a kid go from crying because a subject is 'just too hard' to smiling when they finally 'get it!'"

Student Ambassadors

At many high schools, student ambassadors play a pivotal role in helping new students to make a smooth transition. They also encourage current students to get involved and stay in school and, generally, represent a positive perspective on student life at the school. At independent and parochial schools, student ambassadors often assist in the recruitment of new students by serving as tour guides or hosts to prospective students and their families.

Spirit Club

School spirit is vital to a positive high school environment. Sometimes called pep squads, spirit clubs work to ensure support for school activities, such as athletics. These groups may organize pep rallies or tailgate parties, decorate the school for athletic or social events, or organize fundraising drives. Spirit Club can be hard work, but it is also just plain fun!

COOPERATIVE/DISTRIBUTIVE EDUCATION PROGRAMS

Many schools offer students opportunities to participate in supervised work environments outside of school. Cooperative (co-op) education programs allow students to earn academic credit for work performed in a business setting; distributive education (D.E.) programs supplement specific academic work—which may include vocational instruction—with on-the-job training. Many public high schools offer both co-op and D.E. programs. In both types of programs, students are paid for their work. Below are two organizations that advocate opportunities of this type.

- **National Commission for Cooperative Education (NCCE)**

  Established in 1962, NCCE is a nonprofit organization that promotes cooperative education in the United States. Today, it accomplishes this aim primarily by fostering research partnerships between businesses and colleges. In addition to its various research projects, NCCE offers high school students competitive scholarships. Visit Co-op.edu/scholarships.htm for more information.[24]

- **DECA**

  DECA is a nonprofit distributive education organization that serves teachers, administrators, and more than 200,000 high school and college students. Founded in the late 1940s to enhance students' education and career options, DECA now has over 5,000 chapters building partnerships between business and education. The organization works to prepare students for marketing and business careers by providing leadership training, encouraging self-esteem, and promoting community service. It also offers scholarships and competitive activities for students. Some of its most popular activities are its Sunkist Challenge, Stock Market Game, and Virtual Business Challenge.[25]

  If you are interested in a career in business, distributive education is a fine way to get your foot in the door. Ask your counselor or business education teacher about the possibility of joining or starting a DECA chapter at your school.

OTHER SUBJECT-AREA GROUPS

If you haven't found anything that really piques your interest so far, don't worry! There are literally hundreds of opportunities available in a wide range of fields. Other subject-area clubs take a more specialized approach than the ones mentioned above and focus on a specific subject within a larger discipline. Some even combine two different clubs into one. An example of the latter is the Spanish Chorus and Glee Club at an independent school in Florida. Some musically-inclined students in second- and third-year Spanish started this group in an effort to combine their separate interests in music and Spanish. The result: A *rock en español* band complete with choreographed Latin dance routines!

Activities highlighting a specific area of science, math, social studies, art, music, or another subject may be just the thing to spark your interest. Think about what your talents are and how you would like to develop them. Do some independent research to figure out where your interests and skills might lie.

STUDENT PUBLICATIONS

For the budding writers, poets, and journalists out there, this is your chance to put it in ink!

Literary Magazine

Most schools publish a periodical that includes student and faculty writing as well as art, offering ambitious writers a great opportunity to showcase their work. This activity differs significantly from a literary club in that it involves the publication of student and faculty work as opposed to reading and responding to literature. Students who collaborate on the creation a literary magazine not only exercise their creative skills, they also gain valuable skills in organization, decision-making, research, marketing, and book publishing.

School Newspaper

When high schools need the news, they turn to the school newspaper. More than a quality read, the school paper is a fine opportunity for students to learn and develop journalism and leadership skills. As you would expect, teamwork is the linchpin of a quality paper. With a staff of reporters, copywriters, editors, layout artists, graphic designers, and more, students have to pull together this make this good ship sail. What do they get for their hard work? The satisfaction of making a difference in the school community, earning valuable professional skills, and having a fun experience—all at once.

Newsletters

Similar to the school newspaper, newsletters set their sights on specific departments or activities at a school—such as athletics, the arts, or community service—and provide information about events and issues of interest to the student population. Getting involved with an existing newsletter—or creating a new one—can provide you with an exceptional opportunity for teamwork, leadership, and a deeper engagement in your school community.

Yearbook

Published annually, this publication is an important part of school life. (There's a reason people hold on to these years after they've graduated!) It not only records the year's activities involving each grade level, but includes pictures of each student and faculty member, along with photographs of key events. Generally released at the end of each school year, the senior class is highlighted. The yearbook becomes a paperbound vault of memories and serves as a reference point for many alumni for the rest of their lives. Like other school publications, it affords those who participate great training and production experience.

SPEECH/DEBATE/FORENSICS

These clubs are all talk—literally! If you fancy yourself a town crier or a future orator, the activities described below are great ways to hone your skills.

Speech Club

Speech Club provides a venue for students to combine their creative talents and verbal communication skills. Participating students practice the art of public speaking, learn parliamentary procedure (Roberts Rules of Order), and study performances of history's great orators. If you're interested in a career in law, politics, the media, or another field that relies on public speaking, this type of activity is a great way to test your public voice.

Literary Interpretation Team

In this activity, teams of students compete against each other through oral interpretations of poetry, prose, plays, and film. Students who are also involved in theater often enjoy using their dramatic skills in competition. Some of the most skilled and successful in literary interpreters, however, come from a debating perspective—it's all about convincing your audience of your point.

Debate Team

One definition of forensics is "the art or study of argumentative discourse."[26] Debate, an aspect of forensics, is defined as "a regulated discussion of a proposition between two matched sides."[27] Put these two together and you've got yourself a debate team! These teams engage in competitive argument against other teams on issues of societal and global importance. With skillful discourse, they argue out either side of an issue with factual information, scoring points for accuracy and strength of argument.

Debate is a popular co-curricular activity at the college level. Therefore, skillful debaters who show passion for their experience in this activity are attractive college applicants. If you like to argue—not quarrel!—over issues, this may be a perfect activity for you.

Mock Trial

The College of William & Mary, on its website, explains mock trial as "a competition in which two teams try a criminal or civil case against each other, with one team as the prosecution (plaintiff) and one team as the defense. In competition, the students use the Federal Rules of Evidence, along with a number of case strategies, in order to simulate an actual trial experience. Students play both attorneys and witnesses; attorneys are responsible for direct examinations, cross examinations, openings and closings, while witnesses participate in direct examination and cross."[28]

If you have an interest in studying law, mock trial is a great way to participate in something that will give you insight into the profession while, at the same time, developing your communication skills.

SPECIAL INTEREST GROUPS

In addition to traditional co- and extracurricular opportunities, many schools offer clubs that address students' diverse interests and passions. This section features a number of clubs that you might find at your high school. If a group below interests you but is not offered at your school, why not start it yourself? All it takes is a little initiative.

Amnesty International

Amnesty International (AI) is a worldwide movement of people who campaign for international human rights. AI's vision is for "a world in which every person enjoys all of the human rights enshrined in the *Universal Declaration of Human Rights* and other international human rights standards." Its research and activity center are dedicated to alleviating worldwide human suffering, unlawful censorship and imprisonment, discrimination, and any other human rights offenses.[29]

Schools all over the world have chapters of AI. For more information on how you can help, visit Web.Amnesty.org/pages/aboutai-index-eng.

Chess Club

Think you could give Garry Kasparov a run for his money? How about Deep Blue? Not yet? No worries, you can practice after school.

Cultural Awareness Organizations

Most schools work hard to promote harmony and understanding among students of different ethnic, religious, national, or socioeconomic backgrounds. And for good reason—even in schools where there is little diversity, it's important that students are educated about different cultures. In fact, colleges highly value evidence of cultural awareness and experiences in diversity as it makes for a more well-rounded and mature individual. Cultural awareness organizations are excellent opportunities to learn about the world, demonstrate character, develop leadership skills, and make new friends.

Additionally, some schools support affinity groups—clubs or organizations centered on a particular culture, ethnicity, or religion. One such example is The ASPIRA Association, a national nonprofit organization devoted to the education and leadership development of Puerto Rican and other Latino youth.[30]

Environmental Awareness

Environmental science and environmental awareness clubs are popular activities in many schools. These groups focus their discussions and activities on understanding and resolving major issues such as recycling; forest, wetland, and energy conservation; global warming; and hazardous waste, mercury, pesticide, and pollution control—which are all major issues for the human race, not to mention the planet. For more information on protecting our environment or to learn more about environmental issues, the Wallerstein Collaborative for Urban Environmental Education, located in the Steinhardt School of Education at New York University, is an excellent resource. Their website features a number of links for further information on internships, careers, education, and resources in the environmental field. Check it out at Steinhardt.NYU.edu/wallerstein.[31]

Global Emergency Response

The events of 9/11, Hurricane Katrina, the Indian Ocean tsunami, and other emergencies around the world have made us all too aware of the need for a timely response to such occurrences. While there is no way to fully prepare for these tragic events, we can learn how to better prepare ourselves for—and respond more effectively to—the aftermath of these disasters. In line with this, many students have created groups or started fundraisers to address such issues. Take Jack, an 11th-grade student in the Southeast during the 2004 tsunami. In the aftermath of that disaster, hundreds of thousands of survivors were without drinkable water due to severe contamination of wells and not enough supplies from emergency response teams. In reaction to this, Jack spoke to the school during an assembly and described the tsunami survivors' situation and their need for immediate help. As a result of his actions, the school raised thousands of dollars to buy and transport water to the victims—a truly lifesaving move.

A HOBY alumnus (see the previous section on leadership and citizenship programs), Jack currently attends a prestigious Southeastern university. However, he will be long remembered in his former school community as someone whose compassion and commitment to serving others made a difference through his response to a global emergency.

Patagonia

Patagonia clubs derive their name from the rugged South American landscape famed for its unlimited offering of outdoor adventures. As you'd expect, these clubs focus on seeking exercise in the natural world. Activities like mountain biking, skiing, rock climbing, rappelling, snowboarding, paddling, rafting, hiking, camping, and many more reign supreme. So put on your boots, bring your helmet and board, and have some fun!

Political Groups

High school political interest groups provide an excellent way for students to test their political aspirations. Many schools have chapters or clubs that support political parties or serve to keep the student body informed about what is taking place on the local, state, or national political fronts. Common student-led organizations include Young Democrats, Young Republicans, Young Independents, and Political Awareness Club.

Pre-professional Interest Groups

Pre-professional interest groups and organizations are a great way to explore career options and develop relationships with potential mentors. Through guest speakers, shadow experiences, field trips, and other exciting experiences, students are able to build partnerships with professional organizations—something that comes in very handy when they start looking for jobs.

POPULAR PRE-PROFESSIONAL INTEREST GROUPS

The following are some of the more popular pre-professional interest groups found in high schools:

Future Architects

Future Business Leaders

Future Certified Public Accountants

Future Filmmakers

Future Information Technologists

Future Journalists

Future Lawyers

Future Physicians

Future Playwrights/Screenwriters

Future Teachers

Video Game Club

Video game enthusiasts and those interested in a career in video game design don't usually have much trouble when it comes to forming a group (that's why consoles have at least two controllers, right?). Over the past decade video game clubs have cropped up in many high schools. These groups discuss and swap current games among themselves and sometimes even design new ones. If they're lucky enough to live near a gaming company, well-organized groups can take advantage of opportunities to be new-game testers. Others might organize video game tournaments within their schools or in the local community. If you're an avid gamer, joining or starting a video game club is a must!

World Affairs Council

Some schools in the United States are members of the World Affairs Councils of America (WACA). WACA is a non-partisan foreign affairs forum that serves students, public institutions, and individuals through over 2,500 events, educational activities, international visitor programs, and other experiences designed to foster the understanding of global issues and engagement in international exchange. With nearly half a million active participants and 26 affiliates, WACA provides services to some 20 million people.[32] For more information, visit WACA's website, WorldAffairsCouncils.org.

Local Community Service

The majority of the co- and extracurricular activities outlined in this chapter thus far have been school-sponsored. However, there are also many opportunities to get directly involved with meaningful and educational program in your community. Below are some examples of programs that serve the community-at-large. While these organizations often partner with high schools, in most cases students can participate in these programs independently of their schools.

> "We cannot always build the future for our youth, but we can build our youth for the future."
>
> —Franklin Delano Roosevelt[33]

- **Habitat for Humanity**

    Since its founding in 1976, Habitat for Humanity has built more than 200,000 houses around the world to provide a financially viable and compassionate solution to families faced with housing problems. According to the organization, "5.1 million American families have 'worst-case' housing needs, forced to pay more than half their income for housing, endure overcrowded conditions and/or live in houses with severe physical deficiencies. While the number of families in poverty is growing, the number of affordable rental units is shrinking, and most families who qualify for government housing assistance aren't receiving any aid."[34] In a noble effort to solve this crisis, Habitat for Humanity seeks to eliminate impoverished housing conditions and homelessness by refurbishing or building houses for families in need. The organization is able to do this thanks to a wide support network of volunteers and donors who make shelter a matter of conscience and action. After completion, Habitat houses are sold to partner families at no profit and financed with affordable loans. From there, the homeowners' monthly mortgage payments are used to build additional Habitat houses so that those who have been helped play an active role in those that will get help.[35] You can get involved in your community by going to Habitat.org.

- **Key Club International**

  Founded in 1925, Key Club International is the "oldest and largest service program for high school students" and seeks to provide its members "with opportunities to provide service, build character, and develop leadership." This is achieved through a variety of activities designed to support and enhance members' schools and communities through volunteer work, partnerships, and citizenship. The key to the Key Club is instilling leadership through serving others, in effect learning by doing.

  Today, Key Club exists in more than 5,000 high schools, primarily in the United States and Canada. It is funded by nominal dues paid by every member. Its officers are high school leaders elected by members during district and international conventions. At every high school, Key Club members work to promote respect, self-esteem, fair play, and positive citizenship—qualities that are quick to translate into college admissions upon graduation. Also among the benefits of membership in Key Club are opportunities for college scholarships and vocational guidance.[36] Learn more at KeyClub.org.

- **Red Cross**

  Since 1881, the American Red Cross has played an invaluable role in serving the nation through times of war and peace, providing help whenever and wherever needed. In 1917, the Junior Red Cross was born; today, individuals ages 24 and under comprise 35 percent of all volunteer personnel for the Red Cross. This program's goal is "to provide young people with meaningful opportunities for education, training, and volunteer/community service so that they remain a part of the Red Cross family throughout their lives."

  Junior Red Cross offers many opportunities for service. School-related activities often take the form of Red Cross clubs that engage in "fund raising, organizing blood drives, providing international assistance, and learning about such things as disaster preparedness and HIV/AIDS prevention and education." In addition, there are leadership development opportunities made available through clubs, councils, boards, camps, and centers, as well as through the national policy-making and advisory groups.

Outside of school, Junior Red Cross members take part in "cleaning up streets, planting trees, and organizing food drives. They also serve as mentors to peers and younger youth on substance abuse prevention, teen pregnancy prevention, environmental awareness, violence prevention, and other major youth issues."[37]

- **Ronald McDonald House Charities**

"A strong mind. A strong body. And a safe, supportive place to grow. These are things that every child needs—and deserves. Helping to provide these things is what we do." This is the mission the Ronald McDonald House Charities delivers on with its three core programs: Ronald McDonald House (the founding program which began in 1974), Ronald McDonald Family Room, and Ronald McDonald Care Mobile. Each of these programs goes to great lengths to ensure the comfort and quality of life for seriously ill children and their families, whether it's a place they can be together in or away from the hospital, or it's bringing low-cost medical attention to needy children around the world.[38]

A number of schools have made Ronald McDonald House programs a vital part of their community service projects. Whether it's by planning/hosting a fun event, fundraising, or even gardening, schools and their students can show the community that they care through Ronald McDonald House Charities. In fact, it's likely your school already has a partnership with Ronald McDonald House. If interested, check with your school's administration or visit RMHC.org for more information on how you can lend a hand.

- **Urban Ministries**

Most churches or community organizations welcome the assistance of high school and college students in helping them care for the less fortunate. Schools have shown great responsiveness to issues like homelessness and poverty by encouraging their students to volunteer assistance to urban ministries that aid those in need. These school-community partnerships offer students countless opportunities to develop character and gain experience in community service, leadership, and skill development—all while bettering people's lives.

Augusta Urban Ministries (AugustaUrbanMinistries.org), Wesley Urban Ministries (WesleyUrbanMinistries.com), and the Jewish Council on Urban Affairs (JCUA.org) are but a few examples of organizations that encourage the participation of students in their community service programs. Does your school currently work with such an organization? If not, you can build a partnership between your school and an urban outreach program and help make a difference in the lives those in your community who need your help.

Faith-Based Activities as School/Cummunity Service

Some parochial schools include community service as part of their requirements for graduation. If you are affiliated with a church, temple, or mosque, you may be involved in service on its behalf. Regardless of its source, faith-based service is a great activity to be involved in. Not only does it offer you the chance to put your beliefs into action, it also provides assistance to the religious or local community. Opportunities such as serving as an acolyte; becoming a part of the dance or drama group in your religious community; engaging in community projects sponsored by your temple, mosque, or church; offering your musical talents through the choir or instrumental group; or serving as an usher are just a few examples of ways for you to get involved in faith-based community service. In addition, such service is recognized by college admission officers as meaningful volunteer work.

As you can see, countless opportunities exist for you to get involved in school- and community-sponsored service projects. And more than that, if the opportunity isn't there, you can make it! You may also want to keep in mind that nursing homes, food banks, hospitals, libraries, hospices, government agencies, and numerous other organizations located in your community would be more than happy to have your help. So keep your eyes open for ways you can engage your talents and passions to help others—it's a surefire way to improve the quality of life for every party involved.

Before You Go . . .

By now you should have a fair number of thoughts about the many ways you can maximize your out-of-school time. Take note of the activities and programs that have caught your attention. Can you combine one or more of them? You may create a chess team for underprivileged youth, or you may create a hospital book club. You'd be surprised at the ways you can improve your community—and your college admissions chances—while having fun. Keep these ideas in mind as you continue your journey through this book, looking out for ways to enhance them or new directions to take. Be creative, take initiative, and make sure you enjoy yourself—your after-school experience is what you make of it, so make it great!

Have your journal handy and pen ready to go? There are even more opportunities for academic enrichment, volunteering, travel, and internships—and your summer vacation is a great time to take part in some incredible adventures!

ENDNOTES

1   Mountain Dreamer, Oriah. Your Heart's Prayer: Following the Thread of
    Desire into Deeper Life. Sounds True, 2002, compact disc.

2   Forum for Youth Investment. "About the Forum." Forum for Youth
    Investment. 2001–2007. www.forumfyi.org/_catdisp_page.cfm?LID=124.

3   Forum for Youth Investment. "High School After-School: What Is It? What
    Might It Be? Why Is It Important?" January, 2003. Forum for Youth
    Investment. January 2003. www.forumfyi.org/files//ostpc2.pdf.

4   The University of Chicago Laboratory Schools. "Co-curricular Activities."
    The University of Chicago Laboratory Schools. 2006–2007.
    www.ucls.uchicago.edu/students/activities/.

5   National Association of Secondary School Principals. "About Us."
    www.nhs.us/s_nhs/sec.asp?CID=126&DID=5270.

6   The National Beta Club. "Membership."
    www.betaclub.org/Membership/index.html.

7   The National Beta Club. "Benefits of Membership."
    www.betaclub.org/Membership/benefits.html.

8   The Cum Laude Society, Inc. "General Information."
    http://cumlaudesociety.org/generalinfo.html.

9   The National Conference of Governor's Schools. "About Governor's
    Schools." http://ncogs.org/home/content/category/3/24/44/.

10 Phi Sigma Iota International Foreign Language Honor Society. "Phi Sigma
    Iota." July 18, 2006. www.phisigmaiota.org.

11 Junior Engineering Technical Society. "JETS – Opening the World of
    Engineering the World of Engineering and Technology to Students, Parents,
    and Educators." 2007. www.jets.org/about/index.cfm.

12 Math Forum @ Drexel University. "Virtual Math Teams."
    www.mathforum.org/vmt/students/orientation.html.

13 Devon Arts in Schools Initiative. "Value of Arts in Schools."
    www.daisi.org.uk/values/value.php.

14 Office of the Law Revision Counsel. U.S. House of Representatives. "Armed Forces: General Military Law; Training and Education; Junior Reserve Officers' Training Corps; Sec. 2031." January 3, 2005. http://uscode.house.gov/uscodecgi/fastweb.exe.

15 Blair, Julie. "Report Says JROTC Benefits Students; Calls for More Funding for Programs." Junior Reserve Officer Training Corps. September 29, 1999. www.jrotc.org/jrotc_benifits.htm.

16 Wikipedia Foundation, Inc. "Color guard." January 3, 2007. http://en.wikipedia.org/wiki/Color_guard.

17 Anderson, Mary Lou. "Leadership." GovLeaders.org. April 1970. www.govleaders.org/quotes7.htm.

18 Close Up Foundation. "About Us." Close Up Foundation. 2005. www.closeup.org/why.htm.

19 Hugh O'Brien Youth Leadership (HOBY). "Hugh O'Brien Youth Leadership." www.hoby.org/index.shtml.

20 Hugh O'Brien Youth Leadership (HOBY). "HOBY Leadership Seminars." www.hoby.org/Schools/index.shtml.

21 National 4-H Council. "Frequently Asked Questions About 4-H." www.fourhcouncil.edu/uploadedFiles/News/4-H_FAQS.pdf.

22 Ibid.

23 National 4-H Council. "Programs: Rural Youth Development." www.fourhcouncil.edu/RuralYouthDevProgram.aspx.

24 National Commission for Cooperative Education. "About NCCE." www.co-op.edu/aboutncce.htm.

25 DECA Inc. "High School Division." 1999–2007. www.deca.org/hsd.html.

26 Merriam-Webster, Inc. Merriam-Webster's Collegiate Dictionary, 10th Ed. Springfield, Massachusetts: Merriam-Webster, 1999. 456.

27 Merriam-Webster, Inc. Merriam-Webster's Collegiate Dictionary, 10th Ed. Springfield, Massachusetts: Merriam-Webster, 1999. 296.

28 The College of William & Mary. "W&M Mock Trial Team." 2005. www.wm.edu/so/mocktrial/faq.php.

29 Amnesty International. "About Amnesty International."
    http://web.amnesty.org/pages/aboutai-index-eng.

30 The ASPIRA Association, Inc. "Overview of the Aspira Association."
    www.aspira.org/about.html.

31 Wallerstein Collaborative for Urban Environmental Education—The
    Steinhardt School of Education, New York University. "Our Mission." 2005.
    http://steinhardt.nyu.edu/wallerstein.

32 World Affairs Councils of America. "The World Affairs Council System."
    2007. www.worldaffairscouncils.org/aboutus.

33 Roosevelt, Franklin D. Quotation. 1994–2005.
    www.quotationspage.com/quotes/Franklin_D._Roosevelt/.

34 Habitat for Humanity International. "Why Habitat for Humanity Is
    Needed." 2007. www.habitat.org/how/why.aspx.

35 Habitat for Humanity International. "Habitat for Humanity Fact Sheet."
    2007. www.habitat.org/how/factsheet.aspx.

36 Key Club International. "About Key Club." 2007.
    www.keyclub.org/keyclub/about/.

37 The American National Red Cross. "Youth Services." 2006. www.red-
    cross.org/services/youth/0,1082,0_326_,00.html.

38 Ronald McDonald House Charities, Inc. "About Us."
    www.rmhc.org/rmhc/index/about.html.

CHAPTER 4
SUMMER EXPERIENCES

How Did You Spend *Your* Summer Vacation?

As has been stated earlier, it is important to use your out-of-school time productively. This is particularly true during your high school years, as it's the time college admissions officers look at when evaluating your academic record and personal characteristics. If you do not attend school year-round, you will have a summer break that generally lasts 8 to 10 weeks. This is a great time for you to dedicate yourself to an interesting and productive activity. The idea of just "vegging out" after a busy school year may sound appealing, but it will not do much to help you find your passion, get involved, or get into college. Remember that colleges look closely at all of the activities you take part in, from extracurricular groups at your high school to non-school activities. Your participation in unique and interesting activities—whether work, travel, or school related—can make you stand out as a unique and interesting applicant.

Ian, a 10th grader in Augusta, Georgia, has done something different each of the last four summers. As a rising 7th grader, he attended an outdoor summer camp, where he learned to appreciate nature and developed an interest in environmental science. He says, "Everyone should have an outdoor experience, if possible. Not only did I learn a lot about nature and develop confidence in myself, but [camp] was where I became interested in environmental science."

The next summer, Ian enrolled in advanced classes at a college preparatory school in his community to prepare for the rigorous 8th grade curriculum he would face that fall. While he admits that "classes were hard," at the end of the day he appreciated that he was "challenged to do my best work." He also discovered a new passion. "I enjoyed my English class most," he says. "Though it was the hardest . . . we read some really good literature."

The summer before 9th grade, Ian attended classes at a highly ranked public school in suburban Augusta. He also recognized his passion for swimming. Each of the previous summers he had spent hours perfecting his stroke at the local pool. The summer before 10th grade, in addition to taking classes, he increased the amount he swam to prepare for his high school swim team's tryouts. It wasn't all work and no play however—he also traveled to California with his family and had a great time.

Now a sophomore in high school, Ian comes alive when he talks about the previous summer. "Last summer, I worked as a lifeguard! It was my first job and I loved it! I really intensified my swimming and gained a sense of responsibility. I plan to get a job again next summer at a local pool and continue to swim as much as possible." He continues to look ahead: "I also want to travel to another country during the summer before my senior year and maybe [use] my interest in environmental science to help with some kind of service project in that country. I like traveling and learning about other cultures."

While getting to travel and improve his swim stroke are nice perks, Ian most appreciates the personal growth he's achieved the last several summers as a result of his activities: "Since middle school, some family hardships and different experiences I've had have helped me mature and build character. I am a lot more responsible and have a much better sense of the world around me." With college on the horizon, Ian is already thinking about how he can continue to explore his interests on campus. "As I think about college and my future," he says, "I want to try to balance my interests . . . maybe combining architecture with environmental science as [my] major and swimming on the college team."

Many successful college applicants have spent their summers engaged in a variety of different activities. What sets Ian apart, however, is his insight into the personal growth he achieved as a result of these activities. How you will spend you next summer vacation? Paid work? An internship? An academic program? Summer camp? Community service? Travel? As you think about this, remember: What you do isn't as important as doing it with purpose. Set ambitious goals for yourself and try to accomplish them.

My Summer Activities Wish List

You may be thinking: Sure, I'd like to do something cool and interesting this summer. But how do I get started? That's easy—all you have to do is start with the great ideas in your head. Pick up your journal and see what ideas for a productive summer spring to mind.

Journaling Activity

When thinking about how you'd like to spend your summer vacation, ask yourself the questions listed below. Jot down your response to each question and any other ideas on ways to spend your summer that come to mind. As you read the rest of this chapter, make note of the activities that interest you. Try to come up with ways that you can get involved in them. No matter where your interests ultimately take you, the key to finding a productive summer opportunity is an openness to try different sorts of things. Like Ian, you may discover new passions and interests that will push you to grow in new and challenging ways.

1. What kinds of activities have I participated in over the last three summers?

2. Do I have a summer reading list? If not, what books would I read if I had the time? How many books could I read if I devoted my summer to reading?

3. Would I like to have a summer job? If so, what would I like to do?

4. Would I like to gain knowledge or enrichment in an academic area? If so, which subjects would I take?

5. Which interests or talents of mine might be developed more fully through a summer activity?

6. If I could travel anywhere in the country or the world, where would I go?

7. What social issues concern me? How could I volunteer my time and services to make a difference in these areas?

THE BOOKS OF SUMMER

What if you are needed at home during the summer or have commitments that do not allow you to have a job or participate in a summer program? If this is the case, reading can be a productive way to use your spare time. College admissions officers know the value of a well-read applicant. In fact, some college application essays ask you to discuss books that you have read, and you never know when you might be asked to talk about your favorite book during a college admissions interview.

> "Outside of a dog, a book is man's best friend. Inside of a dog it's too dark to read."
>
> —Groucho Marx[1]

Being well read benefits you way before you begin to fill out your college applications; it enhances your chances for academic success in the present. Make no mistake—in high school, you will be required to read literature in a variety of genres and for a variety of classes. Many of the world's greatest political documents—the U.S. Constitution and the Declaration of the Rights of Man and of the Citizen, for example—are also great works of literature. You'll encounter essays, legal opinions, theorems, and scientific theories in everything from AP Calculus to Honors Physics. A measure of comfort with the English language—attained through reading well and reading often—is incredibly useful. Reading also imparts knowledge of and insight into topics covered by class discussions and assignments. Not only will reading for pleasure benefit you during your high school years, it will also put you ahead of the pack in college.

Let's say you decide to make reading a major project this summer—where can you find resources to help you decide what to read? Below are two places that can help you craft an excellent summer reading list of your very own.

- **Arrowhead Library System**

    A regional library program in the Midwest, Arrowhead has compiled a list of suggested reading for college-bound students, which includes American and world literatures, biographies, histories, and works in the social, natural, and physical sciences.[2] To view this list, visit ALS.lib.wi.us/Collegebound.html.

- **American Library Association (ALA)**

   ALA offers links to several websites with recommended reading lists for college-bound students.[3] It also features author Daniel Pennac's "Reader's Bill of Rights," which can help you get the most out of your literary pursuits.[4] Check out ALA.org/ala/yalsa/teenreading/teenreading.htm for more information.

It may also be helpful to do a Google search for recommended reading lists published by colleges and universities in which you are interested. Not only will this give you some insight into what these colleges consider "essential reading," it will also allow you to do a "test run" of each one's curriculum to see if its academics might be a good match for you. You can also browse the shelves of your local library or check out the bestseller section of your neighborhood bookstore to find recently published and popular books that appeal to your individual taste.

Whether you decide to spend the summer immersed in reading or to take a less intense approach in favor of other activities, remember to record the experiences, feelings, and insights you have as you read each book; your journal is the perfect place to do this. Who knows—by the end of the summer you may have discovered a hidden passion, a new favorite author, or an awe-inspiring story. At the very least you'll have a ready answer for the oh-so-popular college application prompt that begins: "Describe a book that you've read and the impact it has had on your life . . . ."

FOR YOUR EMPLOYMENT

A summer job can be a great way to stay productive while you earn a few extra dollars. You can use your earnings to buy some new clothes or DVDs, or even to put some money away for college, and a summer job can be a boon to your college applications, because good ones demonstrate that you are mature, responsible, and reliable.

Just Mad About 14

When you are 14 years old you are legally eligible to work in the U.S. Though you'll be able to do many types of work, you won't be eligible for *all* positions (you won't be able to do work that involves driving or the operation of heavy machinery, for example).[5] In Canada the working age varies by province and by type of work.[6]

Many students find jobs right in their neighborhood. They might work at a fast food restaurant, drugstore, supermarket, or even the local ice-cream parlor. If local places aren't hiring, talk to your counselor—various summer job opportunities may be advertised in the guidance office. Parents, other relatives, and family friends are also great sources for job leads; they might even be able to help you land a summer position at their place of employment.

If reaching out to your counselor, friends, and family doesn't yield results, you can also consult the want ads in your local newspaper or do an online search (keywords: "teen jobs" or "summer jobs for youth"). The following are some great Internet resources for information on jobs for young people:

- **About.com**

  About.com's web page on teen jobs offers job search tips, links to specific job search websites, and information on labor laws.[7] Check it out at JobSearch.About.com/cs/justforstudents/a/teenjobs.htm.

- **ItsAboutUs.org**

  This fun, youth-oriented site provides tips for young people on understanding youth employment laws, information on how to ace the interview, as well as leads on specific job opportunities. The site also features a scholarship bank, games, contests, and a question-and-answer forum where you can get advice on everything from applying for a job to acing your driver's test.[8] Visit ItsAboutUs.org/employment/Default.asp for more information.

- **National Youth Employment Commission (NYEC)**

    NYEC is a national nonprofit organization dedicated to working with state and local governments to develop local youth employment policies and initiatives. NYEC provides information and resources to youth, families, private organizations, and governmental boards on youth employment policies and programs.[9] Check out NYEC's website (www.NYEC.org) for job search tips and links to specific employment programs around the country.

- **Teens4Hire.org**

    This employment resource for teens age 14 and older provides information on topics such as the "Top 10 Places for Teens to Look for a Job" and the "Top 10 Qualities Employers Want Most in a Teen Candidate." A resource-oriented site, it features several industry-specific job searches as well as information on youth labor laws. Basic membership—which allows you to search the site for jobs and apply online—is free.[10] For more information, visit Teens4Hire.org.

Young people in both the U.S. and Canada may require work permits to do several types of work. You might be able to obtain such a permit through your high school. Talk to your guidance counselor about the steps involved in obtaining one, which usually entail parental permission.

There are also many independent ways to earn money during the summer. You can find a job babysitting, mowing lawns, tutoring, or doing something to help out family members or other people in your neighborhood. Some particularly creative students have even started their own businesses, offering services like the ones mentioned above, or utilizing their skills and talents in other areas. (See Chapter 5 for information on how you can start your own business.)

There may also be a youth work program sponsored and funded by your city, county, or state government that can assist you in finding summer employment. These programs typically work by placing participants in positions with various city agencies where responsibilities run the gamut from administrative work to city clean-up. They often also involve a career development component that teaches students resume-writing and interviewing skills, among other things. To find out if a program like this is available in your hometown, visit your local government's website and search for "youth services."

Those who spend their summer at a paid job are likely to learn valuable skills related to the position they hold, as well as character traits that can be transferred anywhere. The responsibility, perseverance, and commitment developed by a paid job are highly regarded by colleges and future employers alike.

Your Internship Has Come In

An internship is a position that offers practical experience under the supervision of a professional. It's similar to a job, but it's much more about the work you do—and see—than the amount you're paid. In fact, many internships offer only a stipend to cover expenses (such as lunch and travel), and some offer no payment at all. However, even young adults who receive little or no payment for their internships are generally happy to have them because internships are usually much more geared to the participant's specific interest(s) than the average paid job. Opportunities are available for high school students to serve as interns in government, business, the arts, media, and other professions. Those who do gain firsthand exposure to the field and learn what such work entails on a day-to-day basis. Good internship experiences help participants decide if they should pursue academic studies that will lead to a career in that particular field.

The Internet is a great resource for information on the many summer internship opportunities that are available to high school students. The following is a list of some notable programs:

- **Artbarn**

  Interested in theater arts? Artbarn is a nonprofit program based in Brookline, Massachusetts that offers internship opportunities to high school students who are talented in the performing and creative arts.[11] Participants work under the supervision of an Artbarn staff member while they coach, choreograph, and teach technical theater skills and other activities to younger children. Participation is viewed as community service and provides students interested in careers in theater arts with valuable career development and exposure to personal character traits needed for success in the field.[12] To learn more about Artbarn's mission and philosophy, visit ArtBarn.org/about_us.

- **Career Explorations (CE)**

  A nonprofit organization based in Morristown, New Jersey, CE offers rising high school juniors and seniors exposure to a professional work environment via its residential internship programs in New York City and Boston, Massachusetts. Interns selected to participate in CE complete a four- or six-week internship at a well-established company in one of a variety of fields. Working under the supervision of a mentor, interns gain insight into the field and participate in various college planning activities, including visits to schools in the New York or Boston area. The program enables participants to gain a sense of autonomy and responsibility while exposing them to the cultural and recreational opportunities that city life has to offer. Eligible students can demonstrate that they are motivated and hardworking and up for the challenges of living and working in the city.[13] To learn more about this exciting program and to read testimonials from students who have served as CE interns, visit CEinternships.com/experience_whatis.asp.

- **Forest Project Summer Collaborative**

  Wave Hill is a nonprofit cultural institution located in Bronx, New York that has teamed up with Lehman College at the City University of New York to offer an exciting internship program for high school students focused on the natural environment. The Forest Project Summer Collaborative offers both paid and for-credit internship opportunities that engage teens in work that teaches them about the urban ecosystem and how to enhance the urban environment through basic forest restoration. The program seeks to grow interns in the program by offering four levels of internships that bring participants back for subsequent summers. Eligible students reside in or near the Bronx, earn C's or better in their high school courses, and have an interest in environmental issues.[14] Visit Wavehill.org/education/high_school_internships.html to learn more about the Forest Project Summer Collaborative.

- **National Security Agency (NSA)**

  The U.S. National Security Agency's Gifted and Talented Program is a paid summer training opportunity for high school students who have demonstrated an aptitude for math and science and who live in the Baltimore/Washington, DC area. NSA provides program participants with a temporary appointment from June to August. During this time, participants commit to working 32 hours a week. In addition to training, they receive a salary, earn full social security taxes, and accrue sick days and leave time. Each participant is assigned a mentor with whom they work on projects that coincide with their aptitude and interests. To learn more about this opportunity and NSA's year-round high school work-study program, visit NSA.gov/careers/students_3.cfm.[15]

Another good way to find a great summer internship is to create your own. Is there a person, organization, or company for which you've always dreamed of working? If so, you should write him/her/it a letter and offer your services in an ad-hoc internship. Do your research first and make sure your letter conveys why the particular work is exactly the kind with which you want to be involved. Also be sure to include information about any special skills or experience you bring to the table. Chances are the person on the other end of that letter will be so flattered and impressed by your initiative, they'll be offering you your dream summer internship in no time.

WHAT ELSE IS OUT THERE?

So far you've been directed to various books, jobs, and internships that can provide you with great precollege, summer experiences. Each one can help you find your passion, get involved, and get into the college of your dreams! Know, however, that, as a group, these experiences are only a small sample of the great options available. The Princeton Review guide, *The 500 Best Ways for Teens to Spend the Summer*, written by Neill Seltzer, lists scores of specific programs and opportunities that can broaden your experience and test your abilities.[16] If you have some trouble finding the right summer opportunity for you, know that that there are literally hundreds of great programs out there—if you look long enough, you will find the right one!

The rest of this chapter points you to specific summer opportunities in areas you may not have considered, from summer school to travel and volunteer opportunities abroad. In the pages that follow you'll also get some ideas on how to use your summer experiences as a springboard to your college years. Remember: This book is only a starting point. With so many great programs out there, it's up to you to do the necessary research to find the one that fits best.

It's Academic

An academic summer program can take various forms. Among many things, it can: follow a traditional, summer school model; bestow college credit; or involve travel to another country. There's a program for almost every set of interests and needs.

> "I was thinking that we all learn by experience, but some of us have to go to summer school."
>
> —Peter De Vries[17]

But first things first: If you attend summer school to complete a course, improve a grade, or build proficiency in a subject that has given you difficulty, know that it will *not* cast your college applications in a poor light. College admissions offices view summer school courses taken for these reasons as a demonstration good character and initiative on your part. There nothing wrong with needing help if you take the help that is available.

Other summer school programs can give you the opportunity to take a course that might not be offered by your high school or to get a head start on an especially difficult course required in the coming year. If there is a particular course you're interested in taking, the first thing you should do is check with your high school (or school district, if you're homeschooled) to see if it offers the course and to find out what you need to do to sign up. This is the easiest route to enrolling in summer school. Another great option is to check out the offerings at community colleges and other high schools in your area. You can very often find the course you're looking for right in your neighborhood. Your guidance counselor can assist you in this process and let you know whether your high school recognizes any courses you plan to take at other schools, if you plan to take them to earn required credits for graduation.

Online Programs

Accredited online programs are increasingly popular options. The benefit of online courses is that they allow you to participate from home. Many online courses allow students to view lectures and complete assignments on a more flexible schedule. Others work to simulate a real-time classroom experience through tools like videoconferencing, webcams, and specialized chat programs. Although this is a relatively new venture—as recently as the mid 1990s, there were no online educational programs at the high school level—today almost every state has at least one institution with an online learning component for high school students.

Some online offerings at the high school level are for-profit educational ventures. Other offerings are run by state departments of education, local school districts, or private schools. (Some such programs are offered in partnership with online education service providers, but many private schools and public school systems offer their own online educational programs.) The key to finding the right online program for your needs is research. Always investigate a given program's credentials to make sure it is accredited. If possible, talk to other students who have completed the program to find out what their experiences were like. Again, make sure your guidance counselor is in the loop so he or she can advise you on specific programs to consider, as well as give you advice on how to make sure the credits you earn count.

An example of an online educational program that is available to high school students nationwide is Virtual High School (VHS). A non-profit organization, VHS has become a leader in the field of online high school education and offers a varied catalogue of courses across a broad range of levels and abilities. Working in partnership with schools and educational organizations across the U.S., VHS provides a standards-based curriculum and a common grading system. It offers summer school courses for both make-up work and enrichment, plus regular semester and full-year course offerings (including pre-AP and AP). Students may take VHS courses through their high school (if it is a member) or independently by registering online. Transcripts are provided for all independent course work and all VHS courses are approved by the National Collegiate Athletics Association (NCAA).[18] You can learn more about VHS by visiting GoVHS.org.

At the state level, programs that have earned special recognition include the following:

- **Delta Cyber School (DCS)**

    This online public charter school offers courses to Alaska residents ages 5–19. The aim of DCS is to provide students with knowledge and technological skills that will equip them for life in the twenty-first century.[19] Details about the Delta Cyber School are provided at DCS.k12.ak.us.

- **Florida Virtual School (FLVS)**

    The first state-sponsored online school for high school students, FLVS is considered a model program. It offers over 90 online courses, including honors and AP, to students in all Florida school districts. FLVS also serves school districts in New Jersey, Wisconsin, West Virginia, Alabama, Ohio, and other areas within the United States. All FLVS teachers are certified and the program is accredited by the Southern Association of Colleges and Schools. Its courses are also approved by the NCAA.[20] Detailed information is available at the FLVS website, FLVS.net.

- **Kentucky Virtual High School (KVHS)**

    KVHS is dedicated to expanding students' access to a challenging high school curriculum. Its offers a broad range of courses, including four foreign languages, Advanced Placement courses, and dual credit courses. All courses meet national and state standards and all KVHS teachers are fully certified.[21] You can learn more at KVHS.org.

- **Michigan Virtual High School (MVHS)**

    Working under the premise that youth should be prepared to compete in today's global, knowledge-based economy, MVHS offers a broad range of online courses that provide a way for students to improve technological skills while increasing their knowledge of diverse subjects. Operated by Michigan Virtual University, a nonprofit corporation, MVHS partners with school districts to grant course credits and diplomas to gifted and talented students, students who need to make up credits, special-needs students, and home-schooled students. Its services are available to students at both public and private schools.[22] For more information, visit MiVHS.org.

- **Illinois Virtual High School (IVHS)**

  IVHS provides online courses to students throughout the state of Illinois. Students register for classes and pay tuition through their school district. Scholarship opportunities are available and course work is offered for both semester and full-year credit. All courses are taught by fully certified teachers and the curriculum meets both national and state standards. In addition, IVHS offers information about online aviation courses available through the Experimental Aviation Association.[23] More information is available at IVHS.org.

Notable programs at the local and district level include

- **Columbia County Schools**

  The Columbia County School System, located just outside of Augusta, GA, has recently launched its eLearning Academy. Students may, with their counselor's approval, enroll in online courses provided by selected third parties. All eLearning Academy courses are taught by certified teachers and meet district requirements for credit toward graduation.[24] Visit Ccboe.net/elearning/home.html for more information.

- **Fairfax County Public Schools (FCPS) Online Campus**

  FCPS in Virginia began its Online Campus program in 2001. The program's mission is to provide new educational choices to students who need to complete graduation requirements, have scheduling conflicts, or are homebound. The Internet-based curriculum simulates a traditional in-class learning experience. Students are responsible for using Online Campus resources to create a personalized learning experience.[25] For more information, go to FCPSfcps.edu/DIS/onlinecampus/welcome.htm.

- **Northampton Area Senior High School**

  Located in Pennsylvania's Lehigh Valley, this school works with Pearson Digital Learning's NovaNet system to offer its own online courses. Initially implemented to address the needs of students requiring academic help, online courses are now available for remediation or enrichment, during the school year as well as the summer. Students may also enroll in NovaNet courses because of scheduling conflicts, the over-enrollment of a particular class, or a situation where they are homebound.[26] Visit PearsonDigital.com/success-es/novanet/northhampton.cfm for more information.

As mentioned earlier, a number of for-profit online schools also exist—just do an Internet search for online course options to see how many. Unfortunately, it can be difficult to pick out the quality ones. Accreditation by a reputable governing body does not automatically make a school a good option. The key to determining whether a for-profit online school (its website will include ".com") is a viable option for you is to find out if your high school or school district will grant you credit toward graduation for completion of its courses.

Excel High School is a for-profit online school with offices in Minnesota, Louisiana, and Florida. A tour of its website, ExcelHighSchool.com, will give you an idea of what for-profit schools can offer students. Fully accredited by the National Private Schools Accreditation Alliance (NPSAA), Excel offers a complete college preparatory high school curriculum. Under its open admissions policy, students in grades 9–12 can enroll in summer school courses for remediation or enrichment, take regular school-year courses, or earn a diploma through an accelerated program—all online and at their own pace. Scholarships to offset the cost of tuition are available to qualified students and monthly payment plans are also available.[27]

Regardless of the specific platform you choose, online courses generally afford students a great deal more flexibility than a traditional school environment would. As a result, they allow you the opportunity to engage in other summer activities that would occupy you during traditional school hours. (Volunteer work, performing arts programs, athletic camps, and jobs all have a tendency to require your presence during traditional school hours.) Online courses are not right for everyone. As an online student, you must be self-motivated since no one will pester you about turning in your assignments. You must also be disciplined and skilled at managing your time, and able to communicate clearly and effectively in writing. Ready access to a computer and a reliable Internet connection outside of your regular school setting are also essential. You must make sure that the online program you choose is approved by your counselor or principal of your regular high school.

College Programs

Perhaps you are seeking academic enrichment coupled with the opportunity for career exploration or the development of a particular talent or interest. Many colleges and universities offer precollege programs that provide exactly that. These programs serve a dual purpose: They offer particularly ambitious and talented students the chance to gain knowledge (and possibly even earn college credit for it) while, at the same time, getting a taste of what college life will be like. They are usually overnight programs, so students get to experience life in the dorms firsthand. Some are tougher to get into or more expensive than others, but many offer scholarships to eligible students. Your first stop for information about precollege programs should be your high school guidance counselor's office. You can also go online and search for "precollege programs"—a plethora of opportunities will show up. This section discusses some programs that may appeal to you.

PAVE AT VANDERBILT UNIVERSITY

PAVE is a six-week summer program for 11th and 12th graders who plan to take honors or AP courses in the fall and are thinking of studying engineering, medicine, or technology in college. It is designed to enhance students' academic achievement in math and the sciences and to provide exposure to the independence and the challenges of college life—both in and outside of the classroom. Students may apply to PAVE at any time, and an admissions decision will be made based on their qualifications and the space available in the program.[28]

Andrew, now in his third year at a midsized, tech-centric college in the Midwest, got his first taste of college life through Vanderbilt's PAVE program the summer before his senior year of high school. He worked with his college counselor to find a precollege program that suited his needs and he applied to PAVE because he wanted to test his independence in a college setting. He applied in the late winter and was accepted in the spring of his junior year. In PAVE, Andrew learned to apply his study skills, manage his time, and budget his money before going off to college the next year. You can learn more about PAVE by visiting Vanderbilt.edu/pave.

Each summer, the Blair School of Music at Vanderbilt University hosts an International Fiddle School, which is open to students of all ages.[29] Year-round instruction—including private instruction—in various other instruments is also available, and many students enrolled in Blair precollege programs receive high school credit. For more information about these programs, or to schedule an audition, visit: Vanderbilt.edu/Blair/precoll/index.html.[30]

PRECOLLEGE AND DISCOVER HOPKINS PROGRAMS AT JOHNS HOPKINS UNIVERSITY

Nationally renowned for its biological sciences curriculum, Johns Hopkins University offers two main summer programs to high school students. Like Vanderbilt's PAVE program, these summer programs allow students to get a preview of college life, both in and outside of the classroom. Both programs bestow college credit. Students have the opportunity to live in on-campus housing for the duration of the programs and have the opportunity to meet and interact with students from all over the world.[31]

The Precollege Summer Program is a wonderful opportunity for high school students to get inside look at college life and college-level academics. This five-week program gives students an opportunity to earn up to seven college credits while taking classes alongside currently enrolled college students. Students have hundreds of course options to choose from and, depending on the course, students may also have the opportunity to participate in co-curricular activities offered in partnership with educational and cultural institutions in the surrounding area, such as the Baltimore Museum of Art.[32]

Todd, now a sophomore majoring in premed at Wake Forest University, participated in the Pre-College Summer Program the summer after his sophomore year in high school. He remembers the experience as one of the most important milestones in his personal and academic development:

Attending the Johns Hopkins Precollege Program was an amazing experience. I earned seven college credits that summer while gaining valuable exposure to new approaches and dimensions of familiar subjects. I chose a premed focus, taking classes in subjects such as molecular biology and genetics with actual college students. We got to see work on human cadavers and I actually got to place a needle in preparation for a spinal tap. (I was scared to death!) We were involved in computer-assisted work in medical technology. We were written up in the *Washington Post*. It was crazy! It really gave me something to look forward to and I came away from that summer experience more "well rounded" and better prepared for the challenges that college at a prestigious school would bring. As a word of caution, I would advise students to wait until the end of their junior year to have this kind of experience. Though I got along fine and learned all kinds of things, I think I would have been better able to connect it to college life if I had not been so young when I went to Hopkins.

For more information on the Johns Hopkins Precollege Program, visit JHU.edu/summer/precollege/preCollege.html.

Applicants to Discover Hopkins, a competitive residential program at Johns Hopkins University, are screened for both their maturity and their academic achievement. Presented as a series of short-term programs over the course of the summer, Discover Hopkins offers three intense two-week-long programs organized around a particular theme. Summer 2006 offerings included Bioethics in Molecular Biology, Natural Disasters, and the American Civil War. Students may enroll in one or all of the theme-based cohorts, and earn one college credit at the completion of each program.[33] Visit JHU.edu/summer/precollege/discover.html for more information.

The Summer Intensive English as a Second Language (ESL) program at Johns Hopkins University is a full-immersion English language learning program for secondary school students aged 15–18, designed to help them fine-tune their English communication and testing skills. Eligible students must meet Johns Hopkins' TOEFL score requirements and take a placement test once they arrive on campus. The program incorporates 25-plus hours of course work per week, and also includes language lab reinforcement exercises. Students are assigned advisors to help them throughout their five-week term and benefit from social activities that put their language skills to the test. A credit option for students meeting TOEFL score requirements and possessing the required academic qualifications is also available. Students enrolled in the ESL program who meet Johns Hopkins' requirements may also take part in the Pre-College or Discover Hopkins programs.[34] For more information about the ESL opportunities at Johns Hopkins University, visit JHU.edu/ltc/esl/.

SUMMER PROGRAMS AT COLORADO COLLEGE

If you're interested in a pre-college program that will allow you to study against the gorgeous backdrop of the Rocky Mountains, Colorado College (CC) may have just what you're looking for. Located in Colorado Springs, CC offers a summer session reflects the college's deep commitment to liberal arts learning. The emphasis is on total academic immersion with a significant laboratory and fieldwork component.

Colorado College is known for its Block Plan, which emphasizes academic immersion by offering "one course at a time." CC's summer session is organized into three "blocks," offered between early June and early August. High school students are welcomed into CC's regular summer session, and take courses for credit alongside currently enrolled college students. In addition to the regular course work, high school participants are offered exposure to campus residential life and participate in college planning sessions on admissions, college essay writing, and career exploration. Students are also able to take trips into the surrounding Colorado Springs area and participate in other extracurricular opportunities on campus. Highly qualified students may be eligible for merit-based partial scholarships.[35]

CC also offers College Ahead!—a great precollege summer program specifically for rising juniors living in the southwestern portion of the United States. The goal of this two-week residential program is to provide participants with an engaging and supportive introduction to campus social and academic life. Students enrolled in the program may choose a course in either the natural or social sciences taught by CC professors. Outside of class, students participate in reading, writing, and oral communication skills-building activities. They also learn about the college application process. All students accepted to this program receive full scholarships to cover the cost of tuition, as well as a travel stipend and spending money.[36] To learn more about CC's College Ahead! program, visit ColoradoCollege.edu/summerprograms/summersession/collegeahead.asp.

Additional Popular Precollege Programs

The programs discussed above are just a small sampling of what's out there. There are many, many terrific summer academic program opportunities available across the United States. In fact, almost all colleges and universities offer summer school courses; it's just a question of whether they also offer a formalized enrichment program for high school students in tandem with their regular summer school curriculum. You may continue searching on your own by visiting college websites or doing an Internet search. Below is a list of some other popular summer academic programs that may appeal to you. (This list is in no way exhaustive.)

- **Cornell University Summer College for High School Students**

  www.summercollege.cornell.edu

- **Harvard University Summer Secondary School Program**

  www.ssp.harvard.edu

- **Stanford University Summer College**

  http://summersession.stanford.edu

- **University of California—Berkeley Academic Talent Development Program**

  http://atdp.berkeley.edu

- **University of Southern California Summer Seminars for High School Students**

  www.usc.edu/dept/admissions/programs/summer/seminars.shtml

In addition, some high schools publish lists of precollege programs on their websites. The following web pages are two great places to look for information on a broad variety of summer programs:

- **Monticello High School**

  www.k12albemarle.org/monticello/departments/gifted/Summer.htm

- **Moses Brown School**

  www.mosesbrown.org/Page.aspx?id=219144

YOU GOTTA HAVE ART

Do you have a special talent or interest in the visual, performing, or media arts? If so, know that there are many summer programs out there for students interested in exploring their talents and interests in this area. And many fantastic programs can be found right at home in your local community! Contact local art schools and museums, theater companies, dance schools, radio and television stations, colleges, and other organizations and inquire about summer program opportunities available to students. If you already take lessons in any area of the arts, talk to your instructor to see if he or she can steer you toward a meaningful summer experience. Some of the most competitive summer experiences for the artistically inclined require recommendations from instructors, teachers, or coaches, so make sure you are on good terms with yours. If you are interested in arts programs away from home, the programs below may include a few of interest to you.

EXPLORATIONS IN ARCHITECTURE AND DESIGN AT THE UNIVERSITY OF MIAMI

The University of Miami offers several summer programs for high school students. Among its offerings is a residential program housed under its School of Architecture and Design. Explorations in Architecture and Design is an intensive, three-week long program for students interested in a career in architecture or design. The program seeks to familiarize participants with design processes and the role of architects and designers in society. University of Miami professors and advanced architecture students teach all courses. In addition to attending lectures, students engage in extensive studio work, including drawing, model-making, and proposing designs for several projects. The program provides students with drafting supplies and equipment, computer-aided design programming, and photographic equipment. At the close of the program, a school-wide exhibition displays student work. Students may earn up to three college credits for the program, and there are a limited number of scholarships available for extremely qualified students.[37] For more information, visit ARC.miami.edu/programs/Explorations.htm.

JACOBS SCHOOL OF MUSIC AT INDIANA UNIVERSITY—BLOOMINGTON

The Jacobs School of Music at Indiana University's Bloomington campus has graduated some of the world's most successful performers, conductors, composers, music educators, and scholars; it also offers a number of programs for high school students. Among them are a summer academy in ballet, a piano and string academy, and a summer music clinic. Ranging from a few days to over a month, the summer programs offer talented students quality instruction and training by professional musicians and music educators from around the country.[38] To learn more, visit Music.Indiana.edu/special_programs/summer.shtml.

NATIONAL HIGH SCHOOL INSTITUTE AT NORTHWESTERN UNIVERSITY

Northwestern University in Evanston, IL offers several summer programs in the communication and performing arts through its National High School Institute (NHSI). The oldest university program for high school students in the country, NHSI features programs in debate, journalism, forensics, music, digital media arts, theater arts, and film and video production—there is something here for virtually every arts-minded student. Each program track has its own mission, focus, and admission requirements. Participants are exposed to a college environment and professional standards of performance in a residential program. Programs run from mid-June to early August and are generally four to five weeks in length.[39] Read about all of the individual programs by visiting NHSI's website at Northwestern.edu/nhsi/.

Summer Arts Camp at Interlochen Center for the Arts

Located in northern Michigan, the Interlochen Center for the Arts is a world-renowned arts community with over 85,000 alumni. Its Summer Arts Camp annually offers over 2,000 students in grades 3–12 the opportunity to train intensively with world-class instructors. It offers the following areas of concentration:

- Creative writing
- Dance
- General arts
- Motion picture arts
- Music
- Theater arts
- Visual arts

Financial aid (including scholarships) is available for outstanding young performers who demonstrate financial need—approximately 25 percent of Summer Arts Camp participants receive some form of financial aid. You can learn more about this program and Interlochen's other programs by visiting Interlochen.org.[40]

Summer High School Programs at Snow Farm

Located in the foothills of the Berkshire Mountains, near the Five College Consortium (Amherst, Smith, Mount Holyoke, UMass—Amherst, and Hampshire), Snow Farm offers a two- to four-week summer studio arts experience in a bucolic setting. The Summer in Art high school program is taught by master artists, many of whom reside in the vicinity of Snow Farm. Participating students may concentrate in the following areas of study:

- Ceramics
- Drawing and color
- Glasswork
- Jewelry making
- Metalsmithing
- Photography
- Textile art
- Welding

The program curriculum is full and fast paced. Students have the opportunity to take Sunday trips to arts-related sites, such as artists' studios, craft fairs, and museums. High school credit is avialable.[41] To find out more information, visit SnowFarm.org/summerhsprogram.html.

SUMMER INSTITUTE AT BOSTON UNIVERSITY

The Summer Institute, offered by Boston University's School of Visual Arts, is a four-week program open to high school students ages 15–18. Participating students are introduced to a full range of methods and materials used in professional arts practice. Applicants to the program should demonstrate creative ability. If accepted, they'll learn how to more fully utilize their artistic abilities in order to improve and build their portfolio. Studio time is balanced by off-site arts education opportunities, including museum visits and classes with masters in the arts. Students accepted to the Summer Institute have the opportunity to interact with other precollege students in the program and gain firsthand experience of residential college life.[42] Visit BU.edu/cfa/visual/summer-arts/index.htm for more information.

SUMMER PROGRAMS AT UNIVERSITY OF PENNSYLVANIA (PENN)

A wide variety of summer experiences are available to high school students through Penn's precollege programs, from a summer science academy to programs in theater and the arts. All programs feature both residential and commuter options and provide students with exposure to college life and Ivy League academics. Students receive instruction from Penn faculty members and have plenty of time to pursue extracurricular interests outside of class, from the exploration of the historic city of Philadelphia to SAT-prep and college application workshops. Rising high school juniors and seniors may apply to the Precollege Program, Penn Summer Science Academy, or one of the two arts programs described below.[43]

- **Penn Summer Studio: Arts/Architecture Academy**

  If you are a rising junior or senior who prefers learning in an environment not focused on grades and credit, and you are interested in expanding your portfolio, this may be the program for you. Students admitted to this noncredit program engage in challenging work in drawing, painting, ceramics, photography, filmmaking, animation, or architecture. At the culmination of the program, participants receive the opportunity to exhibit their work during the Academy's Presentation Weekend. Successful applicants can demonstrate evidence of creative ability.[44]

- **Penn Summer Theater Workshop**

  This residential four-week program offers participants the opportunity to engage in the intense study and practice of theatrical performance and technique. Course modules are taught by Penn faculty, alumni, and professionals; cover acting, scene study, and the Alexander technique; and conclude in a final public performance. Participants in the program also have the opportunity to attend theater performances in New York City and Philadelphia. Successful applicants can demonstrate interest and experience in theatrical performance.[45]

To get more information on all of Penn's summer programs, visit SAS.upenn.edu/CGS/highschool/index_summerhighschool.php.

TISCH SCHOOL OF THE ARTS AT NEW YORK UNIVERSITY

The prestigious Tisch School of the Arts at New York University offers high school students four-week summer sessions in New York, New York; Paris, France; and Dublin, Ireland. Running from early June to early August, areas of study include: drama, dramatic writing, film and photography (NY); drama (Paris); and drama and film (Dublin). Participants are presented with challenging college-level training under the tutelage of full-time NYU faculty and can earn up to six college credits for successful completion of the fully accredited program. The goal is not only for students to receive a stimulating and enriching summer experience, but to make sure they also come away from the program with a clearer sense of what professional training in the arts entails.[46] Visit Specialprograms.tisch.nyu.edu/page/hsStudents.html to learn more about the Tisch summer experience for high school students.

Camping Around

When you think of summer camp, do images of lakes, log cabins, and people singing songs around a campfire come to mind? Can you practically taste the s'mores and feel the tiny bites of mosquitoes? This may describe summer camp for many students, but the truth is there are many different kinds of summer camps out there—from the traditional outdoors camp described above to athletic camps, computer camps, and more. The DMOZ Open Directory Project (http://dmoz.org/Kids_and_Teens/) is a comprehensive directory of resources on the web for people under the age of 18. There, you will be able to find extensive listings of sports and hobby camps for high school students.[47] A few different types of camps are listed below, with selected examples.

Athletic Camps

If sports are your passion, or if you want to get extra training before trying out for your school's team, summer athletic camps are an excellent option. Talk to the coach or the athletic director at your school—he or she can point you toward programs that might be a good fit for you. You can also inquire about community athletic associations in your area—they may offer summer opportunities for high school students.

Scott, a rising sophomore in Illinois, plays on his high school's basketball team and participates in his local community's basketball program. Since the 5th grade, when he discovered that he was not only good at playing basketball, but that he was also respected by other players as a team leader, basketball has been Scott's passion. (It didn't hurt that he had grown to be over six feet tall by the time he was in middle school.) During the summer, Scott participates in athletic camps sponsored by his local park district that focus on fitness, training, and basketball techniques. He also plays in summer and holiday basketball tournaments against teams in the Midwest and Southeast. Scott has the following to say about his passion for basketball: "Like every player my age, I dream of playing in the NBA, and I am working hard to make that happen. I know not that many people make it that far . . . so I have a Plan B. Even if I don't play 'pro' ball, I will always stay involved with basketball. Maybe I will coach a high school or middle school team. Or a community team, like the one that I played for in 5th grade. Basketball and my coaches have meant a lot in my life. I will never forget that, no matter what the future brings."

Perhaps you feel the same way about a sport in which you are involved. Whether your passion lies with a team sport like football, basketball, or soccer, or a more individual endeavor like gymnastics, golf, or swimming, there are plenty of programs out there that can help you get your game to the next level. Pushing yourself, both physically and mentally, and using your summer to become stronger and more skilled in your sport, is a potentially rewarding experience that colleges look upon favorably. The following are a few summer athletic programs that may be of interest to you.

SummerOnCampus

SummerOnCampus' website (SummerOnCampus.com) provides information on summer camps and summer programs held throughout New York State. More than 100 colleges, college prep schools, and private institutes are indexed in this online directory. A comprehensive resource, it covers over 70 camp/program categories, including the following:

- Baseball
- Basketball
- Cheerleading
- Cross Country
- Diving
- Equestrian/Riding
- Fencing
- Field Hockey
- Football
- Golf
- Ice Hockey

- Lacrosse
- Sailing
- Soccer
- Softball
- Strength and Conditioning
- Swimming
- Tennis
- Track and Field
- Volleyball
- Wrestling

Other programs listed on the SummerOnCampus website focus on adventure experiences, circus training, rock climbing, ropes courses, wilderness experiences, and triathlon training.[48]

Joe Machnik's No. 1 Camps

Offered in more than a dozen locations across the United States, No. 1 Camps are a popular choice for the training and development of soccer players. Specific program options include striker camps, goal-keeper camps, and team camps.[49] To learn more about No.1 Camps, visit No1SoccerCamps.com/about5.lasso.

International Sports Training Camps

International Sports Training Camps, located in Stroudsburg, Pennsylvania, offers students between the ages of 8 and 16 the opportunity to complete one of four week-long programs in different sports areas. Participants are taught sportsmanship and athletic skills through a series of lectures and reinforcement activities The goal is to provide students with a complete appreciation for athleticism and sports, while emphasizing at all times the most important aspect of any sport: sportsmanship! At the end of camp, each student receives a score card charting his or her progress throughout the program. Trophies and certificates are also awarded.[50] Information about ISTC is available at International-Sports.com.

Computer Camps

iD Tech Camps, a Silicon Valley-based company, recently established the iD Gaming Academy, which provides high-quality instruction in a summer-camp format. With locations at UC—Berkeley, Stanford, UCLA, and Villanova, the iD Gaming Academy provides instruction in the design and creation of video games. Courses are three-week programs taught in small groups by experienced game-creation professionals. Each student has the opportunity to operate a workstation where they become familiar with producing 3-D graphics and animation, and work to develop their own game-creation portfolio.[51] To find out more about iD Tech Camps' many summer technology programs for young people, visit InternalDrive.com.

Foreign Language Immersion Programs (Travel Abroad)

Participation in a foreign language immersion program is a great way to spend your summer. These programs typically combine classroom instruction with travel to a host country where the language in question is widely spoken. The locale offers plenty of opportunities for language skills practice in real-life social situations. Below are some examples of these programs.

BAJA CALIFORNIA LANGUAGE COLLEGE

The Baja California Language College offers a wide variety of Spanish immersion programs in Ensenada, Mexico, accommodating everyone from beginners to those who are somewhat fluent and want to become even more so. Options include private instruction, small-group instruction, programs for the whole family, and Mexican cooking lessons.

If your family is interested in spending its summer in Spanish language and Mexican culture immersion, instruction can be coupled with a camping experience or a stay in a local hotel. You can also take the journey alone. If you do, participation in the program can be combined with a stay in the household of a Mexican family, which will complement your daily class instruction.[52] For more information about this program, check out BajaCal.com.

RUSTIC PATHWAYS

Specializing in student travel, Rustic Pathways offers a program that allows participants to combine travel with language immersion in Costa Rica, China, or Thailand. Rustic Pathways also offers programs that focus on community service, life skills development, soccer skills development, and adventure experiences (mountain climbing, surfing, diving, skiing, hiking, etc.). Programs range from eight days to eight weeks and are open to students at every skill level.[53] Details on each Rustic Pathways opportunity can be found at RusticPathways.com.

ABBEY ROAD

An organization founded by Stanford alumni and dedicated to creating opportunities for international student exchange, Abbey Road offers several summer programs for high school students. Students travel to Spain, France, Italy, or Canada for four weeks and participate in a home stay with a family living in the host country. The organization's unique approach to language instruction takes students outside of the classroom, where they engage with locals and participate in activities-based situations that enhance language skills and encourage cultural immersion. In addition to language immersion programs, Abbey Road also offers precollege programs in which students get to take a hands-on approach to the study of a particular topic, for example: studying art and history in the Louvre. While Abbey Road's program in France requires students to have completed 3 years of French, travel to the other countries does not require skill in the languages spoken there.[54] More information on Abbey Road summer opportunities is available at GoAbbeyRoad.com.

INTRAX STUDY ABROAD

Intrax Study Abroad offers summer, semester, or year-long language immersion programs in sixteen countries: Brazil, Costa Rica, Ecuador, Mexico, England, France, Germany, Holland, Ireland, Italy, Spain, Sweden, Australia, China, Japan, and South Africa. In its four-week summer program, participants live with host families in Brazil, France, Spain, or Japan while receiving classroom instruction. The summer program affords a unique opportunity for cultural exchange and does not require participants to have had previous instruction in or exposure to the language of the host country.[55] You can learn more about all of Intrax's opportunities at its website, IntraxStudyAbroad.com.

There are many other summer travel opportunities that may suit your needs and interests. You may even be able to find a program that will allow you to combine your language study with another area of interest, such as the arts, community service, or athletics. In addition to investigating the programs listed above, you should search the Internet to see what you can find. If you're lucky enough to spend your next summer traveling, remember to keep a journal and take lots of pictures—the experience might end up as the subject of one of your college application essays. Bon voyage!

VOLUNTEERING

The activities described above are all interesting and productive ways to spend your summer. However, each one chiefly enriches your own life. While self-improvement is a laudable and respectable aim, "giving back" through community service and volunteerism can also be extremely rewarding. According to the *Merriam-Webster Online Dictionary*, a volunteer is "a person who a person who voluntarily undertakes or expresses a willingness to undertake a service . . . while having no legal concern or interest."[56] In other words, when you volunteer your service to a person or organization, you are making a commitment born of personal conviction to do something you do not have to do. Colleges are almost always interested in seeing that prospective students care about and are involved in helping others. In many ways, volunteering is the easiest summer activity to pursue of all, because no matter where you live or how much time you can commit, there is always going to be someone out there who needs a helping hand. All you have to do is extend yours.

There's literally a world of opportunities for volunteer work, and summer is a great time to make a commitment to serve others in your own community, your place of worship, or even another country. Many of the travel opportunities discussed earlier may be combined with community service activities. And volunteering not only provides you with rewarding, character-building experiences, it can also change lives for the better. The wonderful thing about volunteering is that you get to decide the scale of your involvement. Volunteering can be something simple, like offering to make dinner when the person who usually does so is very busy with something else, or lending a hand to someone with an armload of heavy or cumbersome objects. It can also be a formal engagement in community or religious service, such as working with the Red Cross, Habitat for Humanity, or an Urban Ministries organization (details on activities such as these can be found in Chapter 3). Below is one unique option for involvement

> "You must give some time to your fellow men. Even if it's a little thing, do something for others—something for which you get no pay but the privilege of doing it."
>
> —Albert Schweitzer[57]

this summer. Remember that, as always, it is just a starting point. Chances are you won't have to look any further than your front door for a chance to lend a helping hand.

Laughter Heals

Are you funny? Do you love to laugh? Do you have jokes that you can share? One very special way to serve others is by bringing laughter into their lives. In recent years, several nonprofit organizations have been established for that very purpose. Among them is the Laughter Heals Foundation, whose main objective is to increase awareness of the power of laughter in the physical and emotional healing process. Laughter Heals is currently working to develop "laugh-mobiles" that will bring humor into hospitals, cancer treatment facilities, mental health facilities, and nursing homes through DVDs of classic comedy films and sitcoms, comedic concerts, and other programming. Its newly revamped website provides information on therapeutic humor and features a numbers of jokes and humorous anecdotes.[58] There may be ways for you to help in this important effort. Visit the Laughter Heals website, LaughterHeals.org, learn more about its work and to find out how you can get involved.

Resources for Finding Community Service Opportunities

As stated above, Laughter Heals is just one way to get involved in community service. The DMOZ Open Directory Project, in addition to being a great resource for finding summer sports and hobby camps, is also an excellent resource for locating opportunities to volunteer in the U.S. and other countries.[59] Go to DMOZ.org/Kids_and_Teens/ Teen_Life/Volunteering_and_Service for a list of Internet links to community service organizations and volunteer opportunities that may be right for you. 20 Ways for Teens to Help Others by Volunteering (BYgpub.com/books/tg2rw/volunteer.htm) is another helpful website where you can find a list of tips for creating your own community service opportunity.[60]

STEPS FOR FINDING A GREAT SUMMER PROGRAM

1. **Research**

   Take charge of the situation by using the Internet, school and public libraries, and other resources at your disposal to find out more about ways to get involved in the programs and activities that interest you. Don't hesitate to ask parents, older siblings, teachers, counselors, college students, community leaders, family friends, and others for help in brainstorming ideas or solutions to your concerns.

2. **Timelines, Program Requirements, and Deadlines**

   Keep track of due dates. Apply early to give yourself an edge over other applicants who may be interested in the same types of summer programs as you are.

3. **Contacts**

   Find someone at each organization you are interested in who can answer your questions accurately and give you sound advice about the specific program or experience that interests you. This person may even be able to advocate on your behalf during the application process.

Reading this chapter most likely gave you several ideas about what you'd like to do this summer. What can you do to explore these ideas further? Use your journal to answer this question and to reflect on what you've learned in this chapter.

ENDNOTES

1   Marx Groucho. Quotation. 1994-2005.
    www.quotationspage.com/quotes/Groucho_Marx/.

2   Arrowhead Library System. "College Bound Reading List."
    http://als.lib.wi.us/Collegebound.html.

3   Young Adult Library Services Association (a division of the American
    Library Association). "Good Reads for Teens."
    www.ala.org/ala/yalsa/teenreading/recreading/recommendedreading.htm.

4   Young Adult Library Services Association (a division of the American
    Library Association). "Tips to Encourage Reading."
    www.ala.org/ala/yalsa/teenreading/tipsenc/tipsencourage.htm.

5   U.S. Department of Labor. "Youth & Labor:Age Requirements."
    www.dol.gov/dol/topic/youthlabor/agerequirements.htm.

6   Right to Education. "Canada – [At what age . . . are school-children
    employed, married and taken to court]."
    www.right-to education.org/content/age/canada.html.

7   About, Inc. "About: Job Searching: Teen Jobs."
    http://jobsearch.about.com/cs/justforstudents/a/teenjobs.htm.

8   ItsAboutUs.org. "Get A Job!" 2001.
    www.itsaboutus.org/employment/Default.asp.

9   National Youth Employment Coalition. "What is the National Youth
    Employment Coalition?" www.nyec.org/majoracts.htm.

10 The Forward Group. "Teens4Hire.org." www.teens4hire.org.

11 Artbarn. "Mission and Philosophy." www.artbarn.org/about_us.

12. Artbarn. "High School Internships."
    www.artbarn.org/programs/intern.html.

13 Career Explorations. "Summer Internships for High School Students: Boston
    and New York 2007." 2007.
    www.ceinternships.com/experience_whatis.asp.

14 Wave Hill. "High School Internships." 2007. www.wavehill.org/educa-
    tion/high_school_internships.html.

15 National Security Agency. "Student Programs: High School Programs." www.nsa.gov/careers/students_3.cfm.

16 Seltzer, Neill. *The 500 Best Ways for Teens to Spend the Summer.* New York: Princeton Review, 2004.

17 De Vries, Peter. Quotation. www.quotationspage.com/quotes/Peter_De_Vries/.

18 Virtual High School. "About Us—FAQs." 1996–2007 www.govhs.org/Pages/AboutUs-FAQs.

19 Delta Cyber School. "About: General Information." www.dcs.k12.ak.us/about.html.

20 Florida Virtual School. "FLVS Facts." 2006. www.flvs.net/educators/fact_sheet.php.

21 Kentucky Virtual High School. "General Information: About Kentucky Virtual High School." http://kvhs.org/main.learn?action=about&subaction=information&loc=stud.

22 Michigan Virtual High School. "About Us: What is the Michigan Virtual High School?" 2007. www.mivhs.org/content.cfm?ID=30.

23 Illinois Virtual High School. "Welcome." www.ivhs.org/index.learn?action=welcome&bhcp=1.

24 Columbia County Board of Education. "eLearning Academy." www.ccboe.net/elearning/home.html.

25 Fairfax County Public Schools: Online Campus. "FCPS Online Campus: FAQ's." www.fcps.edu/DIS/onlinecampus/faqs.htm.

26 Pearson Digital Learning - Pearson Education, Inc. "Northampton Area Senior High School, Northampton, PA." Pearson Digital Learning—Pearson Education, Inc. www.pearsondigital.com/successes/novanet/northhampton.cfm.

27 Excel High School. "Excel High School." Excel High School. 2007. www.excelhighschool.com.

28 Veillette, J.R. "PAVE Precollege Summer Program." PAVE—Vanderbilt University. 2003–2006. www.vanderbilt.edu/pave.

29 Plohman, Crystal. "International Fiddle School: Workshops." Crystal Plohman. www.crystalplohman.net/workshops.htm.

30 Blair School of Music—Vanderbilt University. "The Precollege Program." www.vanderbilt.edu/Blair/precoll/precoll_precoll.html.

31 Johns Hopkins University. "Johns Hopkins University Summer Programs: Programs for High School Students." www.jhu.edu/summer/precollege/index.html.

32 Johns Hopkins University. "Johns Hopkins University Summer Programs: Programs for High School Students." www.jhu.edu/summer/precollege/preCollege.html.

33 Johns Hopkins University. "Johns Hopkins University Summer Programs: Discover Hopkins Programs." www.jhu.edu/summer/precollege/discover.html.

34 Johns Hopkins University. "English As A Second Language: ESL Summer Intensive." 2006. www.jhu.edu/ltc/esl/summer_intensive.htm.

35 Colorado College. "Summer Session High School Program." 2006. www.coloradocollege.edu/summerprograms/summersession/precollege.asp.

36 Colorado College. "College Ahead!" 2006. www.coloradocollege.edu/summerprograms/summersession/collegeahead.asp.

37 The University of Miami School of Architecture. "Explorations in Architecture and Design." 2006. www.arc.miami.edu/programs/Explorations.htm.

38 Indiana University Jacobs School of Music. "Precollege and Special Programs: Summer Academies." 2007. www.music.indiana.edu/special_programs/summer.shtml.

39 National High School Institute at Northwestern University. "National High School Institute at Northwestern University." www.northwestern.edu/nhsi/.

40 Snow Farm: The New England Craft Program. "Summer in Arts." 2006. www.snowfarm.org/summerhsprogram.html.

41 University of Pennsylvania—College of General Studies. "Summer Programs for High School Students." www.sas.upenn.edu/CGS/highschool/index_summerhighschool.php.

42 Boston University College of Fine Arts. "Visual Arts Summer Institute." www.bu.edu/cfa/visual/summerarts/index.htm.

43 University of Pennsylvania—College of General Studies. "Summer Programs for High School Students: Penn Summer Art and Architecture Studios." www.sas.upenn.edu/CGS/highschool/summerstudios_hs.php.

44 Interlochen Center for the Arts. "Interlochen Arts Camp." 2006. www.inter-lochen.org/camp/.

45 University of Pennsylvania—College of General Studies. "Summer Programs for High School Students: Penn Summer Theater Workshop." www.sas.upenn.edu/CGS/highschool/summertheater_hs.php.

46 New York University—Tisch School of the Arts. "Tisch: Special Programs: High School Students."
http://specialprograms.tisch.nyu.edu/page/hsStudents.html.

47 Netscape. "Kids and Teens." DMOZ Open Directory Project.
http://dmoz.org/Kids_and_Teens/.

48 SummerOnCampus. "About Us: Summer Camps and Summer Programs for Kids and Teens 8–18+ at Colleges in New York State." 2000–2007.
www.summeroncampus.com/main/AboutUs.asp.

49 Joe Machnik's No.1 Camps. "Mission Statement."
http://no1soccercamps.com/about5.lasso.

50 International Sports Training Camp. "All Sports." 2005.
www.international-sports.com/sports_allsports.php.

51 iD Tech Camps. "iD Gaming Academy: Summer 2007."
www.idgamingacademy.com.

52 Baja California Language College. "Children, Teen and Family Programs."
www.bajacal.com/spanish-immersion-programs/family-program.html.

53 Rustic Pathways. "2007 Rustic Pathways Language Immersion Programs." 2006. www.rusticpathways.com/2007/2007ghtm/language.html.

54 Abbey Road Overseas Programs. "About US." 2006–2007.
www.goabbeyroad.com/aboutus.htm#academics.

55 Intrax Study Abroad. "High School Study Abroad Programs." 2005.
www.intraxstudyabroad.com.

56 Merriam-Webster, Incorporated. "Definition of volunteer." Merriam-Webster Online Dictionary. 2006–2007.
www.webster.com/dictionary/volunteer.

57 Schweitzer, Albert. Quotation.
www.quotationspage.com/quotes/Albert_Schweitzer/.

58 Laughter Heals Foundation—Community Partners. "Laughter Heals." 2002–2003. http://laughterheals.org.

59 Netscape. "Teen Life: Volunteering and Service." DMOZ Open Directory Project.
www.dmoz.org/Kids_and_Teens/Teen_Life/Volunteering_and_Service.

60 Brain, Marshall. "20 Ways for Teens to Help Others by Volunteering." The Teenager's Guide to the Real World Online. Raleigh, NC: BYG Publishing, 1997. www.bygpub.com/books/tg2rw/volunteer.htm.

CHAPTER 5
DO IT YOURSELF!

IT COULDN'T BE DONE

Somebody said that it couldn't be done
    But he with a chuckle replied
That "maybe it couldn't," but he would be one
    Who wouldn't say so till he'd tried.
So he buckled right in with the trace of a grin
    On his face. If he worried he hid it.
He started to sing as he tackled the thing
    That couldn't be done, and he did it!

Somebody scoffed: "Oh, you'll never do that;
    At least no one has done it";
But he took off his coat and he took off his hat,
    And the first thing we knew he'd begun it.
With a lift of his chin and a bit of a grin,
    Without any doubting or quiddit,
He started to sing as he tackled the thing
    That couldn't be done, and he did it.

There are thousands to tell you it cannot be done,
    There are thousands to prophesy failure;
There are thousands to point out to you one by one,
    The dangers that wait to assail you.
But just buckle it in with a bit of a grin,
    Just take off your coat and go to it;
Just start to sing as you tackle the thing
    That "couldn't be done," and you'll do it.

—Edgar Guest[1]

If you watched the *CBS Early Show* in August 2006, you might have learned about an enterprising young man named Bill Bridgers. In the summer before his senior year of high school, he and a friend drove his pickup truck from Atlanta to the West Coast, then to New York, and finally back to Atlanta, spending less than $5.00 on fuel for a 7,500 mile trip. Talk about getting your money's worth! But how'd he do it? Bill took an innovative approach to sidestep obscene gasoline prices by rigging his pickup to run on recycled vegetable oil. Instead of filling up at the pump, he went to restaurants to relieve them of their used cooking oil, effectively using his engine as an environmentally friendly waste disposal service (no toxic fumes here, just the welcome aroma of mandarin chicken).[2] Read more about Bill and his experiment at his website, VegtheUSA.com.

> "Straight vegetable oil . . . runs like diesel fuel . . . no modification to the engine [required,] only add a simple fuel tank . . . . Just a little bit of research, a little know how, and it can be done relatively easily."
>
> —Bill Bridgers[3]

Ever hear the one about the 16-year-old published author? No punch line here, just a very determined young man who, after a few years of research and collecting data, wrote and published *Tips from the Top: Advice for a Young Person from 125 of America's Most Successful People*. Bradley Gallagher spent years interacting and interviewing each of the people profiled in his book, impressing his subjects so much that Max Cleland, former U.S. Senator, wrote the foreword for this inspiring tome. Bradley clearly took his research to heart; he excelled at his studies and currently attends Yale University.[4]

These experiences are just two examples of the many things that inventive and ambitious young people can do to distinguish themselves outside of class and in their own time. Have you always had an idea for a project you'd like to work on but never managed to make it happen? As you'll see, the main difference between students who realize their goals and those who don't is a question of time. By making or taking time to work on your project, you've already won half the battle! The rest is just follow-through.

> **initiative** n (ca. 1793) 1: an introductory step 2: energy or aptitude displayed in initiation of action
>
> —*Merriam-Webster's Collegiate Dictionary*[5]

Warrick Dunn of the National Football League's Atlanta Falcons is a generous humanitarian who uses every resource he has to help out families in need. He can often be seen wearing a t-shirt that says "People say I can't do it. I do it anyway!" This more direct reiteration of the poem at the start of this chapter summarizes the attitude it takes to achieve your dreams and goals. Just like Bill Bridger and Bradley Gallagher, Warrick Dunn succeeds through a combination of determination, initiative, and confidence.

Through exploring the lives of these types of individuals, you will learn tips and techniques to turn your dreams into reality and ideas into action. The first part of this chapter includes many testimonials by courageous, risk-taking, and ambitious young people. As you read them, remember that the only thing between you and amazing things is the willingness to undertake them. Gook luck!

Most Likely to Succeed

When it comes to high achievement, many factors can contribute. For someone with exceptional academic accomplishments, athletic prowess, *and* a desire to make a difference in the lives of others, anything is possible. Brock, who is currently a senior at an Ivy League university, is living proof that such people exist. He shares his story below.

> I guess I first realized that I was good at math in the last years of middle school. It came easy for me, and I always got very positive reinforcement from my teachers and classmates. My family moved from the Northeast to another part of the country during my 7th grade year, and I spent just a short time in 7th-grade-level math at my new school. Almost immediately, I was transferred to an 8th grade class where I continued to excel, even doing 10th grade work! Because of this I was invited to join the high school math team as an alternate for competitions and enrolled in a summer course in advanced math. In the 9th

grade, I officially joined the math team and was a member for all 4 years of high school. During this time, I was entered in the AMC-12 level of the American Math Contests, winning recognition for 3 of my 4 years in high school and coming in second in regional competition during my senior year. (The salutatorian of my senior class won the regionals. We had a very talented and competitive graduating class that won all kinds of honors and awards throughout high school!)

Q: What is AMC-12?

A: AMC-12 is a secondary school mathematics examination offered through the American Mathematics Contest. The test's purpose is to identify and reward students who have outstanding mathematical knowledge and skills. An exceptional score on this multiple-choice exam can lead to further competition, culminating with the participation of finalists in the International Mathematical Olympiad, the most difficult competition of its type in the world.[6]

Math was not the only subject that I enjoyed. I loved school and did well in all of my classes. I particularly liked learning foreign languages, especially Latin and Spanish. The summer after my sophomore year, I was accepted into the Governor's Honors Program in Spanish. (Originally I was named as an alternate; however, following the interview for the program, I was invited to participate in the six-week experience on the campus of one of our state universities.) As a junior, I won the district-wide competition in Spanish and won awards in Latin. I also won my school's 'Student of the Year Award' in foreign languages.

I participated in athletics, as well. In middle school, I played soccer. Coming from the Northeast, I played ice hockey but my new school did not have a hockey program so I played on the city's youth hockey team until high school. (Our team took third in the league while I was on the team.) By that time I was becoming very busy and decided to focus on only one sport. That's when I fell in love with cross-country and track. A parent (who later became our coach) encouraged me to stay with this sport after seeing me run a few times. By 9th grade, I was devoted to running and became a member of the varsity team. In 2000, the coach formed a group of distance runners comprised of myself and three outstanding upperclassmen. The next year, I was named captain of the track team. The school won the state title in cross-country during my junior year and I came in third for the one- and two-mile races in state competition.

My interest in social issues and global awareness led me to join the debate team on which I participated for 4 years. I enjoyed this activity very much. I also served on the discipline and honor council as an upperclassman and, through the school, volunteered as a tutor with the urban ministries program in our area. (My classmates elected me secretary of that community service project during my senior year.)

Despite all I was involved in and all that I had learned, math remained the love of my life. In fact, the most memorable thing that happened to me in high school was related to my love for math. My math teachers were awesome and by my senior year, I couldn't get enough of it. In October of my senior year, I scored 1600 on the SAT and was named STAR [Student Teacher Achievement Recognition] Student by my school and I picked my favorite math teacher as my STAR Teacher. Later that fall, I was named STAR Student for the county. In the winter, I was named STAR Student for the region! I couldn't believe it! As it got closer to state competition in the spring, my parents and I were so excited we could hardly contain ourselves. Finally, the big night arrived and I was chosen as first runner-up for the entire state. This achievement has opened more doors than I ever could have imagined . . . but I'm getting ahead of myself.

As a senior, I applied to MIT, Georgia Tech, and Emory early action and was admitted to all three. (I was also an Emory Scholars candidate that year.) Knowing that I now had some very good choices for college no matter what the outcome, I decided to apply to the most selective Ivy League schools in the nation. When I got into two of them, I knew I had to make some very important decisions that would affect my future forever. I had considered running track and cross-country in college, and both Emory and MIT offered me that opportunity. However, realizing that I was probably not Olympic material, I opted out of attending those schools and decided on one of the Ivies in the Northeast near where I had grown up.

I thought about becoming a psychology major with a math minor, but my love for math made me realize that my heart was just not in psychology. I also realized that I was more interested in applied math than in the theoretical, and I had a serious desire to study economics. As a result, I chose to major in economics on the math track. It is hard work, but I enjoy every minute of it.

Since starting college, I have been involved in many things. For all 4 years, I have tutored incarcerated men for two hours each week at the state prison. (These inmates are seeking a GED in preparation for finding work when they are released.) I participate in intramurals. (I was chosen as captain of the Ultimate Frisbee team in my freshman year.) I have also gotten interested in Indian dance—a relatively new venture for Indian men—and spend about four hours per week in practice. In addition, I am involved in the student association.

My summers since starting college have been busy, as well. I spent my first college summer in Germany, studying the language along with other academic subjects. My second summer, I worked in private wealth management at a Wall Street investment firm. The summer before my senior year, I worked for a New York City bank on the trading floor of the New York Stock Exchange. This experience resulted in my receiving a job offer and I will go to work for the bank when I graduate next spring, putting my passion for math and my knowledge of economics to the test. Right now, I plan to do this for a few years and then go back to school to earn an advanced degree in business or economics. (One of my mentors at the bank informed me that my STAR Student experience was a deciding factor in choosing me for summer employment and in the decision to hire me after undergraduate school. He suggests that I keep that information on my resume for at least 5 years after I graduate.)

My life has been full of exciting opportunities and great mentors (including my parents who are both very successful in the corporate world). I am grateful for my training in all of the areas mentioned above and for the many things I have learned and experienced along the way.*

Success Is a Moot Point

> **moot** adj (ca. 1587) 1: a: open to discussion : DEBATABLE b: subject to discussion : DISPUTED
>
> —*Merriam-Webster's Collegiate Dictionary* [7]

In Chapter 3, you got to know debate as a co- and extracurricular activity. For Isabelle, who entered her first year at a state university in the Northwest in 2006, debate is a true passion. She details her experiences below.

> "Our deepest fear is not that we are inadequate. Our deepest fear is that we are powerful beyond measure. It is our light, not our darkness, that most frightens us."
>
> —Marianne Williamson from *A Return to Love*[8]

I joined the debate team when I was in 9th grade. After attending the first meeting, I was hooked. As I watched passionate, opinionated, intelligent students battle out worldly issues, I knew that I had to take part in that exciting activity. Today, the whole experience of policy debate has shaped many of my beliefs and transformed my whole sense of individuality.

I joined the debate team because of a suggestion from my 8th grade teacher. Having grown up near New York City, I was used to a more liberal take on world events. However, when I moved to another region of the country and joined the newspaper club (an activity in which I had been involved previously), I came to realize that there are more conservative views in this world. I was shocked when, in the first newspaper club meeting where we were discussing the presidential race (Gore v. Bush), there was literally an uproar when I opened my mouth and said that Gore was the best candidate. (To me, it was so obvious!) I then proceeded to write three editorials on topics considered extremely controversial in my new school setting—the adult death penalty, the juvenile death penalty, and abortion. (The abortion piece was returned with the words "inappropriate for middleschool" scribbled across the copy!—my first experience with censorship.) However, this was the beginning of my intense desire to learn more about the issues I cared about. I began researching controversial news items and starting debates in hallways and at lunch tables because I found it immensely disturbing that people could consider *my* views on such subjects as radical and outlandish.

One day we had a project in my social studies class in which we were separated into groups of eight and were assigned the task of having a debate as if we were living during the Industrial Revolution. The debate was to be between a union leader and a factory owner, and the other roles (journalist, union worker, etc.) were supposed to contribute in some way. In my group, I immediately chose to be the union leader. The debate was heated and intense and boiled down to almost a yelling match between me and my opponent. By the end of the confrontation, I had managed to convince all the others involved in the debate, including the factory owner and most members of the class, to accept my side of the argument. Afterwards, my teacher pulled me aside and suggested that I join the debate team when I went on to high school the next year. Little did I know that debate would not only affect many life decisions, it would shape my whole identity.

On the first day of high school, all of the student clubs were introduced, including the debate team. I went to the first debate meeting of the year, as I mentioned earlier, and, once there, fell in love. The members of the debate team were incredibly knowledgeable on both sides of every issue that they discussed. They even had arguments for issues that they did not find particularly important to them but were relevant to everyday discussions. I was especially impressed by one of the members of the debate team, a junior named Monica whose voice could easily fill any room. She spoke with extreme passion and had the kind of knowledge and obvious intellect that I immediately wanted to emulate. Her knowledge on the issues was expansive, and she inspired me to continue with debate. I did not have many wins my first year, but I did make many friends and discovered a great desire to research important issues and improve my critical thinking.

After this first year of getting my feet wet with debate, I decided to go to debate summer camp as Monica had done the previous summer. Like my role model, I decided to attend the Stanford National Forensics Institute. It was this summer that completely transformed me. Before camp, I was somewhat awkward and not particularly up to speed with the arguments and counter-arguments surrounding the issues that I believed in. But when I went to camp, I was introduced to a whole new world.

The debate community has its own unique culture and I had a small taste of it during my first year at debate camp. I met people who argued for fun, who could debate the semantics of an episode of *Family Guy*, who listened to hip-hop because of its politics, and who knew more about European political affairs than my World History high school teacher. I was completely enchanted with this community and wanted desperately to further my involvement in it. I pulled all-nighters researching, and spent weeks developing arguments and endless hours preparing for debates. This was just plain fun to me! I actually enjoyed poring over documents and losing sleep over arguments. Even though I wasn't yet in 10th grade, I already had read Kant, Foucault, Descartes, and other philosophers.

When I returned home after three weeks of being a debate nerd, I had gained a whole new perspective on things. I now stood my ground on every issue. I learned how to argue with "warrants" and how to question the common everyday assumptions that I and everyone around me took for granted.

At debate camp I also met one of the most influential persons in my life—Jewel—who became my mentor and a close friend. She taught me everything from debate to philosophy, and how to make knowledgeable life decisions. There really are no words to describe my respect for Jewel, nor is there really a description of the impact that she has had on my life that could do it justice. It was because of Jewel that I decided to attend the university at which I am now enrolled, to become a lawyer, and to identify myself as an activist.

In 2004 I returned to the Stanford National Forensics Institute, and my debate partner and I won the final round in our debate at the end of the summer. This was the highlight of my high school debate career. Although I really enjoyed debating on my high school team, and have many irreplaceable memories with that team, I had not until that moment had any significant victories at tournaments, nor had I won any significant trophies to hang on my wall.

When I was searching for colleges in my senior year, I decided that debate was not a primary focus for me. Even though it had been my passion, I wanted to look at colleges for their academic reputations rather than for their debate team records. I must say, my involvement with debate probably helped me in the acceptance process. For example, I was accepted by Macalester College, an excellent school, even though I had less-than-wonderful grades. My acceptance was probably based on my extracurricular activities rather than my academic record. In the end, however, I chose a different university at which I was accepted by the Honors Program, even though the school didn't have a policy debate team.

In my first year of college, I joined many activist organizations in my spare time instead of joining the parliamentary debate team. (Policy debate is drastically different than parliamentary, and I wasn't interested in the activity.) However, your passion has a way of finding you and one day, when I was marching in a major immigration protest downtown, the most random thing happened to me. Out of the tens of thousands of people in the crowd, I actually ran into one of my former debate teachers from debate camp, Jen. I had not seen her in over 2 years. A few weeks later, Jen offered me a job as program coordinator of the local Debate Society, which I accepted.

The Debate Society organizes and sponsors "debate across the curriculum" in over 20 schools (elementary through high school) in the area. As program coordinator, I was responsible for facilitating debate programs in schools, conferences, and meetings. Additionally, I helped coach teams when needed, and became the coach of an elementary school debate team in the first-ever elementary school debate tournament in the area. I also helped organize a summer debate camp on my college campus for middle and high school students which incorporated hip-hop into debate.

My experience in the debate community as a leader rather than a student has been a transformative one. I discovered a love for teaching and a renewed love for the debate community. It was a wonderful experience to share an activity that was so significant for me with children who would not have had the opportunity under normal circumstances. Currently, I coach an inner-city school debate team about twice a week. On the weekends, I help organize and judge tournaments.

Though debate was an activity I originally investigated at the suggestion of someone else, it is now an activity to which I devote a great deal of my time through teaching and participation. Thanks to debate, I have become a skilled debater, a devoted activist, and a resourceful teacher.*

The "Write" Stuff

In the following, Esteban relates his story as an example of how unknown talents can emerge from seemingly insignificant experiences and how life can take us places we never dreamed of going.

On Christmas morning when I was 8 years old, I unwrapped my creativity. It appeared in the form of 150 blank pages in plaid binding with a ballpoint pen and colored pencils attached in a pouch on the cover. Not knowing exactly what it was or what I was supposed to do with it, I asked my mom, who explained that it was a journal, my own special book in which I could write or draw anything I wanted. I thought, "Okay! This is a funny present for a little kid," and put it aside in favor of the more interesting things—like toys and games—that had my name on them under the Christmas tree.

Before I went to bed that night, I wrote my name inside the cover and tucked this strange book into my book bag. During the holiday vacation, I decided to write a list of the things I had received for Christmas and what I thought of them. I had also received a joke book and I copied a couple of my favorites to try them out on my friends when I returned to school after the holidays. I had no idea that this "journal" was a harbinger of things to come.

Over the next few months, I used this book to write all sorts of things—thoughts about my older brother when he bugged me, the names of girls that liked me, ideas on how to play tricks on my friends, things I wanted to remember to include in my bedtime prayers, adventures with my best friend, Kenny, and other notes befitting a very active 3rd grader. I also drew pictures of Space Invaders, Pac-Man, and other video game figures, being sure to note the incredible scores I earned. During weekends and school vacations spent in Michigan, I sketched scenes from the porch of my grandparents' home in the country and recorded forays into the woods surrounding their house, which I shared with their dog, Tiger. When I found that the pages were suddenly full, I saved up for a new book, not telling anyone that I really liked this journal.

By the time I was in the 8th grade, journaling and writing had become a passion for me. Then, through the world of rhythm and rap, I discovered a flair for writing poetry. I had always enjoyed hearing it read aloud and the sound of words that seemed to paint pictures in my mind. My family is very verbal and I had long been exposed to the works of poets such as Carl Sandburg, Henry Wadsworth Longfellow, Robert Frost, Maya Angelou, Emily Dickenson, Paul Laurence Dunbar, and Langston Hughes, but I had never thought of writing poems of my own. Then something happened—I don't remember exactly what—and I wrote about it in free verse. I thought it was pretty good, but not wanting to appear corny to my friends or to my brother, I kept it to myself.

In the 9th grade, I began using my journaling habit almost exclusively for writing poetry. By the time I was a junior, I had written rough drafts of several dozen poems in many folders and notebooks. That year, an unexpected turn of events "outed" me as a budding poet and creative writer.

Always the underachiever who viewed good grades only as a way to remain eligible for playing football, I turned in an important assignment for English class in a rare and noteworthy fashion. I chose to do the assignment in poetic form, which was easier for me than writing an essay. Upon reading it, my teacher demanded to know the source of my work and accused me of plagiarism. When I insisted that it was my own original work, she scheduled a meeting with my parents. My stepmother took her side and threatened me with a month's grounding if I did not reveal my source. In my defense, I produced a collection of my work, written in my own hand over the last 3 years, including some of the material I had turned in for the English assignment in question.

The next day, my stepmom called my English teacher to schedule a second meeting. My parents had had a change of heart after reading my poetry and not only wanted to show the teacher my capabilities, they also wanted to demand an apology for her having accused me of plagiarism. The teacher apologized, my punishment was rescinded, and all three of them praised my work. It felt good to be affirmed for my writing, even if it meant that I could no longer keep my talents to myself.

In my senior year, I tried my hand at writing rap and hip-hop lyrics for an up-and-coming group of rappers in Florida. I was even invited to forgo college in order to write for them exclusively. Of course, my parents would not hear of it and I enrolled in a Midwestern university the following fall. I continued writing and in my second year of college, I decided to compile a book of my poems and publish it myself. The finished product included over a hundred poems in rhyme, free verse, and blank verse. This is one of the poems I wrote while I was working on my book.

REPLY

Should I write a book on
            Everything I know
                    Or should I Just
                            Stop lyin'
            Or
Should I write a book on everything I don't know
            But then
                    How would I ever finish?
    See,
            These things say
                    Forget it, man
                            'Cause it will never happen
            All these things say
                    Yeah it can
                            For the superhero
            Yeah it can
                    Tomorrow
                            Signed: The Average Man
                            To: The Superhero
    Dated: Yesterday

I left school at the end of that year and went to work in an environmental research lab, testing water samples. However, I was bored to death in this setting and began to explore careers in the media. I am now pursuing a film/screenwriting major at a Midwestern art school and working on a project for a cable-access television station. Through this circuitous journey, I have learned that my passion for writing is leading me toward doing things the "write" way.*

All Roads Lead to Radio

Sometimes your passions can lead you to use your talents in ways you never thought possible. Natasha loves what she does in the world of music and entertainment, and she attributes her current success to her love of vocal music and her desire to share her talents with large audiences. She describes her journey below.

> "You have to become what you've never been before in order to do what you've never done before."
>
> —Kuwana Haulsey
> from *Angel of Harlem*[9]

One time my parents took me out to dinner at the Anchor Bar ("Home of the Buffalo Wing") in Buffalo, New York. I was only 5 or 6 years old, but I remember getting on stage and singing with the band. When I finished, I took a bow and the audience clapped, whistled, and rose from their seats. I loved every moment of it—the attention, the sound of the applause, the smiles on their faces. I remember it as clearly as if it happened last night.

Even though I never had voice lessons, I sang all the time and always had a solo part in school assemblies when I was in elementary school. On Saturdays, one of our local TV stations featured old movies and musicals and, by the time I was 8 or 9 years old, I watched these instead of cartoons like a normal kid. I imagined myself in these movies, singing, dancing, and acting like Doris Day, Judy Garland, Shirley Temple, and all the other stars. In the 4th or 5th grade, I joined the school chorus. I sang soprano and lived for rehearsals and performances where I almost always sang a solo, sometimes even with a dancing part. I could never seem to get enough of singing and being on stage.

This continued into high school. I was admitted to the magnet high school for high academic achievers. I was a good student all around, but music was my passion. I took as many music classes as my schedule would allow and I sang in the chorus. I also auditioned for every dramatic production, most of them musicals, and landed key roles in all of the musicals.

When it came time to think about college, I decided that I wanted to major in musical theater. My grades had dropped a bit because of my obsession with music, but, on my teachers' recommendations, I was offered auditions at Juilliard, California School of the Arts, and Eastman School of Music at University of Rochester. I chose to attend Cal Arts because I wanted the experience of attending college far away from home and it was there that I began formal vocal training. I was doing well in the program when I got word that my mother had terminal lung cancer. I left school after the first year and returned to Buffalo, where I enrolled in a state university music program with a business minor.

For a while I was sidetracked. Spending time in the hospital with my mom, I developed an interest in nursing. I got a job there as a nurse's aid on the night shift. Working this shift, I was often left to manage many of the duties of the nursing station. I really liked the job and the feeling I got from helping patients and families cope with illness and injuries from accidents. I discovered that I was very good at handling crises and I developed pretty good management, public relations, and leadership skills. For a while I considered becoming a nurse, but in the long run, I could not see myself in a future that did not include music. Also, I was in my third year of college and did not want to have to start all over in another field. Then one day, it happened. A mentor appeared and changed my life forever.

In my music business class, my instructor invited a speaker from a media promotions company who talked to us about music media, advertising, and public relations. I was so inspired by her that I sought her advice about how to get involved. She agreed to meet with me to discuss this further and, after a few weeks, offered me an internship with her company. A couple of months after I began the internship, a member of her staff was discharged, and she offered me that position! Though scared to death, I jumped at this opportunity and accepted the job. Before long, I knew what I wanted to do with my life. Not only did the work just seem to come naturally for me, I liked it so well I decided to pursue a career in it. I stayed with the company for a few years and, because of contacts with local radio personalities and music media personnel, I received an offer from the general manager of the top adult urban music station in Buffalo. By now, I knew that this was my calling. I had no second thoughts about my readiness to take on this new challenge, and with the encouragement and blessings of my employer/mentor I accepted the position.

Unfortunately, 4 years later tragedy struck my family again: I lost my dad to cancer. Soon after his death I decided to leave Buffalo for a warmer climate and new surroundings. The next year, with excellent references from my Buffalo employers, I landed a job in the Southeast with a major radio station. Today, I'm the director of Marketing and Promotions for the premier adult urban music station in my city—it's also one of the top of its kind in the United States!

I still sing all the time and I still love musical theater. However, instead of applauding my personal on-stage performances, my audience now rises to its feet to applaud Grammy-, BET-, and other award-winning performers from all over the world at the concerts and events I plan, promote, and manage. I get my applause from knowing that my marketing and promotions team and I helped to make it all happen.*

The Road to "Break a Leg!"

Are you the proud owner of a Technicolor Dreamcoat? Do you harbor hopes of one day playing gondolier beneath a Parisian opera house? How about just being "*Wicked*?" If so, the following story is sure to inspire you. Delaney's commitment to her talent and passion for musical theater is nothing less than amazing. But that's just the beginning . . .

I can't remember when I didn't have an interest in music. I first took piano lessons when I was 5 years old and this is probably when my interest began. I started thinking about a career in theater after appearing in church plays and getting really positive feedback from people.

When I was 13 years old, I had my first voice lessons. These lessons continued off and on throughout high school. I also took some acting classes, appearing in a summer production of *Grease* along the way. Even then, theater was just a dream for me and not yet a passion. I got involved in the theater program at my high school the next year. It wasn't until the following year, however, the 11th grade, that musical theater took hold of me. I performed in my high school's production of *Gypsy* and everything changed. I don't know why . . . something just clicked. I started taking my voice lessons seriously and was eventually accepted into the precollege drama program at Carnegie Mellon University between my junior and senior years. I took part in the conservatory training experience in music theater, which stresses discipline, skill, and creativity. It was very challenging and I would recommend it highly to anyone who is serious about a career in drama, music theater, or technical theater.

During my senior year, the school presented *Les Miserables* and I was cast in the role of Eponine. We received rave reviews from local newspaper critics and seasoned theater-goers. We were even favorably compared to the professional touring production of *Les Mis*! I received a lot of positive feedback personally, as well. It was really exciting.

Needless to say, I was disappointed when I was not admitted to some of the big-name theater programs to which I had applied, but this helped me become aware of my strengths and weaknesses as they applied to musical theater. I realized that I particularly needed to work on my dancing. I enrolled in dance classes with the top dance school in my area and worked very hard to overcome the frustration I felt at not being to master this craft as easily as I had with voice and acting. Finally, I came to the conclusion that, while I would probably never be chosen to dance in *A Chorus Line*, I had learned to move well on stage. (My hip-hop class still pays off in the clubs on Saturday nights!)

I was accepted into the theater programs at the University of Miami and Elon University in North Carolina, and I chose Elon for the liberal arts experience and because it was relatively close to home. The theater program was very good there, but after my experience at Carnegie Mellon, I realized that I was much more interested in a conservatory program. While at Elon, I spoke often with a classmate who had gone to the University of Miami and discovered that his experience was more focused on musical theater, which was what I wanted. At Elon, I found it hard to balance my studies in math and other required courses with my desire to work on my theater crafts. So, by the spring of my freshman year, I had decided to transfer to the University of Miami. I reapplied and was accepted!

That summer, I teamed up with a group of my classmates—all passionate about the performing arts—and we decided to raise our own production. We chose *The Last Five Years* but had no idea how we would secure the rights to produce it. It took some doing, but we finally convinced a prominent physician in our area, who also shares our love of musical theater, to back us financially and help us secure a venue. He formed a production company and convinced the headmaster at our high school to allow us to use the school's facilities for our production. Our former drama teacher agreed to direct the show and we were on our way. The production was very successful and we even had the opportunity to take it to a nearby major metropolitan area for a brief run at a small theater there. From this experience, I learned that doing it yourself is one way to make things happen in the theater business.

In the fall, I transferred to the University of Miami and I have enjoyed every minute of my time here. The program here is very different from the one at Elon, and being here has turned my passion into an obsession. I now live and breathe theater.

Through the University of Miami, I was able to take part in a month-long training program in music theater that involved acting, dance, and vocal coaching in Italy! This was an excellent program, offering me the opportunity to meet talented and interesting people and to get a new perspective on theater. Last summer, I had a paid internship with the Creed Repertory Theater in the mountains of Colorado. In addition to raising and performing in two productions—*Sweeney Todd* and *Crazy for You*—I gained invaluable experience by working 20 hours per week in the box office. As a senior, I am looking forward to graduation. Over the summer, I hope to find work in summer stock. If I don't, I will move to New York a little sooner and begin pounding the pavement to find the parts that will feed my obsession and bring me closer to my dream—a major role in a Broadway musical.*

A Test of Endurance

Remember Todd, the Wake Forest student who spent the summer following his sophomore year of high school in the Johns Hopkins precollege program? (The story's in Chapter 4.) Wait until you read about what he did the next summer! With his friend Laci, a group of 10 other young people, and half a dozen group leaders, Todd rode his bicycle from coast to coast.

Organized biking trips are becoming more and more popular, both in the United States and abroad, as young people look for new and exciting opportunities to explore the world. Todd and Laci signed up for the trek with Overland, a company that offers 30 different programs for teens and pre-teens, in areas such as community service, overseas language immersion, writing, outdoors experiences, and much more! Opting for the "American Challenge," they joined a biking expedition designed for 15- to 18-year-olds that took them from Savannah, Georgia to Santa Monica, California in six weeks.[10] Leaving the Atlantic Ocean behind, they crossed America's arid flatlands and towering mountain ranges, bound for the Pacific coast on an adventure that changed their lives in a monumental manner.

Laci, who entered a New England liberal arts college in the fall of 2005, describes her experience:

> Every summer, I went to camp in Chattanooga, Tennessee. It was an all-activities camp where I qualified for scuba and became a counselor-in-training. I had always wanted to participate in an outdoor experience on my own, but most of the programs I had heard about were kind of cheesy. You know, "going out into the woods to find yourself . . . ." Then my friend Todd and I heard about Overland and we committed to doing the coast-to-coast bike trip together.
>
> We started training in the spring, taking one or two 20-mile bike rides a week. When we got new bikes for the trip, we began riding three or four days (30 to 50 miles), increasing the mileage, frequency, and intensity of our training as we approached our departure on the trip.
>
> When we arrived in Savannah to join our group and start off across the U.S. by dipping our wheels in the Atlantic Ocean, I was scared to death. I'm not really athletic, I had no idea what

to expect, and here I was about to spend the last six weeks of my summer away from the security of home.

Once we were on our way, I felt a little better. After a couple of days, we started to see change. The farther away from Savannah we got, the more pronounced the changes became—geography, climate, people, everything!

At times, I was really lonely and homesick. I recall one experience in particular, when I had a panic attack. It was raining and I had gotten separated from the group. I remember wanting to crash my bike just so I could stop riding. (I talked myself out of that madness right away!) There were other times when it all seemed very unreal, like the day one of the leaders and I had to hitchhike.

Then one day, it was suddenly over. We were on the beach in Santa Monica, California, heading for the Pacific Ocean to dip our wheels, signaling the end of the ride. When we came out of the water and someone asked me how I felt, I could barely talk. I hadn't realized that I was crying—crying so hard that I was unable to speak clearly for a few minutes.

I kept a journal of sorts. Although I didn't write in it every day, I did record the mileage, speed, and other factors each night before I went to sleep. I also had a map of the United States on which I traced our progress and our routes.

Over time, I have recognized that it wasn't the whole experience that affected me most, but the many things I experienced and learned along the way. I would tell others who . . . tak[e] a trip like this or even those who do something else along their road to college to view their experiences as unique to them. Whether it's a precollege experience or choosing and attending a college, it's important to recognize that you are an individual and someone else's experience may not be the same for you.

Todd agrees with Laci, adding:

I learned so much about myself on this trip and when it was all over I realized that I could do anything that was humanly possible if I was committed and determined in doing it. The Overland trip was an amazing experience and I will remember it for the rest of my life.

For the second half of her sophomore year of college, Laci has decided to take a leave of absence. Her school's small-town New England location is a long way from her urban Southern roots, and she feels that she needs a break from the rigors of academia and time to think about what she wants to do in the future. This past fall, she was offered the opportunity to do an internship in unbiased, fact-based journalism at a nonpartisan institute in Washington, DC. There she will engage in research and writing under the supervision of a mentor among a group of professional journalists. She is very excited about this impending experience and feels, like Todd, that after the Overland trip anything is possible with determination and planning.

GO YOUR OWN WAY

Now that you've read about some young people who have been proactive and succeeded in forging their own path, the rest of this chapter will give you some possibilities for constructing your own "outside-the-box" experience. Participating in a diversity or intercultural experience, starting a business, creating a new program or activity, or taking a "gap year" between high school and college are all ways for you to find yourself that are looked at favorably by colleges.

DIVERSIFY!

College and university admission committees value evidence of intercultural experiences and have a respect for diversity in their applicants. In fact, most institutions of higher learning in the United States make a concerted effort to admit classes that reflect the nation's varied socioeconomic, ethnic, religious, and geographic diversity. Many also spend significant dollars on developing and implementing programs that teach tolerance and respect for different backgrounds and viewpoints and honor young people for individual and group accomplishments in this important area.

Take Princeton University as an example. In 2003, it started a program that offers awards to high school students who have made significant strides in improving race relations in their schools or communities. The first awards—one $1,000 prize and two $500 prizes—were awarded in 2004 to one student from Boston and two others from Washington, DC.

> "If we are to achieve a richer culture, rich in contrasting values, we must recognize the whole gamut of human potentialities, and so weave a less arbitrary social fabric, one in which each diverse human gift will find a fitting place."
>
> —Margaret Mead
> from *Sex and Temperament in Three Primitive Societies*[11]

Nine other students from these metropolitan areas received certificates of recognition for their work as well. "The Princeton Prize in Race Relations" has now expanded to include Atlanta, Houston, and St. Louis, and plans are underway to eventually offer the program in metropolitan areas across the nation.[12]

Additionally, hundreds of independent school students annually participate in the National Association of Independent Schools (NAIS)'s Student Diversity Leadership Conference (SDLC). This conference occurs in conjunction with the People of Color Conference for independent school administrators and faculty, which is designed to promote inclusiveness and to train educators in their efforts to foster multiculturalism and diversity in their schools.[13]

According to NAIS, "Student buy-in and ownership of any diversity initiative is critical to its success," meaning that student leadership is vital in this important work.[14] Through the SDLC, 9th through 12th grade students from a broad array of racial, ethnic, and religious cultures come from all over the nation to live and work together for several days in a fun and inclusive climate. Here they learn from each other, share their concerns and ideas, and engage in activities that will allow them to return to their schools and assist in the creation and maintenance of programs that make for a more welcoming and supportive school community.

There are countless other opportunities for impassioned students to learn about issues related to diversity and to get involved in experiences and activities that will not only benefit themselves but also the surrounding community. For example, students can play an instrumental role in instilling inclusiveness and multiculturalism in their school by encouraging their teachers and administrators to participate in a program called SEED (Seeking Educational Equity and Diversity). The National SEED Project on Inclusive Curriculum has been in operation for more than 20 years, and it has evolved into a highly regarded monthly seminar that utilizes reading, audiovisual media, exercises, and open discussions to promote greater awareness of diversity issues among public and private school staff in order to generate positive change. The program also offers a Summer New Leaders' Workshop, a week-long experience for educators who are interested in being leaders in implementing their school or school district's diversity efforts.[15]

Another way for students to promote diversity in their schools is to encourage the school administration to consider using the Assessment of Inclusivity and Multiculturalism (AIM), "a comprehensive assessment tool that engages your school community in evaluating inclusivity and multiculturalism . . . [delivering] tangible results your school can use to strategically plan for building and sustaining inclusive independent school communities."[16]

Tolerance.org is a website offered under the auspices of corporate sponsors and the Southern Poverty Law Center, a nonprofit organization founded in 1971 to battle discrimination, intolerance, and hate through education and the judicial system.[17] Tolerance.org devotes web pages to teen learning and provides suggestions for activities and grants for combating intolerance in schools and communities. To get a better idea of what others have done to make a difference in their schools and communities, visit Tolerance.org/teens/index.jsp. You can also download posters, get project ideas, and gather information that will enable you to take the initiative to do something meaningful for multiculturalism.

BUSINESS AS USUAL

According to DaVinciMethod.com, many successful entrepreneurs—people who begin and undertake business ventures—are of similar personality types. Among the traits found among successful business owners such as Walt Disney, Thomas Edison, Bill Gates, Oprah Winfrey, and Sean Combs are high energy, the willingness to take risks, ambition, industry, and skill in problem-solving.[18] Do you possess these traits? If you're interested in starting a business or organization, self-awareness is essential. You must have solid ideas about your strengths and weaknesses and how they relate to running your own business before you embark on this experience.

Once you have decided that you're suited for the entrepreneurial experience, there are some key steps to take to get your business up and running. These include:

- **Assessing of your suitability, energy, and passion for the work of starting and running a business.**

  As mentioned before, this step is essential. Without it, the other steps may prove futile. DaVinciMethod.com and About.com are two online resources that provide entrepreneurial tests you'll find helpful for self-assessment.

- **Identifying the nature of the business.**

  This involves brainstorming ideas for the business and doing research to learn all you can about the service or product your business will provide. Included in this step is deciding whether your business will be for-profit or nonprofit, and whether you will be the sole owner or it will be a partnership.

According to About.com, the term *nonprofit* applies to an organization that is bound, legally, to restrain from distributing company earnings to anyone who is in a position of control over the organization, including its founders, board members, or general membership. It may, however, compensate them financially for the provision of goods or services.[19]

In the U.S. Small Business Administration's *Handbook for Small Business*, "sole proprietorship" is defined as "a business owned and operated by one person," while a "partnership" is "an association of two or more people as co-owners of a business for profit."[20]

- **Getting advice and assistance.**

  It's important to gather and consult resources that can provide you with vital information about the necessary licenses or permits you may need to start up your business (name copyrighting, insurance, zoning codes, etc.). Government agencies, chambers of commerce, and owners of similar businesses are among the resources at your disposal.

- **Developing a Business Plan.**

  Look at it this way—you can't build a house if you don't have the blueprint. It's the same way with a business. Luckily, you have the good people at the U.S. Small Business Administration on your side. Check out the website they created specifically for young entrepreneurs, SBA.gov/teens/myplan.html. You can also find help in this area from your local chamber of commerce.

- **Finding Funds for Start-up and Operations.**

  Businesses are generally financed with personal funds, investments from other organizations (AKA "venture capital"), and business loans. To ensure at least a shot at success, you must be able to make fairly accurate projections of start-up costs and the funds needed for operations in the early stages of the business.

Business is all about ambition, action, and exploration—if you're an aspiring entrepreneur or hopeful boardroom titan, get out there and see what you can make happen!

GETTING ENGAGED

Of course, starting a business isn't the only way to initiate something new. If you have an idea for a new activity, why not start it (or organize a group for it) yourself?

Just as with business-oriented endeavors, if you want to get something started, you need a little help from those who know the ropes. Think of adults or organizations that have similar interests or goals as you (several such organizations may be found in the pages of this book). The following list features additional places to take your search for sponsors.

- Chambers of commerce
- Churches, temples, and other religious organizations
- Libraries
- Local and national youth organizations
- Nonprofit and community service organizations (United Way, Junior Achievement, Boys and Girls Clubs, Girl Scouts, Boy Scouts)
- Schools

You may want to call these organizations to find out who there would prove your best contact. Get the names, titles, addresses, and phone numbers of these people and write them a letter or email; then follow up on this correspondence with a phone call. Remember: Be persistent. They may not get back to you the first, second, or tenth time for any number of reasons, but be sure they understand clearly your goals and how they could help you in pursuing them. If possible, it's best to make an appointment to speak with them in person. However, before you meet them, think through your approach carefully, and have a solid idea of what you're going to say. Be prepared to discuss your proposed project in detail. Also, be sure you indicate your willingness to take the lead in turning the ideas into practice should the opportunity presents itself.

> Note: Older teens, college students, and young adults may be able to obtain help from the United States Junior Chamber (U.S. Jaycees), a nonprofit organization that provides support for 18- to 40-year-old American entrepreneurs. The Jaycees offer assistance in business development, training, and other key areas to enhance opportunities for success among this segment of the population. More information on the Jaycees and its programs is available at USJaycees.org/learn_more.htm.[21]

Mind The Gap

Sometimes a student may decide to take a year off between graduating from high school and starting college. This is called a "gap year" (or an "interim year") and is a common practice among young

Europeans. For American students, this decision may, in some instances, reflect the desire to improve on the academic record earned in high school in order to gain admission to a more selective college, or to become more comfortable with the transition to postsecondary education and the independence of living away from home. Usually students use their year off to travel, volunteer, work, or engage in other experiences that will broaden their perspectives and heighten their global awareness.

If you're interested in having a gap year, but are unsure of what you could do, visit The Center for Interim Programs, LLC at InterimPrograms.com for an idea. Of course, many recent high school graduates who opt to take a year off look for their own unique way in which to spend this time.

> For nearly 100 years, Young Judaea has served Jewish youth with programs and activities that promote pride in their heritage, encourage their identification with Jewish and Zionist values and teaching, and foster commitment to the support of Israel.[22]

Jeremiah, an independent school graduate who is now enrolled in college, requested a 1-year deferment of his admission so that he could travel to Israel with Young Judaea. Because Jeremiah is currently studying abroad in South Africa, he asked his mother to tell his story on his behalf.

> Throughout Jeremiah's life, he has spent at least two weeks of every summer visiting family and friends in Israel. Since the 8th grade, he has also spent several weeks at a Jewish summer camp in the mountains of North Carolina. In high school, he played soccer on his school's varsity team, winning numerous athletic awards in conference, regional, and state competitions. As a result, he was appointed Sports Director of the camp for the summer prior to his junior year. Each year since then, he has worked at the camp as a counselor, supervising a division of 13-year-old boys.

As a senior in high school, Jeremiah applied and was admitted to several selective colleges, and decided to enroll at his first-choice institution. However, feeling that what he actually wanted was a year off from traditional academic study, he applied for the Young Judaea program. When he was accepted, he sought the advice of his college counselor who suggested that he request deferment of his enrollment at the university he planned to attend and follow his heart. He was granted the deferment and, that fall, embarked on a life-changing experience.

Arriving in Israel in late summer, he visited family for a few days, then, along with some 200 other Young Judaeans, he began 3 months of Judaic studies in the Hebrew language in Jerusalem. On weekends, the group engaged in sightseeing, outdoor experiences such as hiking and canoeing, and interaction in Israeli everyday life. Each month, the group was granted some time off to do as they chose, and Jeremiah used this time to deepen his relationships with family members, friends, and other Young Judaea participants, building important, lasting relationships.

In December, the academic portion of the program ended and Jeremiah moved on [to] the Absorption Center in Gennaret, near Tiberias, where he assisted teaching English to Ethiopian children until March. Following this experience, he was enrolled in the ROTC, a youth division of the Israeli Army, engaging in basic military training. There, he learned the principles of military discipline and was trained in military tactics and the use of artillery.

In May, he was released from his duties with the Army and spent the next six weeks of the program in activities and interaction related to his particular area of interest—international relations. A high point of his Young Judaea experience occurred during this period when he was chosen, among the 200 participants, as one of 11 students to meet and spend time with Ariel Sharon, the Israeli Prime Minister. Another high point was his experience living and working as a ranger in the Negev Desert with the Druse, an Israeli minority group whose responsibility is the maintenance and preservation of the Nature Preserves. There he engaged in archaeological digs, paving roads, and other work required in the desert canyons.

When his experience with Young Judaea ended, he was joined by a childhood friend and classmate for travel to London and Prague, returning home on July 4. The next week, he went to work at the North Carolina summer camp, serving again as a counselor, for the rest of the summer.

Jeremiah started college in the fall, after having deferred enrollment for the previous year. However, he met with unanticipated frustrations and challenges. To start with, at 19, he was a year older than most of his classmates. In addition, he had been away from the formal classroom for almost a year and had been on his own for most of his time in Israel. Now, living in the dorm with the rules and the characteristic behavior of young college students, he was often frustrated. But, having learned the importance of adapting to unfamiliar surroundings during his year in Israel, he got through that first semester and finished the year with great success. During the spring semester he also discovered his true passion through interaction with a professor from the International Studies program.

Learning of Jeremiah's athletic accomplishments in soccer, the professor began talking frequently with Jeremiah about international sports. From there, they developed a relationship that was centered on discussions of international politics and economics. Because Jeremiah had been considering economics as a major, he was fascinated by these conversations. By the end of the year, he was sold on the idea of combining international studies and economics—majoring in economics and enrolling in the four-plus-one program. This option would allow him to earn a master's degree in international relations with a concentration in economics after 4 years of undergraduate studies and just 1 year in graduate school.

Now, nearing the end of his first semester as a junior in college, Jeremiah will soon return from South Africa, where he had the awesome experience of climbing Mt. Kilimanjaro. In South Africa, he says that he was constantly aware of the political climate there and was disturbed by the poverty, health, and education issues he observed and by the vestiges of apartheid that remain in that country. He now believes that he views race relations with a new perspective.

On his way back to the United States, Jeremiah will spend three weeks in Israel where he will rest for a brief time before returning to college life. He has matured significantly as a result of his experiences during his gap year, all of which have helped him to develop into a happy, self-assured young man who is doing well in his college studies and looking forward to a future in international relations.*

Although the gap year is becoming increasingly popular in the United States, it is still unusual for several students from the same class at one school to take a year off. However, eight—that's right, eight!—students from a prestigious college preparatory school in the Southeast opted to defer college enrollment in 2001 in favor of a gap year. Their college counselor shares their stories below.

> The Fulbright Scholar Program is the premier academic exchange experience of the U.S. government. This program is administered by the Center for the International Exchange of Scholars (CIES), a private arm of the Institute of International Education (IIE). The Institute works to foster and support educational relations between United States and countries abroad, creating and promoting links between colleges and universities around the world.[23]

- "Melody traveled with James (another student highlighted below) to Mexico and Latin America in the fall. During the second semester she went on a wilderness expedition with the National Outdoor Leadership School (NOLS), an organization recognized worldwide for two 12-week offerings in outdoor experiences. She enrolled at Kenyon College in the fall of 2002, graduating in the spring of 2006. Winning recognition as a Fulbright Scholar, she then went to South Korea where she began teaching. She did very well at Kenyon and was very involved in getting the college to buy food from local farmers rather than from vendors outside the local area. According to admission officers at Kenyon, Melody distinguished herself as one of the college's most visible and influential students."

- "James traveled with Melody (above) in Mexico and Latin America. In the second half of the school year he traveled throughout Asia and other parts of the world. He enrolled at the University of Virginia in the fall of 2002."

- "Cassie worked in a soup kitchen sponsored by the Brethren Church in Washington, DC, where she was paid $50 a month plus room and board. In the fall of 2002, she went to Oberlin College. She graduated in 2006 and currently works in Philadelphia."

- "Simon went to Colby College but left after one semester. He came back home and painted houses until he entered Wake Forest in January 2003. He graduated from there in 2006."

- "Jack went to Australia, where he operated a camp for children. He entered Colorado College in the winter of 2002, later transferring to a college in the Southeast."

- "Diana went to Switzerland where she worked as a nanny for children in a French-speaking household (her goal being to improve her French). She entered Middlebury in the fall of 2002."

- "Alan hiked the Appalachian Trail—a scenic national trail extending from Maine to Georgia—during his gap year. He entered Appalachian State University in the winter of the next year."

- "Bill went to Georgia Tech for two weeks. He had enrolled there to study environmental engineering but found that the program did not match his needs and expectations. He spent the winter of that year working at a ski resort in New England and then applied early decision to Bowdoin College the next year. Bill graduated from Bowdoin in spring 2006."

The counselor also told us about a more recent gap year participant from her school:

- "Charisse (2004) took a year off to travel to Thailand with GlobalQuest, an experiential academic study abroad program for high school and interim year students. After a rewarding experience with this program, she matriculated into Middlebury College in the fall of 2005."*

As you can see, taking a gap year offers more than just an adventure—it gives you invaluable opportunities to grow as a person and discover the world. If you're considering taking a year off, it's recommended that you still complete your college search and the application process as detailed in Chapters 2 and 7. That way, once you're admitted to college, you can request deferment for 1 year by writing the admissions office—you'll have a year to explore life without the stress of not knowing where you're headed after. Most colleges will honor your request, but will likely require a deposit to hold your place in the class for the following year. (Note: Some public colleges may ask you to reapply to the institution for the year you plan to enroll.) Needless to say, in a situation like this it's better to be safe than sorry, not to mention much easier to apply to college and obtain the necessary supporting documents (transcripts, teacher and counselor recommendations, etc.) and apply for scholarships while you are still in high school. Simply put, good use of your time now will ensure that you enjoy all of your experiences later.

Feeling inspired? Ready to storm the corporate world, start up your own nonprofit, or travel everywhere from Shanghai to Sheffield? Go for it! This would be the perfect time to get your journal and write some entries. Think about particular experiences that have encouraged you to use your talents or ideas more fully. Examine how you've gone about realizing goals in your life to this point and how you could build on that experience now. Make a list of questions you might have about the things you've read in this chapter and a list of helpful websites and resources. Also be sure to include reflections on the stories and information you've read. When you have finished writing, you should have a good amount of material to use in conjunction with the next chapter, which can help you plan next steps in getting involved and developing your talents.

*This text was taken directly from interviews transcribed by the author. While it was edited for clarity and grammar, the interviewee's voice and message remain intact.

ENDNOTES

1   Guest, Edgar Albert "It Couldn't Be Done." Poetry Foundation.
www.poetryfoundation.org/archive/poem.html?id=173579.

2   CBS News, CBS Broadcasting, Inc. "7,500 Miles on $5 In Gas, Veggie
Oil." August 18, 2006.
www.cbsnews.com/stories/2006/08/18/earlyshow/main1910319.shtml?
CMP=ILC-SearchStories.

3   Holopirek, Jemelle. "Teenager Going 'Veg' Across the U.S.A." Gray
Television.
http://media.graytvinc.com/documents/Teenager_Going_Veg_Across_US
A.htm.

4   Wikipedia Foundation. "Bradley Gallagher."
http://en.wikipedia.org/wiki/Bradley_Gallagher.

5   Merriam-Webster, Inc. *Merriam-Webster's Collegiate Dictionary*, 10th Ed.
Springfield, Massachusetts: Merriam-Webster, 1999. 602.

6   The MAA American Math Competitions. "What's What: AMC's Programs
and Contests." 2006. www.unl.edu/amc/whatswhat.shtml.

7   Merriam-Webster, Inc. *Merriam-Webster's Collegiate Dictionary*, 10th Ed.
Springfield, Massachusetts: Merriam-Webster, Inc., 1999. 756.

8   Williamson, Marianne. *A Return to Love*. Harper Collins. 2004. compact
disc.

9   Haulsey, Kuwana. Angel of Harlem. New York: Ballantine, 2004. 202

10 Overland. "Biking Trips: Introduction: American Challenge."
www.overlandsummers.com/article/view/6145/1/765/.

11 Mead, Margaret. Quotation.
www.giga usa.com/quotes/authors/margaret_mead_a001.htm.

12 Princeton University, Office of Communications. "Three High School
Students Win Princeton Prize in Race Relations." April 20, 2004.
www.princeton.edu/pr/news/04/q2/0420-prize.htm.

13 National Association of Independent Schools. "Equity and Justice Initiatives
Team: Student Diversity Leadership Conference (SDLC)."
www.nais.org/equity/index.cfm?Itemnumber=147342&sn.ItemNumber=14
7355&tn.ItemNumber=147377.

14 National Association of Independent Schools. "Equity in Action: Student Voices."
www.nais.org/equity/index.cfm?itemnumber=146095&sn.ItemNumber=14 7382.

15 Wellesley Centers for Women, Wellesley College. "Our Work: National SEED Project on Inclusive Curriculum (Seeking Educational Equity and Diversity)." 2006. www.wcwonline.org/projects/title.php?id=36.

16 National Association of Independent Schools. "Assessment of Inclusivity and Multiculturalism (AIM): Take Aim!"
1997–2006.
www.nais.org/equity/index.cfm?itemnumber=147587&sn.ItemNumber=14 7832.

17 Tolerance.org. "Mix It Up." www.tolerance.org/teens/index.jsp.

18 Media for Your Mind. "The DaVinci Method." 2005.
www.davincimethod.com/entrepreneur-
test/?gclid=CKHi1Yml_IgCFRO6SgodLi39pg.

19 About, Inc. "About: Economics: Definition of Nonprofit." 2007.
http://economics.about.com/cs/economicsglossary/g/nonprofit.htm.

20 U.S. Small Business Administration. *Handbook for Small Business*. 1989.
www.sba.gov/library/pubs/mp-31.pdf.

21 The United States Junior Chamber (Jaycees). "About the Jaycees."
www.usjaycees.org/learn_more.htm.

22 Young Judaea, The Zionist Youth Movement Sponsored by Hadassah. "About Young Judaea." 1999–2006. www.youngjudaea.org/html/overview.html.

23 Council for International Exchange of Scholars. "Traditional Fulbright Scholar Program." www.cies.org/us_scholars/us_awards/.

CHAPTER 6
TOOLS OF ENGAGEMENT

As a part of your growth with this book, you've been encouraged to keep a journal. You've also been encouraged to collect your ideas, discoveries, and records of past achievements to create a personal profile of your character traits, interests, and goals. You should be ready, at this point, to take the necessary strides toward actual engagement in the activities you have identified as right for you.

This chapter offers you "tools of engagement" to further pursue your goals. It should serve as a "tool box" from which you can draw various instruments that will solidify the previous work you've done and facilitate your ongoing work.

The first tool is a mentor. Mentors are role models who can help you to cultivate your interests and talents more fully. They can also offer professional and moral support as you plan the path ahead.

The second tool is networking. You can activate your role in the community by building a network of people and organizations that share your interests and can help you to pursue your goals. They may become lifelines in your future career development. Your network can also ease your involvement into activities—many people will know of good activities for you or be willing to participate in activities with you.

Perhaps the most valuable tools discussed in this chapter are a portfolio and a resume that can present a range of your skills to college admissions officers, program administrators, and potential employers.

The final tool is a list of opportunities—scholarships, awards, and honors—that will reward you for your unique experiences, hard work, and fine character development.

With the support of your community and the websites suggested, you should have a firm jumping-off point for the road ahead: Choosing your college and orienting yourself toward a specific set of interests. The creation of a portfolio and resume will present an authentic and affirming portrait of you that will serve you well when applying to college.

MENTORS: TOOLS FOR SUPPORT AND DIRECTION

At this point, perhaps you are thinking, "I have read the first five chapters of the book and started this one. I completed the Self-Assessment Surveys and followed all of the suggestions. I have started a journal, written all sorts of reflections, and I have created a file the size of a small encyclopedia. Now I'm lost. What do I do with all of this stuff? I *need help!*" Relax. Help is on the way. It could be that what you need is a mentor—or maybe a few of them.

> "The [mentor] . . . gives not of his wisdom but rather of his faith and his lovingness. If he is indeed wise, he does not bid you enter the house of his wisdom but rather leads you to the threshold of your own mind."
>
> —Kahlil Gibran[1]

What Is a Mentor?

According to Mentor Alabama, a mentoring initiative started by that state's attorney general, "A mentor is an adult who, along with parents, provides young people with support, counsel, friendship, reinforcement, and [a] constructive example. Mentors are good listeners, people who care, people who want to help young people bring out strengths that are already there."[2]

In light of this definition, a number of individuals in your life may already serve as mentors to you. If not, it is likely that many adults with whom you interact regularly—such as teachers, counselors, relatives, family friends, and the adults who supervise the extra- and co-curricular activities in which you are involved—would be glad to help you in any way they could. (You may also be involved in "peer mentoring" relationships, either as a mentor *or* as a mentee. While this section is only concerned with traditional mentors, peer mentors can be a good source of empathetic support.) As always, the key to getting help is letting people know that you need and want it.

> Mentors are most valuable when you realize the choices you make today may affect all of your tomorrows.

You can start by talking to one or more of these people about your interests and ideas. Ask questions and share your ideas and your desire to get involved in something meaningful. Explain that you'd like to take your current talents and interests to another level. Just by using someone as a sounding board, your sense of direction may become clearer.

A mentor can, among other things, provide tutoring, assist you in exploring career options, or share experiences with you by accompanying you to events or getting involved with you in mutual interests, such as art or sports. If you don't know of any good candidates, mentors can be found through many high schools. Mentors found in this way may meet with you during or following the school day to assist you in developing conflict resolution, interpersonal, and time management skills, among others. You may also spend time with them developing your portfolio. They may further assist you in school or community projects, building a sense of teamwork while you both work for the benefit of the local community. Such a person may also be instrumental in putting you in touch with others who can assist you in specific ways, opening additional doors of opportunity or providing additional knowledge and perspectives pertinent to your aspirations.

> Many young people have gone further than they thought they could because someone else thought they could.

Beyond your personal network and school, there are many other avenues to take in finding mentors. There are many corporations and government agencies, as well as civic and religious organizations, with programs that encourage the development of mentoring relationships with young people in their communities. The organization MENTOR (Mentoring.org) is a wellspring of information on youth mentoring programs. Identifying itself as "a trusted voice for the power of mentoring . . . [that] work[s] to ensure that every child who wants and needs a mentor has the right one," MENTOR provides information on various ways that mentoring relationships can be developed.[3] MENTOR is also a safe resource for young people to check up on the authenticity of mentoring programs they learn about. (You want to be sure that any mentors or mentoring programs you find online are legitimate and endorsed by reputable organizations.)

MENTOR notes that most volunteers in faith-based organizations consider "instilling spiritual values and moral strength [to be] key elements in mentoring." Faith-based mentoring programs generally occur at a house of worship on weekends or during afterschool hours. They usually reflect the beliefs of the religious organization offering the program and may serve students from a particular congregation or the local community. Such programs can allow you to put your faith in practice while engaging in role play, receiving tutorial assistance, exploring careers, participating in sports or art activities, and attending various events.[4]

E-mentoring is also very popular. It utilizes the Internet to make the connection between mentors and young people. Teens and their mentors communicate through online chats and e-mail as they develop a relationship. Though it is very likely that they will meet face to face on occasion, e-mentoring allows people to interact regularly at their mutual convenience and when they might be unable to meet in person. This type of interaction also offers the opportunity for adults to work simultaneously with more than one young person. Hailed by many as the future of mentoring, e-mentoring also affords young people the chance to improve their written communication skills and increase their knowledge in communicating via modern technology.[5]

To give you a more concrete idea of the kinds of youth mentoring programs available, let's look at some specific programs and see what they're all about.

Corporations and Nonprofit Organizations

Youth mentoring has become an increasingly popular way for employees of corporations to show commitment to and to help young people, in the words of Youth Mentoring Connection, develop "character and capabilities."[6] There are also many nonprofit organizations created expressly to oversee mentoring programs or programs with a strong mentoring component.

Programs run by corporations or nonprofits can allow a young person to interact with a variety of adults while exploring careers, participating in job shadowing or role-play, or engaging in other activities provided by administrators. Many also help the youth they serve to gain knowledge and develop skills in a specific area of interest. Numerous companies, foundations, and philanthropists without their own mentoring programs provide funding and in-kind support to outside programs.

The following list features a selection programs that have received wide recognition for their success:

100 BLACK MEN OF AMERICA

100 Black Men of America is a nonprofit organization dedicated to enriching the lives of youth through academic and social support with the goal of "economic empowerment of the African American community." There are more than one hundred chapters of 100 Black Men throughout the United States, and each chapter operates a number of community service activities, including youth mentoring programs such as "Mentoring the 100 Way" and "Collegiate 100."[7]

- **Collegiate 100**

  This program is driven by male and female African American college students. Collegiate 100 organizations can be found operating on college campuses across the country. Volunteers mentor and tutor young African American males in the community in which their college is located. Each Collegiate 100 chapter has an advisor who is an active member of 100 Black Men and a member of the administration or faculty of the college at which the chapter is located.[8]

- **Mentoring the 100 Way**

  This program provides youth between the ages of 8 and 18 with activities and guidance to meet their social, emotional, and cultural needs. Mentors are members of 100 Black Men who have been trained and certified to work individually and in groups with young residents of their communities. The chief aim of the program is to assist these youth in intellectual and personal skill development and to act as role models who will lead them toward productive citizenship.

Among the activities provided through Mentoring the 100 Way are workshops on topics such as:

- Positive self identity/personal vision
- Lifelong learning
- Work ethic
- Life skill development

All of the goals, strategies, and activities of the program are informed by the acronym SMART, which stands for "Specific, Measurable, Attainable, Realistic, and Target-driven."[9]

Big Time Sports 24/7

Big Time Sports 24/7 is a relatively new nonprofit venture. The organization offers programs that are designed to inspire, mentor, and motivate young people in communities throughout the U.S. These programs include a variety of sports camps, cheerleading camps, high school all-star games, golf tournaments, health and wellness activities, and scholarships. Big Time Sports 24/7 regularly works with players from the National Football League and the National Basketball Association; each year more than 5,000 young people participate in its collaborative experiences. You can learn more about the organization and find out how you can participate in its exciting programs at Bigtimesports247.org.[10]

Other sports-related youth mentoring programs run by corporations and nonprofits operate in communities throughout the United States. You can ask the athletic director at your school or your coach about mentoring opportunities for student athletes in your area.

Camp Coca-Cola

The Coca-Cola Company spends millions of dollars each year to support programs that benefit young people, including mentoring programs. Camp Coca-Cola is one of the more recent programs offered by the company. It operates year-round to offer educational, community service, and leadership development opportunities for young people in grades 8–12.

Included in the program is a unique experience that provides four weeks of outdoor education. Participants engage in rock climbing, swimming, and other activities, while building relationships with peers and mentors and learning new skills.[11]

THE EARL BAKKEN SCIENCE PROGRAM

The Bakken: A Library and Museum of Electricity in Life in Minneapolis, Minnesota offers a program where young people "brainstorm, design, and make their own inventions to take home." With a 4:1 student-mentor ratio, it is a great opportunity for students with an interest or a curiosity in science. While there is a fee associated with the program, scholarships are available.[12]

EXPLORER POST PROGRAM

Each fall, students from North High School in Minneapolis have the chance to participate in the Explorer Post Program offered by General Mills. Through this program, students are able to gain knowledge about and insight into careers available in the field of technology. They engage in various learning activities, such as classes in Microsoft Excel, Java programming, and web page construction. The experience benefits not only the youth who participate but also the mentors involved; longtime organizer Mike Ruesewald calls the program "a great opportunity for information systems professionals to gain experience in public speaking, mentoring, planning, and organizing."[13]

GIRL SCOUTS OF THE USA

Girl Scouts of the USA is the worldwide leading organization focused solely on girls. Adult volunteers with Girl Scout organizations provide acceptance, nurturance, guidance, and support for young women with interests in business, medicine, the arts, technology, sports, government, and other enterprises. Young women are guided through career exploration experiences and are offered workshops and activities designed to promote the development of their skills and interests. The central aim of all Girl Scout programs is to help "girls develop qualities that will serve them all their lives, like leadership, strong values, social conscience, and conviction about their own potential and self-worth."[14]

The division of Girl Scouts for girls ages 11–17 is STUDIO 2B. More information is available at Studio2b.org.[15]

Serving roughly seven million students in grades K–12, Junior Achievement Worldwide (JA) is the largest international organization committed to providing activities related to economics, free enterprise, and the world of business to prepare youth "to succeed in a global economy."[16]

JA provides its services outside of school time in venues all over the U.S. and in nearly 100 countries. The programs offered by JA cover areas including citizenship, financial awareness, economics, business, entrepreneurship, career development, and ethics and character development. At the high school level, students focus on economics and business, engaging in student-led enterprises and gaining experience in the workplace. Mentors, teachers, and other volunteers work with these students on the real-life applications of their learning.[17]

You can learn more about JA and the programs it offers in your area by visiting JA.org. You can read about some of JA's mentors by going to JA.org/programs/programs_supplements.shtml and clicking the "Online Mentor Discussions" link.

PROJECT FOR PUBLIC SPACES

Project for Public Spaces (PPS) is a nonprofit "dedicated to helping people of all ages create the kinds of places that build communities." Through its website PPS connects young people with programs that provide education, technical assistance, and training to assist them in creating spaces in which they can be comfortable and feel a sense of ownership. It also believes strongly that "examples of teens' success can provide inspiration to other youth who are struggling to make a difference."[18] A few programs with mentoring components that PPS connects young people with are below.

- **New Urban Arts**

  New Urban Arts is a nonprofit arts organization and studio for high school students and emerging artists in Providence, Rhode Island. The philosophy of the organization holds that the arts can transform lives.[19] Its three core programs are the following:

  Artist Mentor Development: Artists receive challenging professional development that trains them to assist the young people who participate in New Urban Arts' community arts programs.

Youth Mentorship: Artist mentors work with four to eight high school students in an after-school program through which they develop creative projects.

Teaching Artist Residency: Artists and young people involved with New Urban Arts for at least 1 year collaborate on the design and implementation of workshops for staff and other artists in the community. Through these workshops, artists have the opportunity to create and exhibit new works and share information with the public about community art.[20]

- **Community Film Workshop of Chicago**

  Established by the Community Film Workshop Council of New York (an outgrowth of the American Film Institute), the Community Film Workshop of Chicago (CFW) offers participants from a diverse range of ages, educations, and backgrounds the opportunity to engage in training and hands-on activities in media arts.[21]

  A premier program of the CFW is the Media Arts and New Technologies Project, which focuses on every facet of media production and business development. The project teaches computer and digital skills to youth from some of Chicago's most disadvantaged neighborhoods. Students create video diaries, narratives, and documentaries that are presented at an annual youth and community forum. As a group, these young people work with mentors to design and implement a small business venture and produce work that addresses a pressing community or school problem.[21]

- **Totally Cool, Totally Art**

  In this Austin, Texas afterschool program, sponsored by the city's Parks and Recreation Department, teenagers receive free classes in arts education in community centers throughout the city. There they work alongside professional artists who serve as mentors to create original work and express themselves. TCTA, as the program is called, helps teens connect with role models, make positive choices, build relationships, and gain a deeper appreciation for art and its creation.[23]

YOUTH ATHLETIC ADVOCACY OF CENTRAL TEXAS

The Youth Athletic Advocacy of Central Texas (YAACT) is a nonprofit organization serving college-bound athletes in Central Texas communities. It offers youth mentoring and academic support to student athletes who need college scholarships as well as college planning services to the students, their parents, and coaches. The program also fosters positive lifestyle choices among the students involved.[24]

State-Sponsored Mentorship Clearinghouses

If a mentorship program seems like a good fit, there's nothing preventing you from calling, e-mailing, or writing it. Contact at the interest stage can be very productive: You can gain information that may not be found on the program's website, such as specific eligibility requirements or options for required travel. You can also talk with someone involved to get a feel for what the program's environment may be like. If you're still looking for a program that meets your needs, interests, and abilities, you may be able to use a state-sponsored mentorship clearinghouse to find additional programs. Many states offer these go-betweens, which connect young people with appropriate mentorship opportunities in their area. Such an organization can be an excellent way to get a broad view of many of the mentorship opportunities in your state.

A by-state index of organizations serving as mentorship clearinghouses can be found at Mentoring.org/leaders/partnerships/index.php. The following list features organizations in three states:

CALIFORNIA GOVERNOR'S MENTORING PARTNERSHIP (GMP)

Backed by strong partnerships with more than 700 community-, faith-, and school-based mentoring programs—such as Big Brothers/Big Sisters, Boys and Girls Clubs, and regional mentoring coalitions—this program works to encourage and facilitate collaboration in support of mentoring. To find mentors and learn more about mentorship opportunities in California, visit Mentoring.ca.gov.[25]

THE CONNECTICUT MENTORING PARTNERSHIP (CMP)

This program is an outgrowth of Connecticut's Governor's Prevention Partnership, an agenda focused on discouraging underage drinking and drug use and promoting safe schools and communities. CMP's top goal is to "increase the number of mentoring relationships and mentoring programs across the state and to assure the quality and safety of those programs." It has created more than 300 new mentoring programs since its inception.[26]

> ## CONNECTICUT CAREER CHOICES (CCC)
>
> The state of Connecticut also sponsors this initiative. CCC provides a range of activities to expose students to activities involving science, information technology, health, and medicine. These activities include classroom visits/speakers, company visits/tours, job shadowing experiences for students, teacher externships, and a Tech Expo.[27]

MARYLAND MENTORING PARTNERSHIP (MMP)

MMP serves as "an advocate, clearinghouse, and expert resource for the advancement of youth mentoring statewide." Founded in 1988 as RAISE Inc., MMP aims to develop and support high-quality, sustainable youth mentoring programs that will assist all youth in Maryland in reaching their fullest potential. Considered a leader in the mentoring movement, MMP operates a number of programs that provide: training and technical assistance; targeted recruitment of mentors from the corporate, higher education, and religious sectors; research and evaluation; and public awareness and advocacy.[28]

A NATIONAL INITIATIVE

One of several initiatives by the Department of Labor's Office of Disability Employment Policy (ODEP), the High School/High Tech (HS/HT) program is designed to provide students with all types of disabilities the opportunity to explore jobs and or post-secondary education leading to careers in science, engineering, or technology. It links youth to a broad range of academic, career development, and experiential resources that enable them to meet the demands of a twenty-first century economy and help them to make the transition to employment and economic self-sufficiency. Technical assistance and support to HS/HT sites nationwide is provided by the ODEP-funded National Collaborative on Workforce and Disability for Youth (NCWD/Youth). Community-based partnerships at HS/HT sites are forged between rehabilitation agencies, school systems, colleges and universities, disability service providers, employers, and families.[29]

To learn more about HS/HT or NCWD/Youth, visit DOL.gov/odep/programs/high.htm or NCWD-youth.info.

"Mentoring programs can provide . . . students with emotional support, encourage them to be more involved in schooling, and help [them] as they transition from school to work . . . . Mentors offer friendship, guidance, and positive role models while instilling the social skills needed in the workplace . . . . The most successful mentoring programs [are] highly structured [and] driven by the needs of the youth involved."

—Welfare Information Network[30]

In addition to the resources described above, it is likely that community and religious organizations in your area can connect you with appropriate mentoring programs. You can also learn about youth mentoring opportunities by visiting websites such as Mentoring.org and Mentoringworks.org (or doing an Internet search for "youth mentoring programs").

NETWORKING: A TOOL FOR STAYING CONNECTED

What Is Networking?

In her article "Savvy Networking: Who You Gonna Call?" Susan RoAne writes, "Networking is a reciprocal process . . . [an] exchange of ideas, leads, and suggestions that support[s] both our professional and our personal lives."[31] As such, networking is crucial to getting the most out of your engagement in purposeful activities.

You're probably already quite familiar with social networking. You may even excel at it. Telecommunication and the Internet connect you with people all over the world in a matter of seconds. It is likely that you have a ton of e-mail addresses and phone numbers, and that you use many of them quite frequently. This will help you as you develop broader networks related to your activities, college planning, college attendance, and career.

Carin, a first year student at a Historically Black College/University (HBCU) in the Mid-Atlantic U.S., is a good example of how networking can have an impact on your college search. Carin's college search was initially driven by the quality of the marching band programs at the schools she considered. During her junior year in high school, she learned in an informal discussion with a friend about NASA's Summer High School Apprenticeship Research Program (SHARP).

Though suspended at the time of this book's publication, NASA's SHARP was, during Carin's junior year, an academic summer program created to encourage interest and increase the involvement of high school students in STEM (science, technology, engineering, and mathematics) fields. In particular, the program sought to involve youth who had been traditionally underrepresented in these fields. Offered annually, SHARP operated for eight weeks at various NASA Field Installations and at selected American colleges and universities. Participants earned an hourly stipend. The program had two parts: a commuter component and a residential component. In the former, students worked in direct contact with NASA researchers. In the latter, students worked at a designated college or university location under the supervision of faculty and staff and were mentored by a professional or academician as they engaged in laboratory research.[32]

Carin looked into this opportunity, found it interesting, applied for it, and became one of 25 students chosen from metropolitan Atlanta to participate that year. After a couple of weeks in SHARP, it became apparent to Carin that she had found her passion! That summer, she worked closely with a professor in research focused on "the DNA of pine cones." In the fall, she applied to colleges with a very different focus in mind, deciding to major in chemistry. Through her involvement in SHARP, she established numerous relationships with professors, researchers, professionals, and students, expanding her network—or the people the networks with—to include individuals who share her interest in science. This network will provide Carin with invaluable help as she applies to grad school with an eye toward becoming a forensic scientist.

This kind of thing can happen in your life! A conversation with someone in your social network has the potential open doors to new areas of interest and new possibilities for your future. It can also allow you to expand your network in a new area. Below are some tips to aid you in developing your networking skills.

Ten Networking Tips

1. Understand the concept of networking as described above.
2. Project a positive image—be courteous, approachable, and competent when interacting with people you know and meeting new people.

3. Initiate conversation, discuss common interests, and show appreciation.

4. Ask pertinent questions, listen well, and digest what you hear.

5. Exchange contact information and record the information you receive in a permanent file or address book.

6. Make plans for further contact, when appropriate.

7. Follow-up on first meetings with a note, e-mail, or phone call thanking your new acquaintance.

8. Stay in contact as much as appropriate and possible.

9. Establish trust and reciprocation as key elements of the relationship.

10. Be realistic about the nature of each relationship and with your expectations for it. Everyone in your network will not become your best friend or a mentor. Some you may only encounter from time to time or in specific settings.

I'd Like to Thank . . .

A great deal of networking can take place around the experiences described in this book and the others you will try as you search for engaging activities. Put forth the effort to establish and maintain reciprocal relationships. If you are in frequent contact with and help others in your network, it won't feel unnatural when you ask someone to help you. Relationships based on mutuality not only have the potential to enhance your personal and professional life well into the future, they're also a lot of fun!

JOURNALING ACTIVITY

Take a moment to list the names of a few people who are or who could become a part of your network. Ask yourself how your relationship with each person could be mutually beneficial in school time, out-of-school time, or college planning activities. Note this next to his or her name.

RESUMES AND PORTFOLIOS: TOOLS FOR IMPRESSIVE PRESENTATION

In Chapter 1 you were encouraged to start a personal profile, or a collection of your insights, awards, contacts, and academic successes as well as other information useful to you as you engage in meaningful activities with an eye towards college admissions. If you didn't do so then, it's not too late to start one now! Refer back to the "Starting Your Personal Profile" section of Chapter 1 and Appendix A: My Personal Profile for direction in doing so. A personal profile will give you easy access to all the materials you will need to build an impressive resume or portfolio, which will be key to making a good impression when you apply for a program, activity, or job—or you solicit funding for your own project, program, or business venture.

Developing Your Resume

A resume offers those who are considering you for a position a realistic but positive snapshot of who you are and how your qualifications suit the position you are seeking. When done effectively, a resume should quickly capture the attention of the reader; it is not necessary to list every experience you've had up until now. In fact, until you have 10 years or more of work experience, it should be limited to one page.

That being said, your resume should always include:

- Contact information (name, current address, telephone number, and e-mail address)
- Education history
- Volunteer, internship, and/or work experience

If relevant to the program, activity, or job, it can also include:

- Skills, abilities, or accomplishments (for example: computer skills, fundraising, child care, leadership, business ventures, publications, program development, research, or performances)
- Memberships, awards, or honors
- Personal interests or hobbies (While you can include this category in a resume submitted for participation in a program

or activity, you should omit it from the resumes you submit for jobs or funding—it may detract from the professional tone you wish to convey.)

The appearance of your resume is crucial to its effectiveness. Use a standard font—such as 12-point Times New Roman—when typing your resume. Organize the content neatly and avoid cluttering the page. It is wise to use a model resume or resume template until you are comfortable with formatting your resume properly. Many word-processing programs, such as Microsoft Word, feature built-in resume templates. You can also find sample resumes at your guidance or college counselor's office.

> "A portfolio is your best foot forward—a representative sample of your work that demonstrates through language and image your greatest strengths and accomplishments. Formerly reserved for artists, models, and architects, today's portfolios are used by a variety of . . . [people] to demonstrate . . . skills, achievements, and professional goals . . . . A portfolio is all about showcasing your great ideas and your best thinking."
>
> —Creative Change Center[33]

When you have completed a draft of your resume, ask a mentor or a trusted adult to proofread it and offer suggestions for improvement. Make corrections, proofread the revised copy, and then offer it to someone else you trust for a second reading. Once you are satisfied with it, save it (with your full name in the title) on a CD, DVD, or jump drive, and print it on clean, good-quality white or off-white paper. Place the hard copy in your personal profile.

A cover letter, tailored to the position you are seeking, should always accompany a mailed, faxed, or e-mailed resume. Done well, this is another way to make a good impression. PrincetonReview.com provides excellent how-to advice on cover letters. Written for job seekers, this advice can be used for to cover letters with a variety of intentions. For some proven tips, go to PrincetonReview.com/cte/articles/hired/greatletter.asp.

Packaging Your Portfolio

While a resume and cover letter are sufficient to apply for positions in many areas, a portfolio is requested in an increasing number of fields. An impressive portfolio will highlight your abilities, talents, and skills; clearly indicate the quality and range of your preparation and experience; and outline your accomplishments.

Your portfolio can include following items, as applicable to the position for which you are applying:

- A copy of your resume
- An official copy of your transcript
- A list of your skills and interests, with an explanation of each, where necessary
- A list of experiences not included on your resume
- Letters of nomination to honor and academic organizations
- Certificates and letters of commendation for special training, honors, and awards
- Documentation of technical or computer skills
- Newspaper articles that address achievements of yours
- Programs from events in which you were involved through performance, technical assistance, or planning
- A list of programs, workshops, and conferences in which you have been involved, with an explanation of each, where necessary
- Samples of your creative work

Where appropriate, you should also include visuals of your accomplishments and experiences. The completed portfolio should be organized into sections that are labeled appropriately and may be submitted manually or electronically (if the former, it should be compiled in a sturdy binder or case), dependent on the wishes of the organization to which you are applying.

Saginaw Valley State University, which offers valuable information to help its students apply for positions of interest, posts two sample portfolios—one for an education major and one for an occupational therapy major—at SVSU.edu/careers/portfolio.cfm. These samples can give you a more tangible idea of the power of a portfolio to present a complete picture of your abilities, experience, and accomplishments.

SCHOLARSHIPS, AWARDS, AND HONORS: TOOLS FOR OPENING NEW DOORS

The excerpt to the right is from *Oh, the Places You'll Go,* a fun book that speaks directly to the subject at hand—opening doors, making choices, doing things, and becoming who you are. You can be certain that,

> "Out there things can happen and frequently do to people as brainy and footsy as you."
>
> —Dr. Seuss[29]

even with this roadmap, life will take you places you never would have imagined going.

As was the case with Carin, who you read about earlier in this chapter, a single opportunity can take your life in a new direction. The activities discussed in Chapters 3, 4, and 5 are great venues for potentially transformative experiences. This can also be the case with scholarships, awards, and honors. They can give you confidence (which can alter your general outlook and increase your willingness to try new things), add prestige to your list of achievements (which can tip a close college admission decision in your favor), and bolster your resources (which can make a greater number of colleges potentially affordable to you and your family); in short, they can open countless new doors for you. The remainder of this chapter is devoted to specific scholarships, awards, and honors and how you can position yourself for each one.

Arts Recognition and Talent Search (ARTS)

The National Foundation for Advancement in the Arts (NFAA), a nonprofit organization based in Miami, Florida, works to aid emerging artists in their professional growth and to increase awareness and appreciation of the arts among Americans. Each year it offers some $3 million in scholarship opportunities and more than $500,000 in cash awards to budding artists in every art form. NFAA's ARTS program offers scholarships and awards to high school seniors who are talented in writing, music (including jazz), dance, theater, visual arts (including photography), and film and video to continue an arts education.[35]

If you are driven toward the arts, NFAA is a terrific resource. You can learn more about it and its various programs at NFAA.org.

Make A Difference Scholarships

According to the Green Mountain College website, the school "is conducting an ongoing national search to find students who have somehow made a significant contribution to a fellow human or to society." Recipients of the college's Make A Difference scholarship are granted full tuition, room, and board for 4 years. "We want to reward this contribution and encourage the leaders of tomorrow with a full scholarship," the school's website states, "to . . . a college that will foster their ideals and their desire to give back."

Students may apply for this scholarship themselves or be nominated for it by a friend, teacher, counselor, family member, or mentor. You will find a video presentation highlighting the positive traits exhibited by recipients at GreenMtn.edu/makeadifference/index.asp. There you will also find information on how to apply for the Make A Difference scholarship and more information about Green Mountain College.[36]

Discover Card Tribute Award Scholarships

Discover Card's Tribute Award is a college scholarship opportunity for high school juniors. Up to 10 national scholarships of $25,000 and 300 state scholarships of $2,500 are awarded each year. Eligible students

- Are enrolled in an accredited public or private high school in the United States.

- Possess at least a 2.75 cumulative grade point average (GPA) on a 4.0 scale for the 9th and 10th grades.

- Are accomplished in the areas of leadership and community service.

- Have faced a significant roadblock or challenge in their lives.[37]

You can download an application and information about recent state and national winners at the Discover Financial Services website: DiscoverFinancial.com/data/philanthropy/tribute.shtml.

Do Something BRICK Awards

You were introduced to Do Something—an organization that believes young people can make a difference in the world—in Chapter 1. To this end, it offers support and recognition for those who take initiative to get things done. To date, Do Something has granted nearly $2 million directly to youth for their efforts.

Its $25,000 BRICK Awards are Do Something's largest grants and are given in recognition of "social change-makers" under the age of 25. Applicants should understand the problems and needs of their community, be able to communicate their vision, and demonstrate how they have passionately dedicated themselves to generating change. The organization is looking for leaders in the form of social entrepreneurs and community leaders.[38]

Gloria Barron Prize for Young Heroes

Recognizing and rewarding the remarkable accomplishments of young people who have made a difference is the aim of the Gloria Barron Prize for Young Heroes. Ten recipients from across the United States are chosen for this honor annually—five of them for their work in aiding their communities or other human beings and five for doing something significant to protect the environment or promote health and wellness here and abroad. Past award winners have come from diverse ethnic, geographic, religious, and socioeconomic backgrounds.

- Michaella organized a rodeo for disabled kids.
- Carter led the effort to conserve a local river.
- Ashley created a scholarship fund for African girls.

- Kyle organized a reading mentorship program.
- Joying cleaned up South Carolina's beaches.
- Ryan helped provide clean drinking water to more than 70 African villages.
- Barbara created a successful oil recycling project in Texas.

According to T. A. Barron, founder of the Gloria Barron Prize for Young Heroes, the prize's goal "is to celebrate such heroic young people—and to inspire others to do their part."[39]

Visit BarronPrize.org to learn more about this program, find information on the nomination process, and read about past winners.

Hispanic Heritage Youth Awards

The Hispanic Heritage Foundation (HHF) is a nonprofit organization that focuses on identifying and preparing Latino youth to serve as role models in their communities and in society. Through partnerships and sponsors it provides a variety of year-round programs involving leadership development, education, cultural experiences, and other activities related to the aims of the organization. Among its annual events are the presentation of the Hispanic Heritage Awards (HHA) and the HHYA.

The HHYA program began in 1998 to honor young people for their achievements in the classroom and in the community. Recipients are given educational grants and opportunities for leadership. HHYA presents more the $600,000 in awards to students in 12 regions of the United States. High school seniors of Hispanic descent compete for these awards based on their academic achievement, community service, and an essay about their heritage. Categories of focus related to the students' accomplishments are also considered; these include: academics, arts and culture, community service, education, engineering and mathematics, healthcare, journalism, leadership, and athletics.

At a local awards ceremony, Gold and Silver Medallion winners receive $3,000 and $2,000 educational grants, respectively. Gold Medallion recipients automatically become candidates for National HHYA. National winners receive an additional $5,000 educational grant; a laptop computer; an all-expenses-paid trip for two to Miami, Florida to attend the national presentation event; and recognition at the annual HHA event.[40]

Visit HispanicHeritage.org/index.php to learn more about opportunities provided by HHF.

NetAid Global Action Awards

NetAid is a nonprofit organization that works to encourage, educate, and empower youth for lifelong involvement in addressing global poverty. Each year, the organization honors American high school students who have demonstrated outstanding initiative and leadership in projects to aid residents of poor countries or to raise awareness of global poverty by granting them the Global Action Award. Winning projects may address, but are not limited to, HIV/AIDS prevention, feeding the hungry, and increasing educational opportunities among the poor.

To qualify for the Global Action Award, you must be in grades 9–12 and have attended high school in the United States during the academic school year for which the awards are given. Recipients are awarded $5,000 to be used to pursue college attendance or to support a charitable organization of their choice.[41]

To learn more about eligibility requirements, the selection process, and timelines, explore the Global Action Awards FAQ at NetAid.org/global_action_awards/faq.html.

Presidential Awards

The following awards are presidential initiatives:

- **Presidential Scholars Program (PSP)**

    Established in 1964 by an executive order from the President of the United States, the PSP recognizes, according to its website, "some of our nation's most distinguished graduating high school seniors." The program was extended in 1979 to recognize "exceptional talent in the visual, creative, and performing arts." Up to 141 students are named Presidential Scholars each year and it is one of the top honors a high school student can receive.[42]

    Presidential Scholars are invited to participate in National Scholars Recognition Week in the nation's capital. For five full days, Presidential Scholars are provided with learning, social, and cultural experiences and the opportunity to meet and network with academics, artists, government officials, fellow Presidential Scholars, and other noted individuals. The week culminates in a ceremony at which the Scholars are awarded the Presidential Medallion.[43]

- **President's Volunteer Service Award**

  In 2002, President George W. Bush challenged each American to devote at least 4,000 hours (or 2 years) over the course of their lives to volunteer work. In 2003, he formalized his challenge by creating the President's Council on Service and Civic Participation, which, in turn, created the President's Volunteer Service Award "as a way to thank and honor Americans who have, by their demonstrated commitment and example, inspired others to engage in volunteer service."

  To date, nearly half a million awards have been given to deserving volunteers. Award categories include children, young adults, adults, and families and groups, and are given either for service performed over a 12-month period or a lifetime.

Recipients are awarded:

- An official President's Volunteer Service Award pin
- A personalized certificate of achievement
- A letter from the President of the United States
- A letter from the President's Council on Service and Civic Participation
- Potential awardees are required to document their volunteer service in journals and submit this documentation to the Council on Service and Civic Participation periodically.[44]

SIEMENS AWARDS FOR ADVANCED PLACEMENT

The Siemens Foundation gives annual awards to the students with the greatest number of scores of five (out of five) on Advanced Placement (AP) exams in the sciences and mathematics taken prior to the senior year of high school. All American high school students—including homeschooled students—are eligible.

A college scholarship in the amount of $2,000 is given to the male student and the female student in each of the 50 states who has earned the greatest number of scores of five. In addition, one male and one female student nationally each receive a $5,000 scholarship. Recipients of either award must be in high school when the award is given. Students do not apply for this competition—College Board determines the winners.[45]

More information is available at Siemens-Foundation.org/awards/AboutSAAP.htm.

SIEMENS COMPETITION

The Siemens Competition in Math, Science & Technology provides early recognition of outstanding academic talent and encourages students to take on the challenge of scientific research. High school seniors submit original science and math research projects as individuals or in two- or three-student teams. Projects are judged at both the regional and national level; the competition offers national recognition for winning projects. More details are available at Siemens-foundation.org/competition.[46]

START SOMETHING

"Dream . . . Achieve . . . Learn . . . Reach . . . Believe . . . Create . . . Inspire . . . Explore . . . Imagine . . . Discover." These action words introduce the Start Something program, a collaboration between The Tiger Woods Foundation and Target. Inspired by the book Start Something—written by Tiger Woods' father, the late Earl Woods—the program focuses on activities and community service experiences generated and implemented by young people ages 8–17. Start Something provides tools and resources—including grants—that help program participants turn their dreams into action. Participants gain self-awareness, develop their skills and talents, explore careers, and do something of significance. Go to Sites.target.com/site/en/spot/page.jsp?title=startsomething to learn about volunteer opportunities in your area, view career profiles, and find out how to apply for grants.[47]

YOUNG SCHOLARS PROGRAM

The Virginia-based Jack Kent Cooke Foundation identifies and supports American high school and college students of exceptional promise, application, and character who have demonstrated excellence in academics extracurriculars and have significant financial need.[348] Through its Young Scholars Program, the Foundation awards about 60 scholarships annually.

Services, guidance, and financial assistance for Young Scholars include, but are not limited to:

- Augmentation of schooling with online courses
- Summer academic or enrichment programs
- Technological equipment to enhance learning
- Development of artistic and academic skills
- A nationwide network of Young Scholars
- Career-goal exploration
- College admissions counseling (if applicable)[49]

To find out more about the Foundation and its programs, go to JackKentCookeFoundation.org.

Youth For Understanding (YFU)

YFU is a nonprofit student exchange organization that offers educational opportunities to young people around the world. Students who are open to new experiences and interested in experiencing and learning about other cultures may spend a summer, semester, or year with a host family in an exchange program. In most YFU opportunities, it is not necessary for participants to be fluent in the language of the host culture, although the ability to communicate in that language is advantageous.

Among YFU's many opportunities is its scholarship program, funded by numerous individuals, corporations, foundations, and governments. These scholarships provide funding for recipients to participate in one of YFU's student exchange programs.

To be eligible for a YFU scholarship, you must meet the eligibility requirements listed at YFU-USA.org/ao/scholarship_facts.htm and on the Scholarship Information Sheet of the specific program for which you are applying. General requirements oblige applicants to be in good physical and emotional health, to be between the ages of 15 and 18, and to maintain a GPA of 3.0 or better during year or semester programs and 2.0 or better during summer programs. All applicants are expected to have a personal interview with a YFU representative.[50]

Browse the Youth for Understanding website—YFU-USA.org—to discover which YFU program is most suited to your interests and needs, what the eligibility requirements are, how to apply for it, and other important information about YFU.

For Further Research . . .

Below you'll find additional organizations that administer (or compile) scholarships, awards, or honors. A brief explanation of each is included. Be sure to check out the websites of any that seem like a good fit for you. Each one could be a boon to someone with the right talents, skills, or experiences.

- **Associated Male Choruses of America Music Scholarships**

  http://amcofa.net/scholar.shtml

  High school seniors or college freshmen who plan to major in vocal music are eligible for awards ranging from $200 to $1,200.[51]

- **Casey Family Scholarships for Foster Care Youth**

  www.Orphan.org/casey_scholarship.html

  Casey Family Programs works in collaboration with the Orphan Foundation of America to provide scholarships of up to $10,000 to young people under the age of 25 who have spent at least 12 months in foster care and who were not subsequently adopted.[52]

- **Coca-Cola Scholars Foundation**

  www.Coca-ColaScholars.org/cokeWeb/jsp/scholars/MissionStatement.jsp

  High school seniors with outstanding achievements in the classroom and the community compete for fifty $20,000 and two hundred $4,000 scholarships annually.[53]

- **Council on International Educational Exchange (CIEE)**

  www.CIEE.org/study/scholarships.aspx

  Each year CIEE awards scholarships and grants to students who want to study overseas but do not have the resources to do so.[54]

- **The Heart of America Christopher Reeve Award**

  www.HeartOfAmerica.org/scholarships.htm

  This award is presented to an extraordinary youth who has demonstrated tremendous courage and compassion in serving his or her community. An awards review committee selects one student each year for the award, which includes a $1,000 scholarship.[55]

- **Hitachi Foundation's Yoshiyama Award for Exemplary Service to the Community**

  www.HitachiFoundation.org/yoshiyama/index.html

  This annual award recognizes ten U.S. high school seniors for admirable service and community involvement.[56]

- **The Kyoto Scholarship**

  www.KyotoPrize.org/scholarship.htm

  High schools in the City and County of San Diego as well as high schools in and around Tijuana, Mexico participate in the Kyoto Scholarship competition. The scholarship is awarded each year in three categories: advanced technology, basic sciences, and arts and philosophy. Six winners—two in each category—are chosen to receive scholarships of up to $10,000 each. The competition is limited to high school seniors.[57]

- **Michigan State University's List of Pre-College Scholarships**

  www.Lib.msu.edu/harris23/grants/3precol.htm

  This resource provides a broad list of grants and scholarships that can be used for college and precollege programs. It links directly to the funding sources, which are listed alphabetically and in categories of interest.[58]

- **Ohio Newspapers Foundation**

  www.OhioNews.org/students.html

  The Ohio Newspapers Foundation provides a variety of scholarships and internships aimed at helping students to learn and achieve the highest standards of excellence and professionalism in all aspects of journalism and newspaper publishing.[59]

- **The Prudential Spirit of Community Awards**

  www.Prudential.com/overview/0,1468,intPageID%
  253D4141%2526blnPrinterFriendly%253D0,00.html

  This program honors young people who attend middle or
  high school and exhibit outstanding community service.[60]

- **The Rotary Foundation Ambassadorial Scholarships**

  www.Rotary.org/foundation/educational/amb_scho/

  Since 1947, the Ambassadorial Scholarship has been The
  Rotary Foundation's flagship program. It is one of a range of
  awards and scholarships offered by the Foundation that
  enables youth leaders to serve and study abroad.[61]

- **The Tylenol Scholarship**

  www.Tylenol.com/page.jhtml?id=tylenol/news/subptyschol.inc

  Tylenol awards higher-education scholarships to students
  pursuing careers in health care. In 2006, 20 $5,000 schol-
  arships and 150 $1,000 scholarships were awarded.
  Awards decisions are based on applicants' leadership qualities and academic achievements.[62]

- **Veterans of Foreign Wars (VFW) Scholarships**

  www.VFW.org/index.cfm?fa=cmty.levelc&cid=1836&tok=1

  Each year, VFW grants more than $3 million in scholarships
  and incentives to America's youth through the annual Voice
  of Democracy and Patriot's Pen contests.[63]

Many opportunities for scholarships, awards, and honors are often
advertised in your school's guidance or counseling office. Talk to your
counselor to find out what information is available through your school's
resources. You may also want to visit the website of the Foundation
Center (FoundationCenter.org)—the nation's foremost authority on volunteerism, fundraising, and other aspects of philanthropy—to ensure
that you've done satisfactory research on this topic. You don't want to
miss any doors that may open still more doors to a bright future.

The next chapter revisits the subject of college admissions in detail. Once you've completed it, you should have a solid idea of where each aspect of your high school experience fits in the picture of your college application. You're almost there!

ENDNOTES

1   Gibran, Kahlil. *The Prophet.* "On Teaching." New York: Alfred K. Knopf. 1923. 56.

2   Mentor Alabama. "Frequently Asked Questions: What is a Mentor Anyway?" www.ago.state.al.us/mentor/faq.htm#a.

3   MENTOR. "Connect with the Power of Mentoring." 2006. www.mentoring.org.

4   MENTOR. "Mentoring Settings." 2006. www.mentoring.org/mentors/about_mentoring/mentoring_settings.php.

5   Ibid.

6   Youth Mentoring Connection. "What is Mentoring?" 2002. www.youthmentoring.org/03ment.html.

7   100 Black Men of America, Inc. "Welcome to 100 Black Men of America, Inc." 2006. www.100blackmen.org.

8   100 Black Men of America, Inc. "Mentoring." 2006. www.100blackmen.org/index.php?option=com_content&task=view&id=40&Itemid=63.

9   Ibid.

10 Big Time Sports 24/7. "Programs." www.bigtimesports247.org/programs.html.

11 Camp Coca-Cola Foundation. "Camp Coca-Cola." www.campcocacola.org/main_home.asp.

12 The Bakken Library and Museum. "Earl Bakken Science Program." November 2006. www.thebakken.org/education/ebsp/index.html.

13 General Mills, Inc. "General Mills 2006 Community Action Report." www.generalmills.com/corporate/commitment/corpCit2006.pdf.

14 Girl Scouts of the United States of America. "Who We Are." 1998–2006. www.girlscouts.org/who_we_are/.

15 STUDIO 2B, Girl Scouts of the United States of America. "STUDIO 2B." 1998–2004. www.studio2b.org/profile.asp.

16 Junior Achievement, JA Worldwide. "Who We Are." 2007.
www.ja.org/about/about.shtml.

17 Junior Achievement, JA Worldwide. "High School Programs Overview."
2007. www.ja.org/programs/programs_high_overview.shtml.

18 Project for Public Spaces, Inc. "Community Builders: Teens Turning Places
Around." www.pps.org/tcb/about.htm.

19 New Urban Arts. "The Basics: Who We Are."
www.newurbanarts.org/basics.html.

20 New Urban Arts. "The Basics:
Programs."www.newurbanarts.org/basics_programs.html.

21 Community Film Workshop of Chicago. "About CFW: History." 2005.
www.cfwchicago.org/history.htm.

22 Project for Public Spaces (PPS). "More Programs by and for Young People."
www.pps.org/tcb/tcblinks.htm.

23 Austin City Connection, Parks and Recreation Department. "About Totally
Cool, Totally Art." 1995. www.ci.austin.tx.us/tcta/history.htm.

24 Youth Athletic Advocacy of Central Texas. "YAACT Programs." 2005.
www.yaact.org/programservices.htm.

25 Governor's Mentoring Partnership, State of California. "About the
Governor's Mentoring Partnership." 2003.
www.mentoring.ca.gov/about_gmp.shtm.

26 The Governor's Prevention Partnership, Connecticut Mentoring Partnership.
"Welcome." 2006. www.preventionworksct.org/mentor.html.

27 Connecticut Career Choices. "CT Career Choices." 2005.
http://ctcareerchoices.org.

28 The Maryland Mentoring Partnership. "About Us."
www.marylandmentors.org/about.html.

29 U.S. Department of Labor–-Office of Disability Employment Policy. "High
School/High Tech." www.dol.gov/odep/programs/high.htm.

30 Welfare Information Network. "Mentoring Programs for High School Aged
Youth." Vol. 7, No. 13. October 2003.
www.financeproject.org/Publications/mentoringprogramsRN.htm.

31 RoAne, Susan. "Savvy Networking: Who You Gonna Call?" The RoAne Group.
    1999–2005. www.susanroane.com/articles/savvynet.html.

32 National Aeronautics and Space Administration (NASA). "Learning Resources: NASA Summer High School Apprenticeship Research Program." March 4, 2006. www.nasa.gov/audience/forstudents/9-12/learning/NASA_SHARP.html.

33 Creative Change Center (C3). "Preparing a Portfolio; Showcasing Your Strengths." www.c3va.org/html/resources/readable_articles/preparing-a-portfolio-vis.shtml.

34 Dr. Seuss (Theodore Geisl). *Oh, The Places You'll Go.* New York: Random House, 1990.

35 Arts Recognition and Talent Search, National Foundation for Advancement in the Arts (NFAA). "Awards for Young Artists: Empowering the Arts in America." 1996–2006. www.nfaa.org.

36 Green Mountain College. "Green Mountain College Make A Difference Scholarship." www.greenmtn.edu/makeadifference/index.asp.

37 Discover Financial Services, Discover Bank. "Philanthropy: Discover Card Tribute Award Scholarship—Recognizing Excellence in High School Juniors." Discover Bank. 2006. www.discoverfinancial.com/data/philan-thropy/tribute.shtml.

38 Do Something. "Brick Awards: Eligibility and Guidelines." www.dosomething.org/brick/guidelines.html.

39 The Barron Prize. "The Gloria Barron Prize for Young Heroes." Thomas A. Barron. 2006. www.barronprize.org.

40 Hispanic Heritage Foundation. "Youth Awards." www.hispanicheritage.org/youth.php.

41 NetAid. "NetAid Global Action Awards: Frequently Asked Questions." 1999–2007. www.netaid.org/global_action_awards/faq.html.

42 U.S. Department of Education. "Presidential Scholars Program." www.ed.gov/programs/psp/index.html.

43 Presidential Scholars Foundation. "About Us." www.presidentialscholars.org/about_us.htm.

44 President's Volunteer Service Award. "About the Award." 2006. www.presidentialserviceawards.org/tg/pvsainfo/dspAboutAwards.cfm.

45 Siemens Foundation, Siemens Corporation. "2006–2007 Siemens Competition National Finals: About the Competition." 2005. www.siemens-foundation.org/competition.

46 Siemens Foundation, Siemens Corporation. "Eligibility." 2005. www.siemens-foundation.org/awards/AboutSAAP.htm.

47 Tiger Woods Foundation, Target Brands Inc. "Start Something." 2006. http://sites.target.com/site/en/spot/page.jsp?title=startsomething.

48 Jack Kent Cooke Foundation. "About the Foundation." 2003. www.jackkentcookefoundation.org/jkcf_web/content.aspx?page=AboutFo &_redir=627.

49 Jack Kent Cooke Foundation. "Young Scholars: The Program." 2003. www.jackkentcookefoundation.org/jkcf_web/content.aspx?page=YounSch.

50 Youth for Understanding USA. "Scholarship Facts." 2000–2007. www.yfu-usa.org.

51 Associated Male Choruses of America. "AMCA Music Scholarships." http://amcofa.net/scholar.shtml.

52 Orphan Foundation of America. "Scholarships: Casey Family Scholars Scholarships." 2006. www.orphan.org/casey_scholarship.html.

53 The Coca-Cola Scholars Foundation. "Mission Statement." www.coca-colascholars.org/cokeWeb/jsp/scholars/MissionStatement.jsp.

54 Council on International Educational Exchange (CIEE). "CIEE Scholarships." www.ciee.org/study/scholarships.aspx.

55 The Heart of America Foundation. "Scholarships: The Christopher Reeve Award." www.heartofamerica.org/scholarships.htm.

56 The Hitachi Foundation. "Yoshiyama Awards." 2001–2006. www.hitachifoundation.org/yoshiyama/index.html.

57 The San Diego Foundation. "The Kyoto Scholarships." www.kyotoprize.org/scholarship.htm.

58 Harrison, Jon. "Grants for Individuals: Precollege Scholarships." Michigan State University Libraries. www.lib.msu.edu/harris23/grants/3precol.htm.

59 Ohio Newspaper Association. "Welcome Students." www.ohionews.org/students.html.

60 Prudential Financial, Inc. "The Prudential Spirit of Community Awards."
    2007.
    www.prudential.com/overview/0%2C1468%2CintPageID%25253D4141%
    252526blnPrinterFriendly%25253D0%2C00.html?furl=%2Fcommunity%2Fs
    pirit%2Fawards.

61 Rotary International. "Ambassadorial Scholarships." 2003–2005.
    www.rotary.org/foundation/educational/amb_scho.

62 Tylenol, McNeil Consumer Health care, a Division of McNeil PPC. "The
    Tylenol Scholarship."
    1998–2007.
    www.tylenol.com/page.jhtml?id=tylenol/news/subptyschol.inc.

63 Veterans of Foreign Wars of the United States. "VFW Scholarship
    Programs." 2007.
    www.vfw.org/index.cfm?fa=cmty.levelc&cid=1836&tok=1.

CHAPTER 7
GETTING ADMITTED
(AND FINANCIAL AID)

In the previous chapters, you learned that precollege experiences can enrich your life while preparing you to be a more attractive applicant during the college admissions process. You were also able to explore various options for such experiences. In light of what you've learned, it's time to delve into the specifics of the admissions and financial aid processes. This chapter will show you how to make your application shine and how to secure the financial aid you'll need to pay for the amazing school you choose to attend.

ADMISSIONS OVERVIEW

We provided an outline of the college admissions process in Chapter 2, but because finding the right schools to apply to is important, a review is in order. Each application should go to a school you have researched thoroughly, and one you would be happy to attend. As mentioned earlier, considering only one college as the "right" choice is unrealistic and unfair to yourself; you've tried hard to maximize your postsecondary school options and focusing on just one school constricts your options. The quality of the education you receive in college is largely dependent on your desire to learn, your involvement in the college community, and your overall attitude toward the experience. Consider a variety of schools with careful consideration of the positive attributes of each. You may choose to apply to a number of prestigious institutions, but those schools won't necessarily be where you'll best fit in or where you will have the best college experience. Your ability to research schools and how they measure up to what you want and need from your time in college is the most critical part of the college application process.

You may remember from Chapter 2 that, once you send an application, it will be evaluated largely on the information you provide in two fundamental categories: academic performance and personal characteristics. This is because colleges, especially fairly selective ones, are interested in several things: your ability to handle the work required in the classroom; whether you will profit by the college's educational teaching style; and your potential to contribute to the campus community in positive and meaningful ways. Admissions officers want their admitted students to be happy, successful, and integrated into life on campus for the duration of their college years. The different elements of your application will work together to give admissions officers a clear picture of whether you, your academic potential, and your unique personality will make a harmonious match with their school.

TIPS FOR COLLEGE-BOUND SENIORS

1. **Make academic success a priority.**

   Continue to give 100 percent in the area of academics. Senior-year grades count! A strong first semester can tip an admission decision in your favor. A strong second semester can move you from a spot on the wait list to a spot in freshman orientation.

2. **Stay organized.**

   Develop a file for all correspondence to and from the colleges to which you apply.

3. **Stay on schedule.**

   Use the College Planning Checklist in Appendix C to stay on track. Procrastination can quickly put you at a disadvantage. You should begin working on a college application a *minimum* of six weeks before the deadline so you have sufficient time to write a quality essay and secure the necessary recommendations.

4. **Submit secondary school reports and requests for your transcript promptly.**

   Give your counselor and the counseling staff of your high school sufficient time to produce the application materials you need from them. Adhere to the deadlines your schools has for submitting these requests.

5. **Meet with your counselor regularly.**

   Don't wait for him or her to make an appointment with you. Make regular appointments with your counselor. Discuss your progress with your applications and allow him or her to answer your questions.

6. Register for standardized tests early.

The timetables for SAT and ACT registration will be posted in your counseling office, in various other places around your school, and usually on your school's website. Information regarding testing may also be found at CollegeBoard.org and ACTstudent.org. Register early to avoid a late fee.

Criteria for Acceptance

As you approach your senior year, make sure you understand fully the criteria for acceptance used by the vast majority of colleges and universities. These criteria, outlined below, will help you—along with your needs, interests, and precollege experiences—to determine which colleges would be most suitable for you.

1. Academic Performance

Your academic record will be viewed in the context of your high school's academic reputation (and ability to challenge students) and the opportunities it provides versus those you took advantage of during your years there. Taking the easiest road you can find is not a good idea; selective colleges want to see a challenging course of studies (including honors and AP courses, if they are offered at your school) throughout your transcript and a grade point average that reflects dedication and effort in each class. Colleges can spot students who took easy-breezy classes as GPA boosters. More prized are students who opted for tougher classes and earned good grades, even if that didn't translate into straight A's.

In addition to an academic transcript, many colleges and universities require applicants to submit standardized test scores (e.g., from College Board or ACT) and will consider your scores as another part of your academic profile. College entrance exams are universal instruments used to measure precollege achievement and future potential, even though the decision to admit or deny a student is rarely based on a specific score. Colleges that use standardized test scores as part of their admissions processes attest that higher scores indicate applicants who have the makings of a successful college student, specifically in terms of tackling college-level course work.

2. Extracurricular and Co-Curricular Activities

Athletics, student government, visual and performing arts, school and community service, and other activities that complement the curriculum—Math Counts, JETS, debate, Close-Up, etc.—are often considered during the review of your application. Colleges that are more selective tend to put more weight in this area. Regardless of the weight they place here, however, admissions officers look to a student's activities for concrete examples of his or her interests, talents, and leadership capabilities. You want to be a well-rounded person in this area, but you also want to demonstrate a level of devotion to one or two extracurricular activities, especially after your first year of high school. Chronic dabbling—that is, minimal involvement in a broad range of activities over the course of 4 years—might be enjoyable, but it's not the right way to get noticed by college admissions officials. Rather, a deep and continued involvement in a few areas is an indication of true commitment, and, in many cases, the presence of real passion. Though colleges usually won't admit a student with poor grades just because he or she was president of the student council or captain of the basketball team, a nice set of grades is always enhanced by a nice set of activities to which you gave of yourself. Not only will admissions officers see that you are an involved and interesting person, they will see that you were able to balance your studies with your activities—and excel in both areas.

3. Essays

Some colleges may require one or more essays as part of their application. Others make the essay an optional submission. Still others do not require an essay at all. Know that if a school requires essays, their admissions officers will read them carefully—both to assess your skill in written expression and to gain insight into you, the person behind the application. Borderline applicants to a particular college—and only the college knows for certain who they are—may be able to sway decision-makers to their side by crafting a thoughtful and well-presented essay. As such, it is smart to spend significant time on both required and recommended essays, fine-tuning the topic, tone, and writing. Be sure to proofread your essays before sending them off. Have a teacher or counselor read them and offer suggestions, too.

4. Letters of Recommendation

Most colleges require at least one letter of recommendation. This recommendation—written by a college counselor or a teacher—is a summary of who you are from someone who believes you are a strong candidate for the college. Because colleges look at recommendations for support of your transcript and other data submitted, each one should be in agreement with the academic, extracurricular, and social profile presented throughout your application. Choose recommenders who know you well and follow directions carefully—every college has its own criteria for who should write your letters of recommendation, in what format, and how many you need to submit.

5. Special Categories

Colleges and universities attempt to "admit a class of distinctively different types" of students, according to a former Dean of Admissions who served at several selective institutions. Talent (artistic, athletic, etc.), diversity (geographic, socio-economic, ethnic, gender, etc.), and other unique aspects of an applicant are considered by admissions officers in their efforts to admit such a class. Being honest and upfront about who you are on all portions of your application will give you the best chance for admission to schools that would be excellent, long-term fits for you as a student and as an individual.

6. Demonstrated Interest

As some students apply to large numbers of colleges just to see where they can get in, demonstrated interest in a school is a significant plus to some admissions officers, who are charged with determining which applicants would bring the most to their school. Visiting the campus, meeting with a professor or advisor, sitting in on a class, participating in an interview (discussed below), and applying Early Decision (also discussed below), are all ways to communicate sincere interest in a particular institution. It is wise to discuss this aspect of the application process with your guidance or college counselor to choose which methods of demonstrating interest are considered appropriate for your top-choice colleges, as they vary by institution.

Your Final Search List

Your final search list is the list of colleges to which you will ultimately apply. In Chapter 2, we promised to provide you with more information about categorizing the colleges on your search list as "reach," "good match," and "safety." Bearing in mind the criteria used by admission officers for reviewing applicants, reach, good match, and safety can be defined in the following ways:

- **Reach schools** are those for which you may appear qualified by the numbers (your grade point average and SAT or ACT scores), but because of the institution's level of selectivity—the number of qualified applicants relative to the number of openings in the first-year class for which you are applying—or other factors outside of your control, there is uncertainty regarding your admission. In other words, your chance of being admitted may be marginal, regardless of your strong qualifications. As an example, Ivy League schools are commonly found on applicants' reach lists: These schools receive many more outstanding applications than they have places for in their incoming classes. Even students at the very top of their high school class are not admitted to Ivy League schools.

- **Good-match schools** are ones for which you are fully qualified in comparison with the overall profile of students admitted over the course of the past several years. Your grades and scores fall right in line with those of other applicants. Based on the institution's selectivity, you believe you have at least a 50 percent chance of being admitted.

- At **safety schools**, your chances of admission are excellent since your qualifications exceed those of students admitted to the institution in the previous year and likely exceed those of most other applicants. If you scored a 29 on the ACT and graduated with a GPA of 3.8, one of your safety schools might report that students in its most recently admitted class averaged a 25 on the ACT and held an average high school GPA of 3.5.

Understand that college admission is not an exact science and that the above method of organizing your final search list is only meant to help you keep a realistic perspective on each school on your list. You should put schools into the three categories above only *after* you have chosen ones that fit your needs, interests, and preferences as discussed in Chapter 2. Factors including a school's location, size, and academic and social offerings should already have been considered by this point. All schools on your final search list should be those you believe would offer you a positive college experience if you were accepted and decided to attend.

As a good guideline, it is wise to devote no more than a third of your final search list to the reach category. You should also have at least one safety option and be reasonably certain, based on your research (campus visits, the use of guidebooks, conversations with college representatives and current students, etc.) that you could be happy at it, even if it isn't your top choice. You may need to fall back on a safety school if, in the end, you do not get enough financial aid from your top-choice school, or if you aren't admitted to the other schools on your list. If the latter happens, don't be discouraged: You can always reapply to those schools as a transfer student if you excel during your freshman year.

Admission Options

As you research colleges, you will notice that different schools offer different options for the admissions process. There are five basic ways to apply to college, and a given school may utilize one or more of them.

1. Regular Admission

Most of your applications will fall into this category. The majority of these deadlines are between December 1 and March 1 for entrance the following autumn. Students generally receive notification of regular admission decisions in March or April, depending on the application deadline. Check each college's application for information about its regular admission deadlines and notification dates.

2. Early Decision*

Under this option, you must apply by a deadline that is earlier than the regular deadline. While some colleges have more than one Early Decision deadline, most Early Decision deadlines fall between mid-October and mid-November. Students generally receive notification of the college's decisions by mid to late December. The benefit to applying Early Decision is that, unless you receive a "deferral"—meaning that the school has neither admitted or rejected your application, but rather has moved it into the applicant pool for regular admission—you won't need to wait until spring to find out if you got in. Another benefit is the favorable light Early Decision casts on your application: It's an indication of extreme interest in a particular institution. If you are accepted through Early Decision, however, you will be expected to accept the offer at once and withdraw your applications to all other colleges. *Applying Early Decision is an obligation to attend if accepted.* It's basically putting all your eggs in one basket. Therefore, it is crucial that you are absolutely certain you want to attend the college to which you apply by Early Decision. If you are unsure or feel that your college search is incomplete, choosing to apply Early Decision is unwise. Discuss this option seriously with your parents and your guidance or college counselor to determine if it is the best one for you. Some counselors discourage applying Early Decision because—though colleges look favorably on Early Decision applicants—this first pool of applicants tends to be filled with top students, which can, in some cases, actually make the odds even stiffer than in regular admission. If you are going to need financial aid for college, you should also know that applying Early Decision does not give you the chance to compare financial aid offers from different schools—you will be limited to the aid package from your Early Decision school. Of course, if this school is your top choice in every way, you may have a letter of good news before the new year, while your friends are still waiting it out.

* Unless the colleges involved indicate otherwise, it is extremely unethical to file an Early Decision application to more than one college.

3. **Early Action***

This admission plan is offered by some Ivy League schools and other selective colleges. Similar to Early Decision, Early Action entails deadlines that fall, generally, between late October and mid-November, and applicants are usually notified by mid-December as to whether they have been accepted, deferred, or denied. As with Early Decision, Early Action tends to attract strong students. Candidates should be able to present very impressive records and applications. The way this strategy differs from Early Decision is this: Applicants who are accepted through Early Action are not obligated to attend the college and can wait until May 1—the universal notification deadline—before notifying the college of their enrollment decision. This offers applicants the opportunity to compare financial aid offers from other schools that send acceptance letters and to take some time in making their final decision. As it indicates interest of a lesser magnitude, however, it does not give you the same edge in the admission process that Early Decision does.

Financial aid is still, most often, awarded much later in the school year. As in other admissions options, a student admitted through Early Action may find that their aid award is not adequate to cover the cost of attending the college. The benefit here is that there is no obligation to attend simply because an offer is made.

*Unless a college indicates otherwise, you may file more than one Early Action application. Many colleges, however, discourage this practice. To this end, several schools have begun to offer a plan called "single-choice Early Action," which does not allow you to apply early to any school but theirs. (You can still, however, apply to other schools through regular admission and give your decision in the spring.)

4. **Rolling Admission**

Colleges using this plan process and review applications as they come in, instead of all at once. As soon as all components of a prospective student's application have arrived (transcript, standardized test scores, essay, recommendations, etc.) admissions officers consider the applicant and decide whether to make an offer to attend. Decisions are made in a relatively short period of time—normally two to four weeks. However, if a college has questions about your academic qualifications, you may be asked to submit first-semester grades from your senior year before they make their decision. Though most schools that offer rolling admissions have a final application deadline, you should submit any rolling admission applications well in advance of that date. With the more popular or selective schools using this plan, spaces allotted for the next year's class fill up quickly—even if you are qualified for admission, there may be no more openings if you apply too close to the deadline. Additionally, if you are denied admission in this way, there may not be enough time to submit applications to other schools that appeal to you.

5. **Early Notification/Early Evaluation**

   Offered by some selective colleges, this is less of an admission strategy than a courtesy extended to applicants. Under this plan, colleges send applicants an estimate of their chances of acceptance in advance of the regular notification date. This estimate, generally sent prior to March 15, provides candidates with a rating that falls into one of three categories: likely, possible, or unlikely. Although a final decision still hangs in the balance at the time of the estimate, colleges that offer early notification give candidates some idea of their chances in advance.

YOUR APPLICATION

It's time to dig deeper into the various components of your application. You'll find the impact of your high school transcript, standardized test scores, letters of recommendation, essays, and interview—and the context each will be viewed in—discussed below. You'll also find sound advice for making the most of your situation.

- **High School Transcript**

  Your high school transcript—including the courses you have taken, your grades, and your class rank—will, for better or for worse, speak volumes about you to admissions officers. Again, admissions officers want to see that you have challenged yourself and have done well. A couple of bad grades will do less damage if they occurred freshman year and you have since improved; conversely, a steady, year-by-year decline in your academic performance won't be viewed favorably. Do your best to keep up your grades in every class. And remember that there are many excellent colleges out there for many different people. By applying to schools that are a good fit for you, you will be able to find a college that accepts the complete you.

- **Standardized Test Scores**

   As we have mentioned, scores on the SAT, ACT, and other entrance exams give admissions officers a look at how you might fare in a college classroom. While it might seem unfair to base this on one test—or, at most, a handful of tests—these tests have been refined through the years to measure aptitudes crucial to college-level work, such as comprehension skills and reasoning abilities.

   A college won't make a decision based on standardized test scores alone, but it will view scores in the context of your entire application. It is worth your time to prepare for these tests in order to earn the highest possible scores. You can find many helpful tools, resources, and articles on PrincetonReview.com. Once you take the test(s), your scores will be sent to the schools you are interested in on your behalf. If you take the SAT, each time you take the test your schools will be sent every score you receive on it. If you take the ACT, you can choose which scores schools will see. While some colleges prefer or require one test over another, many do not have a preference. Check the applications of those schools to which you are applying to be sure.

- **Letters of Recommendation**

   Some colleges will require that you obtain a recommendation specifically from a guidance or college counselor, or from a teacher in a specified group of subjects; others will allow you to choose the recommender(s) you believe would be best. If you plan to play an intercollegiate sport or to utilize a specific talent in college, a recommendation from a coach, teacher, or advisor in the area of your sport or talent is advisable.

Recommendations should support other data submitted with the application, such as your academic achievement, extracurricular involvement, and personal characteristics. Teachers who have had you in class recently and know you well (regardless of the grade you earned in the class) are good choices for recommendations. You should request recommendations early in the application process and provide the teacher, coach, or advisor with the required recommendation forms (some colleges provide a form, others do not), the names and addresses of the colleges to which his or her recommendations will be sent, and the application deadlines. It is also helpful to type up some information on yourself including what you hope to study (if you know), extracurricular activities in which you have been involved, academic and leadership achievements, and so on. Even if a recommender knows you well, he or she will probably be writing recommendations for a handful of students at once. Having a refresher will help him or her to write a stronger letter. Be sure to follow up to ensure that he or she can meet the deadline, and always send a thank-you note to anyone who has taken the time to write you a recommendation.

Recommendations will be mailed directly to the colleges you specify or, if it is your school's policy, submitted to the guidance or college counseling office for mailing with your other application material. (Check each application for any specific instructions.) Either way, the recommendation should be placed in a sealed envelope bearing your school's letterhead, with the words "Recommendation for (your name)" written on the front of the envelope. The teacher, coach, or advisor's signature should be written across the seal. This will ensure that the recommendation reaches the proper application file in the Admissions Office and inform the admission officers that the recommendation is, most likely, confidential. In your application, you are given the option to waive the right to read your recommendations. Doing so ensures confidentiality in the application process. While you certainly have the legal right to read these important documents, conventional wisdom and standard college counseling practice suggest signing the waiver. Admission officers look askance at recommendations that are not confidential and it is unlikely that anyone would agree to write anything but a positive recommendation for you. So, although you will not have the privilege of reading recommendations written about you before they reach the school, if you have chosen appropriate recommenders, and they have agreed to go to bat on your behalf, you should trust that their letters will provide colleges with helpful information that will enhance your application.

Secondary school reports and counselor recommendations should be completed by your guidance or college counselor. The secondary school report usually includes a recommendation section; however, your counselor may wish, additionally, to write a letter of recommendation that is more comprehensive than the space on the form allows. (Many colleges rely heavily on these counselor recommendations.)

- **Essays**

  You should approach the college essay as a way to create a personal impression, as if you were speaking with admissions officers face to face. You want this first impression to be, above all else, intelligent. The writing should an example of your very best work—succinct, well-crafted, and dazzling.

  Parents and teachers can be extremely helpful essay readers. They can offer their opinions on your topic and point out spelling, grammatical, or typographical errors. They should not, however, be involved in the actual writing; their assistance must be limited to critical comments. The writing must be your work alone. In fact, your candidacy for admission may be compromised if your essay is not your own work.

  During your junior year, class meetings, advisory sessions, or other school activities may be devoted to the topic of college essays; some junior or senior year English classes may even include essay-writing practice as part of the curriculum. (Most senior-year English teachers are more than willing to offer advice or assistance in this area, as well.) There are also various books on the market and information on the Internet to which you can refer to for help in writing a quality college essay. As mentioned in Chapter 2, *College Essays that Made a Difference,* written by the staff of The Princeton Review, is a terrific resource.

The following are suggestions as you prepare to write your essays:

1. Don't use the essay to repeat what you have already stated in other parts of the application. You may wish to elaborate on a particular activity in the body of your essay, but a topic that shows a broader view of your life and personality is often more effective.

2. Don't write too much or too little on the topic. If the college gives specific instructions on length, follow them.

3. Never rush to complete an essay. Start early so that you will have the opportunity to revise and edit your work several times. Once you're happy with a draft, put it aside for a few days. After coming back to it, you will undoubtedly find ways to improve it. With every successive draft, your work is likely to get better.

4. Unless a college requests that an essay be submitted in your own handwriting, type it.

5. Don't misspell words. With spelling and grammar tools on every word-processing program and the opportunity to proofread your essay, there is absolutely no way for an admissions official to justify or overlook misspellings.

6. In most cases, you should not use the essay to explain academic or disciplinary problems. You may find the opportunity to address these issues somewhere else in the application. The essay should be used to emphasize your strengths.

7. In the same vein, think twice about discussing sensitive topics. Religion and politics can be tricky, and certainly anything suggestive is out of the question. When in doubt, choose a safer topic, or at the very least, run it by your counselor.

8. Even with open-ended essay prompts, make an effort to avoid using the exact same essay for different college applications. Wherever possible and appropriate, tailor your essays to fit the requirements, programs, and strengths of the college to which you will submit it.

9. Don't try to be cute or clever—as in, don't submit your essay in the form of a poem or on a balloon that must be inflated to be read. Admissions officials have seen everything already, probably more than once. Stick to the format and write a good, solid essay—and don't send it off with home-baked cookies, for goodness's sake. Your writing should speak for itself.

- **Interview**

  While certain colleges require an interview for admission, most do not. They are very time consuming for the school and can be very inconvenient for applicants. For this reason, many colleges and universities make the interview an optional part of their application. You may be given the chance to be interviewed on campus by a faculty or staff member, in your own town by an alum, by a traveling college representative, or even over the phone. If given the chance to interview with a college, take it. Chances are the interview will neither make nor break a potential acceptance, but it can add a face and personality to your application and give you some insight on the school. Dress nicely (but not too formally). Wear something in which you feel comfortable and confident but nothing that makes an overly loud statement. Prepare for the interview by reading up on the school and use the opportunity to put a few intelligent questions to someone on the inside. Most interviews will last about 30 minutes, give or take. Interviewers are on a tight schedule, so be respectful of their time. Follow up with a brief but sincere handwritten thank-you note when you get home.

The Total Impression

In their book, *Your College Application*, Gelband, Kubale, and Schorr write:

After you understand the purpose of each individual document, it is important to consider the picture . . . how your application will appear as a whole. With such limited space, you want to be sure that each document conveys a message.[1]

As you work on each application, try to put yourself in the reader's place. You want to give admission officers a reason to accept you. Think about the total impression you wish to create and ask yourself the following questions:

1. Does my application communicate my strengths, interests, and other personal qualities effectively?

2. Have I shown that my strengths, interests, and other personal qualities would be a good match for the academic environment, extracurricular offerings, and social climate of the college?

3. What do I bring to the table that makes me attractive to those who will determine whether I will be admitted or denied? Have I demonstrated that I would make a positive and unique contribution to the campus?

If you want to present yourself in the best possible light to admissions officers, details are important. Below is a summary of some the more important points made earlier, along with some other suggestions for preparing your application. You should record these points in your journal or somewhere else they can be easily referenced during the application process.

1. Start early. Recognize that when you postpone an application until the last minute, it will be evident in the quality of your essay and other parts of the application. A hastily prepared application will thwart your aim to make the most positive impression.

2. Follow all application instructions to the letter.

3. Photocopy the original application and work from the copy until the application and essays have been completed, proofread, and revised. Transfer the information to the original form once you are satisfied with the results. If you apply online, schools will allow you to save your application each time you work on it until you are satisfied and ready to submit it. Read and reread each piece of it, just as you would if

you were applying on paper. (Know that no magical spell-check tool will filter it before it reaches the school!)

4. If you handwrite an application, print neatly and legibly. Typing it is better. Even if admissions officers don't come out and say it, their eyes prefer it. If you decide to handwrite an application, use a black ballpoint pen that won't smear or bleed.

5. Waive your right to read recommendations written for you. College admission officers prefer confidential recommendations. If you have chosen your recommenders wisely, there should be no reason for you to see what they have written. Many teachers and counselors will discuss, informally, what they have written about you, but most are more comfortable writing recommendations that will be handled confidentially.

6. Carefully organize all of your application materials. Keep a separate file for each college.

7. Photocopy or print out each part of your completed application before you submit it to your counselor or you mail (or e-mail) it yourself.

Putting It All Together

Once your application is complete and has been proofread by your counselor or another reliable adult, it is wise to mail all of its components as a package. This minimizes the possibility that one of the documents may be lost in the mail or that the college may misfile one of them. You or your counselor (according to your school's policy) should mail it and record the date, time, and location it was mailed from. If you mail different sections separately, you should record this information for each section you mail. If you file your application online—many colleges make it safe and easy to do so and encourage their applicants to consider this option—you will receive periodic updates on the status of your application materials via e-mail. Colleges give no preference to applicants who apply a certain way; students who mail their application and students who apply online are considered equally. The only difference is that students who apply online enjoy instant confirmation of receipt of their materials. The choice is yours—you should apply in whichever manner makes you most comfortable.

Review of the Application

When your application materials begin to arrive at an Admissions Office, a file is created in your name. This file, when completed, will contain your application, high school transcript, letter(s) of recommendation, official standardized test scores, and essay(s), as well as any other data submitted to support your candidacy. Once a school has all of your components on file, your application will begin to wend its way through the evaluation process.

Some institutions utilize mathematical formulas (usually based on a combination of the applicant's grade point average, test scores, and other pertinent factors) when evaluating students, and the task of accepting or denying a specific applicant will often be in the hands of just one or two admission officers. At these situations, borderline applications may be referred to a committee (which may include members of the faculty) for further consideration.

At other colleges, each application will be read by several admission officers or by an admissions committee comprised of admissions officers, faculty, and even, in some cases, students. With each reading, admissions personnel jot down their thoughts as to whether the applicant would be a good fit for the school. In committee meetings, the admission officer who has responsibility for and expertise in the applicant's state, region, and school—and who, therefore, knows the area and local schools well—may "present" the applicant. Some committees work toward consensus in regards to each potential newcomer; others take a vote after some discussion. More often than not, final decisions—especially at the nation's most competitive colleges—are made not by a single person but by a group of people who bring somewhat different perspectives to the process and aim to make a fair and comprehensive decision.

ADMISSION DECISIONS

By December of your senior year, students who have applied Early Decision or Early Action, or submitted rolling admission applications early in the fall, will begin to hear back from colleges. The majority of students, however, will receive the bulk—if not all—of their admissions decisions in late March or early April, when most non-open-admission colleges mail their regular admission decisions.

For many seniors, the days and months before these decisions arrive is filled with great anticipation and a dose of anxiety. You should make sure that you—rather than a parent, sibling, or roommate—open the decision letters as they arrive. If you are accepted at your top-choice schools you will want to be the first to share the good news with those you care about; you will receive praise and congratulations and feel a real sense of accomplishment. If you don't receive the news you had hoped for, you will be understandably disappointed. This disappointment may be difficult to handle, particularly if you achieved at a high level throughout your high school years. If this is the case, you deserve the opportunity to share this information with others in your own way and when you feel you are ready to do so. This is a time when you, your classmates, and your friends need to be sensitive to and supportive of each other. In the same way, parents, teachers, and counselors should be aware that the waiting involved in and the results of the application process can be anxiety-provoking and frustrating. Hopefully those around you will make every effort to reduce the stress of this process.

The Wait List

Based on an estimate of how many students will accept their offers of admission (colleges admit many more students than they have room for, knowing that some will choose to enroll elsewhere), many colleges place a certain percentage of their applicants on a wait list. This percentage acts as a buffer zone in the event that the above estimate is too high—it ensures that the college will be able to enroll a full class for the coming year, one that meets its fiscal, academic, extracurricular, and demographic goals.

Students placed on a wait list are generally those who are well qualified for admission and who would be, were space available in the acceptance pool, readily admitted. That said, it is important to understand that wait-listed applicants are admitted only if a larger-than-expected number of the students who were originally admitted decide to enroll elsewhere. Larger schools tend to offer admission to more wait listed applicants than smaller schools. Regardless of size, however, only a tiny percentage of any school's freshman class gets in through the wait list each year. Students should avoid holding their hopes too high if they find themselves in this position.

Should you be placed on a wait list at a college you very much want to attend, you should make an appointment to discuss this situation with your counselor as soon as possible. If you and your counselor decide that it is practical for you to remain on the list, return the card indicating your intent and follow it up with a letter to the Director of Admissions at the college. This letter should state why you want to attend the college enough to remain on its wait list and, if possible, provide positive information regarding your qualifications for admission that were not included in your application. (If you have recently earned an important award or received grades that may impress the admissions committee, be sure to include this information.) While you wait for the school's decision—which could come as late as August—commit to an institution you have already been accepted to. You will be required to make a non-refundable deposit at this college by May 1, the universal notification deadline for most U.S. colleges.

The Final Decision

Once you have received decisions from all of the colleges to which you applied, you will need to identify, from your pool of acceptances, the school you will attend. For some, this is an easy decision; others need more time. Here are some steps to take as you make your final decision.

- Review the notes and marketing materials you used to when deciding which colleges to apply to. Consider the academic and social environment of each college you've been accepted to and the compatibility of each with your needs and interests.

- Discuss your options with your parents, counselor, and if possible, alumni of your high school who have attended the colleges you have been accepted to. Try to see your options from a variety of perspectives.

- If you have trouble deciding between two attractive colleges, make a list of the pros and cons associated with each. If a decision still doesn't come, visit the colleges again, if at all possible. Such a trip may be costly, but, given the investment in your postsecondary education that you and your parents will make over the next several years, it is certainly worthwhile.

- Trust your instincts. In the face of two or more seemingly equal choices, go with the option that *feels* right.

- Unless you've decided to remain on a wait list, make only one deposit. It is unethical to do otherwise. The National Association for College Admission Counseling (NACAC)'s "Statement of Students' Rights and Responsibilities in the College Admission Process" states clearly that multiple deposits are not appropriate.[2]

As soon as you make a final decision, notify your counselor so he or she can prepare to send your final transcript to the proper institution. Once you have sent your deposit to the college of your choice, write a brief note to the Directors of Admissions at each of the other colleges to which you have been accepted. Thank them for accepting you or placing you on their wait list and let them know which school you plan to attend (of course, if you plan to *remain* on a given school's wait list, *don't* send it this letter). Colleges collect this information as part of their detailed records of each year's admissions cycle.

FINANCIAL AID

TIPS FOR APPLYING FOR AID

Many high schools offer a college financial aid workshop for students and parents. If yours does, you should make a point of attending it with your parents. It will most likely feature experts who can explain the financial aid application process and answer questions about the various types of aid. Numerous resources can also be obtained from your school's college counseling office where—in addition to essential financial aid forms, such as the FAFSA and CSS PROFILE—you'll find guidebooks such as *The College Cost and Financial Aid Handbook,* published annually by College Board. The following tips are adapted from the 20th edition of that book:

- Become familiar with the various sources of financial aid.

- Request financial aid materials when you request your college applications.

- Know what forms are required for the financial aid application process.

- Complete the College Scholarship Service (CSS) PROFILE and the FAFSA as early as possible, listing all college programs and agencies to which you want the results of your need analysis sent.

- Fill out all forms accurately and legibly.

- Keep copies of everything.

- Respond promptly to requests for additional information.

- Don't hesitate to ask questions.[3]

Earlier it was suggested that cost shouldn't be a major factor as you compile a list of colleges in line with your needs, interests, and abilities. There is substantial basis for that advice: In the U.S. there is a plethora of financial aid that is need based, or determined by how much you and your family can pay for college.

According to Calvin King, Senior Financial Aid Consultant at the Georgia Student Finance Commission, "Most financial aid programs focus on . . . [what] is known as the 'expected family contribution' or EFC." Such programs will cover college expenses beyond your family's means with grants and loans. "Even though a college may seem too expensive," King adds, "the rule of thumb is, 'The higher the cost, the higher [your] need.'" Using the EFC, which doesn't change according to the expense of a given school, your family won't be expected to pay more while you attend a more expensive school.

That doesn't mean, however, that cost can be completely ignored in the admissions process. Higher costs generally mean greater loans and greater debt for the student and his or her family. According to College Board, in 2006–2007 tuition and fees at 4-year private colleges averaged $22,218; with room and board, total costs averaged $30,367. At 4-year public institutions, tuition and fees averaged $5,836; with room and board, total costs averaged $12,796.[4]

Those are large numbers, and they can really add up over the course of 4 or 5 (or 6) years. The College Board, however, provides some encouraging facts:

- Forty-two percent of students who attended 4-year schools paid less than $6,000 for tuition and fees.

- Only 5 percent of all students attended schools where tuition and fees exceeded $33,000.[5]

- Financial aid in grants and tax benefits averaged about $3,100 per student at public four-year colleges and about $9,000 per student at private four-year colleges.[6]

Sources of Financial Aid

There are two basic types of financial aid—grants (AKA scholarships, gifts that do not require repayment) and self-help (loans and student employment). There are four primary sources: the institution itself (i.e., the college), private third parties, the state government, and the federal government.

MERIT SCHOLARSHIPS

Many colleges offer scholarships to the most academically talented students in their applicant pool. These awards range from a fraction of the school's tuition to a "full ride." Most of these scholarships are competitive, and many require essays, interviews, or other tests as a means of identifying which students should receive them. Some require a nomination by the secondary school from which the student will graduate. You may be a great candidate for a merit scholarship—check college catalogues, websites, and applications for more information.

The amount of institutional aid available varies according to the fiscal capacity of the college. Institutional aid can include merit scholarships and need-based awards. It can also include an offer of on-campus employment outside of Federal Work-Study (discussed below). In recent years, some colleges have taken innovative approaches to helping families find ways to finance an education. If, based on an aid package, you do not think you will be able to afford a given school, you should call its financial aid office—it can spur a productive conversation about your options.

Private third-party aid sources include corporations and foundations, as well as community, religious, cultural, and fraternal organizations. (Chapter 6 features lists of third-party aid sources.) While private aid is most often an outright gift, it may also come as a low-interest loan. The myriad sources of private aid give you a chance to be creative in locating funds to pay for your college education. If you're a student who does not qualify for financial aid from other sources but needs assistance in meeting college costs, private aid is a great option. You should know up front, however, that eligibility for many of these scholarships is outside the realm of possibility for most people—certain restrictions clearly limit the number of students who can take advantage of them. For example, the Swift Export Co. may offer one $5,000 scholarship a year to a left-handed, Lilliputian female with one blue eye and one hazel eye. While most real-life examples aren't as extreme, the ratio of available aid to the aid you potentially qualify for will be high. Viable options do exist, but they will take time to find. Visit websites such as Fastweb.com and CollegeBoard.org—the latter's Scholarship Search is a terrific resource—to start your search. Guidebooks such as *Paying for College without Going Broke* by Kalman A. Chany (with Geoff Martz) and *The Scholarship Book* by Daniel Cassidy are also helpful in this area.

PRIVATE PRIZE: IS IT FOR YOU?

It's important to remember that *all funds accepted by financial aid recipients—from any source—must be reported to the college*. Private grants and loans are considered by the institution as it determines its own financial aid package. Unfortunately, in many situations—particularly those in which your aid package is driven solely by your family's need (rather than the quality of your application)—private aid simply prompts an institution to decrease the amount of grant aid it gives you from its own treasure chest. It is wise to speak with financial aid officers at the schools you are applying to for their policies on private aid before investing time and energy in a search for it.

Additionally, each state has an array of financial aid programs to help its residents pay for college. For more information on your state's programs, visit its student aid website. You can find many of these sites through a Google search with the key words "(your state) state student aid department."

While substantial aid can be found through other sources, the federal government is, by far, the largest source of financial aid for college. Federal aid programs include the following:

1. *Grants*

   Federal Pell Grant: The size of this award depends on several factors, including the student's enrollment status (full- or part-time), his or her family's financial need, and the cost of the school. The ceiling for this award changes each year and depends on program funding. (In 2005–2006, the largest possible Pell Grant was $4,050.) Schools can apply this award to costs, pay the student directly, or split the award between the student and his or her outstanding costs.[7]

   Federal Supplemental Educational Opportunity Grant (FSEOG): Students with considerable financial need—i.e., those with the lowest EFCs—can receive a FSEOG in addition to their Pell Grant. Awards range from $100 to $4,000, depending on when the student applies, his or her EFC, and the fiscal resources of the school and the policies of its financial aid office. The FSEOG has the same options for disbursement as the Pell Grant.[8]

2. *Loans*

   Funds associated with the loans below are disbursed through the college, in at least two installments. No installment can be greater than one-half of the total loan. Loan money is first applied to school costs—tuition and fees, room and board, etc. Any remaining loan money is paid to the student.[9]

   Federal Perkins Loan: A low-interest need-based loan; the interest rate for the Federal Perkins Loan is currently just 5 percent. Repayment starts nine months after a student graduates. No interest accumulates while the student is enrolled or during the nine-month grace period. For college students, the maximum annual loan is $4,000; the cumulative limit is $20,000.[10]

   Stafford Loan: Depending on which Stafford Loan program a college participates in, the federal government may directly provide the funds for this loan or it may guarantee funds provided by a private lender. If you qualify, based on need, for a subsidized Stafford Loan, the government will pay the interest (the interest rate varies annually, but it is capped at 8.25 percent) on your loan while you are in school, during the six-month grace period, and during any deferment periods. You are responsible for paying all of the interest that accrues on an unsubsidized Stafford Loan. [11]

The maximum annual sum a dependent—an individual provided for by another, usually his or her parents—can borrow is currently $3,500 in the first year of college, $4,500 in the second year of college, and $5,500 in the third year of college and beyond. Independent students are eligible for additional loans: $4,000 in each the first and second years of college and $5,000 each year of college afterwards. These additional loans are never subsidized. Total borrowing is capped at $23,000 for dependents and $46,000 for independents. [12]

PLUS Loan: A loan for the parents of college students—the maximum amount disbursed each year is the cost of attendance minus other financial aid (including loans for which the student is directly eligible). There is no limit to PLUS Loan borrowing. [13]

3. *Work-Study*

Federal Work-Study (FWS): This program provides students with jobs that allow them to earn money to cover expenses associated with their education. Many students work on-campus for the institution they attend. You can work at your school's library, for example, to cover the cost of your books, lab fees, and living expenses. Many students also work off campus. As off-campus work must be in the public interest, this work is usually with a nonprofit organization or a public agency. Participants are paid directly and at least one a month. The amount earned, however, cannot exceed the total FWS award. [14]

A Note of Caution

Beware of companies that offer to find you money for college for a nominal fee. Most will simply supply you with lists that you can find yourself via the Internet. Financial aid professionals suggest that you check with your counselor before responding to any such offer.

The Financial Aid Award Package

File the FAFSA as soon as possible after January 1 of your senior year. We'd suggest submitting it even sooner, but it requires your family's tax returns from the previous calendar year. The College Scholarship Service (CSS) PROFILE may be submitted as early as fall of your senior year.

Both the FAFSA and the PROFILE assume that your parents will take primary responsibility for the cost of your college education. Such forms also assume that students will bear some responsibility in helping to meet the cost. With these assumptions in mind, they evaluate the EFC. This information is then forwarded to college financial aid officers who determine your demonstrated need by assessing the difference between your educational expenses (tuition, fees, books, personal expenses, and room and board) and your EFC.

Of course, what the FAFSA or the PROFILE determines to be a reasonable family contribution and what a family feels it can actually contribute may differ. To help fill the gap, many colleges turn to their own resources. This is why it behooves you to start this process as early as possible—financial aid offices are less likely to be hindered by diminishing resources when coming up with "extra money" if it is early in the application season. As a rule, college financial aid officers try to keep loans at a level that allows for reasonable repayment after college and work-study hours at a level that does not detract from a student's success while in school.

Compare your awards carefully to determine the best aid package for you. You have the option to appeal the aid package at a favorite school if it does not meet your needs.

There are many great possibilities for your remaining years in high school. The experiences you choose and the information you've learned about college admissions can work together to aid you in identifying places where you can *continue* to build on your abilities, skills, and talents—and, perhaps, discover new passions. If college is your destination, remember that it is just that: a port of call, a stopping place, a goal on your journey to becoming who you will be in the future. It is not the journey's end.

> "And will you succeed?
> Yes! You will, indeed!
> (98 and 3/4 percent
> guaranteed.)
> KID, YOU'LL MOVE
> MOUNTAINS!
> So . . .
> be your name Buxbaum or Bixby
> or Bray
> or Mordecai Ali Van Allen
> O'Shea,
> you're off to Great Places!
> Today is your day!
> Your mountain is waiting.
> So . . . get on your way!"
>
> —Dr. Seuss[15]

Life is sure to offer you countless choices and opportunities, along with twists and turns that you would never anticipate. Continue to work at self-awareness and build character. Keep journaling and reflecting on your experiences. Continue to set realistic goals for yourself, utilize the "tools of engagement" that are available to you, and make every effort to be as prepared as possible for the next big leap.

ENDNOTES

1   Gelband, Scott, Catherine Kubale, and Eric Schorr. *Your College Application*. New York: College Board, 1992. 95.

2   National Association for College Admission Counseling (NACAC). "Prospective Students Have the Right to Know: Students' Rights and Responsibilities in the College Admissions Process." 2006. www.nacacnet.org/NR/rdonlyres/FA91A978-7D6A-496A-976F-2BB5B8A53BD8/0/StudentsRtsNEW.pdf.

3   College Scholarship Service. *The College Cost and Financial Aid Handbook*. New York: The College Board, 2000. 25–6.

4   College Board. "Press Releases: Tuition Increases Continue to Slow at Public Colleges According to the College Board's 2006 Reports on College Pricing and Financial Aid." 2007. www.collegeboard.com/press/releases/150634.html.

5   College Board. "Trends in Higher Education: Trends in College Pricing." 2006. www.collegeboard.com/prod_downloads/press/cost06/trends_college_pricing_06.pdf.

6   College Board. "Trends in Higher Education: Trends in College Pricing." 2006. www.collegeboard.com/prod_downloads/press/cost06/trends_college_pricing_06.pdf.

7   Federal Student Aid, U.S. Department of Education. "Federal Student Aid for Counselors: Federal Pell Grant." www.fsa4counselors.ed.gov/clcf/PellGrants.html.

8   Federal Student Aid, U.S. Department of Education. "Federal Student Aid for Counselors: Federal Supplemental Educational Opportunity Grants (FSEOG)." www.fsa4counselors.ed.gov/clcf/FSEOG.html.

9   Federal Student Aid, U.S. Department of Education. "Federal Student Aid for Counselors: Loans." www.fsa4counselors.ed.gov/clcf/loans.html.

10 The Office of Student Financial Aid, The Ohio State University. "Loan Programs: Federal Perkins Loan." 2007. http://sfa.osu.edu/loans/index.asp?tab=b#pagecontent.

11 Federal Student Aid, U.S. Department of Education. "Federal Student Aid for Counselors: Loans." www.fsa4counselors.ed.gov/clcf/loans.html.

12 The Office of Student Financial Aid, The Ohio State University. "Loan Programs: Federal Direct Stafford Loans." 2007. http://sfa.osu.edu/loans/index.asp?tab=e#pagecontent.

13 The Office of Student Financial Aid, The Ohio State University. "Loan Programs: Federal Direct Parent Loan for Undergraduate Students (Parent PLUS Loans)." 2007. http://sfa.osu.edu/loans/index.asp?tab=f#pagecontent.

14 Federal Student Aid, U.S. Department of Education. "Federal Student Aid for Counselors: Federal Work-Study." www.fsa4counselors.ed.gov/clcf/workstudy.html.

15 Dr. Seuss (Theodore Geisl). *Oh, The Places You'll Go.* New York: Random House, 1990.

APPENDIX A
MY PERSONAL PROFILE

This form can be used for multiple purposes.

1. To assist you in creating a portfolio or resume
2. To distribute to teachers and others who agree to write letters of recommendation for you
3. To assist you in completing sections of applications for programs, activities, employment, and/or college

===

Name_____

Name or nickname by which I prefer to be called_____

Social Security #_____Date of birth_____

Address_____

_____

_____

Names of Parents or Guardians

_____

_____

_____

Names and ages of siblings

_____

_____

Religious Affiliation _____Ethnicity _____

Name and Address of School

_____

_____

_____

Grade _____   Type of Program_____

Academic Record

What courses have I found to be the most enjoyable over the last 2 years? What has made them enjoyable for me? What grades have I earned in these courses?

_____

_____

_____

_____

_____

_____

What subjects or courses have I found to be the most challenging over the last 2 years? What has made them difficult for me? How have I handled it?

_____

_____

_____

_____

What academic awards and/or honors have I earned? When did I receive them?

_____

_____

_____

_____

_____

In what specific ways would I like to improve as a student (study habits, reading skills, etc.)?

_____

_____

_____

_____

_____

What are my strongest skills as a student (writing, research, problem-solving, etc.)?

_____

_____

_____

_____

_____

_____

How are my personal potential and my academic performance related? Have there been any specific circumstances that enhanced or hindered my performance? If so, what were they and how have they affected me?

_____

_____

_____

_____

_____

_____

What's the best learning or work environment for my skills, abilities, and personality? What would I like most to learn or do in this environment?

_____

_____

_____

_____

_____

_____

Which teachers, counselors, coaches, etc. know me best? Three people I could ask to write recommendations for me are:

Name   Position/Subject or Program

_____   _____

_____   _____

_____   _____

Co- and Extracurricular Activities

Athletics—My participation history

Include varsity (V), junior varsity (JV) or other level of involvement, where appropriate, and the year of participation.

Fall	Winter	Spring	Summer
_____	_____	_____	_____
_____	_____	_____	_____
_____	_____	_____	_____
_____	_____	_____	_____

Leadership roles or awards I earned in the above activities:

_____

_____

_____

The Arts—My participation history

Include the activity and the year of participation. If there are theater productions, indicate the name the production and the role played.

_____

_____

_____

The clubs and organizations I have been involved with and the grades during which I participated in them are:

_____

_____

_____

_____

_____

The activities outside of school I am involved in (including church, synagogue, or community service) are:

_____

_____

_____

_____

Leadership roles or awards I earned in the above activities:

_____

_____

My Personal Interests

Be specific and indicate the depth of involvement.

_____

_____

_____

_____

_____

Significant travel experiences I have had include:

_____

_____

_____

What has made them significant to me?

_____

_____

_____

Favorite Places   Least Favorite Places

_____   _____

_____   _____

Last Book Read (Include author's name)

_____

Favorite Book (Include author's name)

_____

Favorite Film

_____

Favorite Type of Music

_____

Favorite CD

_____

Favorite Type of Game (video, board, card, etc.)

_____

Favorite Games

_____

_____

Immediate Goals

Long Range Goals

_____

_____

_____

_____

_____

Two activities or experiences that have affected me positively are:

_____

_____

_____

_____

_____

_____

_____

Two people who have had a positive impact on my life are:

_____

_____

How their influence has made a difference in my goals for the future:

_____

_____

_____

_____

_____

_____

_____

Independent study or research I have done that went beyond the regular requirements of an academic course:

List the reasons for undertaking this work as well as the outcomes.

_____

_____

_____

_____

_____

_____

_____

What community, civic, societal, or global issues are important to me and why?

_____

_____

_____

_____

_____

_____

_____

What are my personal strengths (energy, personality, initiative, sense of humor, leadership skills, character traits, etc.)?

_____

_____

_____

_____

_____

What five words would describe me and why?

_____

_____

_____

_____

_____

My Future

What academic disciplines have I considered studying in college?

_____

_____

_____

What extracurricular activities do I expect to pursue in college?

_____

_____

_____

_____

What do I see myself doing ten years from now?

_____

_____

_____

_____

What could I do now to help me achieve these goals?

_____

_____

_____

_____

My "Bio"

Write a brief autobiographical sketch (approximately 300 words).
Attach this bio to the answers to the questions above.

_____
_____
_____
_____
_____
_____
_____
_____
_____
_____
_____
_____
_____
_____
_____
_____
_____
_____
_____
_____
_____
_____
_____
_____
_____
_____
_____
_____
_____
_____

APPENDIX B
MY COLLEGE PLANNING PROFILE

Personal Data

Date_____ Year in School_____

Full Name_____ Nickname_____

Date of Birth_____ Soc. Sec. #_____

Grade Point Average_____

Type of Program _____

(college preparation, general, vocational, etc.)

My Academic Strengths:

_____

_____

_____

My Academic Challenges:

_____

_____

_____

My Talents:

_____

_____

_____

My Interests:

_____

_____

_____

My Extracurricular Activities

9th grade	10th grade	11th grade	12th grade
_____	_____	_____	_____
_____	_____	_____	_____
_____	_____	_____	_____
_____	_____	_____	_____
_____	_____	_____	_____
_____	_____	_____	_____
_____	_____	_____	_____

Awards and Honors that I have Received   Year in School

_____

_____

_____

_____

_____

_____

My Goals and Dreams for the Future:

_____

_____

_____

_____

_____

_____

_____

Ideal College Environment:

Location

Northeast _____ Mid-Atlantic _____ Southeast _____ Midwest _____

Mid-South _____ Southwest _____ West Coast _____ Northwest _____

Preferred States

_____/_____/_____/_____

Other_____

Urban_____ Suburban_____ Rural_____

Residential_____ On- or Off-Campus?_____ Commuter_____

Distance from home _____miles or _____hours

Size (Student Population)

Small (less than 1000)_____ Moderate (1,000–3,000)_____

Medium (3,000–10,000)_____ Large/Very Large (10,000+)_____

Public or Private? _____

Majors that interest me:

_____

_____

Activities, sports, and clubs that interest me:

_____

_____

_____

_____

Fraternities and Sororities?   Yes____   No_____   It doesn't matter_____

What academic and social experiences am I looking forward to in college?

_____
_____
_____
_____

Attach a brief autobiographical sketch that addresses at least two of the four ideas listed below.

- Who am I? (Don't describe yourself by according to what other people say you are. This is your opportunity to reflect on your life and say who you think you are. What makes you a unique individual?)
- What have I learned about myself since the 9th grade?
- What do I want the college admission staff to know most about me?
- What are my best talents and skills?

_____
_____
_____
_____
_____
_____
_____
_____
_____
_____
_____
_____
_____
_____
_____
_____
_____
_____

Write a mock college essay that answers one of the following questions:

- What traits must a person possess to be a productive citizen in the twenty-first century?

- What do I see as one of the most significant challenges of our time? What can I do to help overcome that challenge?

- What does it mean to think critically? Is critical thinking a valuable characteristic in today's society? Why or why not?

- Who is the funniest person I know? Why do I think this person is so funny?

_____
_____
_____
_____
_____
_____
_____
_____
_____
_____
_____
_____
_____
_____
_____
_____
_____
_____
_____
_____
_____
_____
_____
_____
_____
_____

APPENDIX C
COLLEGE PLANNING CHECKLIST

9TH GRADE—AWARENESS

- Talk with my parents/guardian about my future (interests, dreams, plans, their expectations, etc.).
- Make academics my priority.
  - ☑ Challenge myself.
  - ☑ Discover my learning style.
  - ☑ Develop good study habits.
  - ☑ Learn to manage my time wisely.
  - ☑ Always give my best effort.
  - ☑ Seek help when I need it.
- Maintain good attendance.
- Practice good citizenship.
- Make wise social choices.
- Get involved in co- and extracurricular and class activities.
- Volunteer for community service.
- Develop my talents.
- Discover new interests.
- Meet regularly with my advisor.
- Participate in advisory group activities.
- Get acquainted with my counselor and/or advisor.
- Attend area or school college fairs with my parents/guardian.
- Parents/guardian should attend the parents' programs offered by my school.
- Take the PLAN assessment given in October.
- Begin keeping a file/record/portfolio of my work and achievements.

- Talk with my parents/guardian about my progress and future plans (including my college search and financing my post-secondary education).
- Continue making academics my priority.
  - ☑ Give attention to course selection and academic progress.
  - ☑ Stretch myself to meet new challenges.
  - ☑ Take stock of my strengths and weaknesses.
  - ☑ Practice wise time management.
  - ☑ Practice good study habits.
  - ☑ Always give my best effort.
- Continue to maintain good attendance and practice good citizenship.
- Make wise social choices.
- Continue involvement in school activities and community service.
- Attend the area or school college fairs or college nights with my parents/guardian.
- Take the New PSAT/NSMQT in October, if possible. (Just for practice! You don't have report your scores to colleges yet.)
- Meet regularly with my advisor.
- Participate in advisory group activities.
- Parents/guardian should attend the parents' programs offered by my school.
- Meet occasionally with my counselor.
- Explore my school's College Resource Room.
- Begin to build a personal college resource library.
- Take the PLAN assessment in October.
- Take the Myers-Briggs Personality Type Inventory (MBTI) and Campbell Interest and Skill Assessment (CISS), if possible.

- Explore summer program options.
- Continue building a file/record/portfolio of my work and achievements.

11TH GRADE—GROWTH

- Continue to make academics my priority.
  - ☑ Review my academic progress and achievement to date with my counselor or advisor.
  - ☑ Continue to assess my strengths and weaknesses.
  - ☑ Continue to stretch and challenge myself.
  - ☑ Continue to give attention to course selection.
  - ☑ Continue to practice wise time management and good study habits.
  - ☑ Continue to always give my best effort.
- Continue involvement in school activities and community service.
- Continue to maintain good attendance and to practice good citizenship.
- Make wise social choices.
- Attend presentations by visiting college representatives.
- Attend the area and school college fairs and college nights.
- Parents/guardian should attend parents' programs offered by my school.
- Take the PSAT/NMSQT in October.
- Meet regularly with my advisor.
- Participate in advisory group activities.
- Take the SAT in March/April and May.
- Take the ACT in April.
- Meet with my counselor in the spring for an individual family conference to develop a college search list.
- Begin visiting colleges during spring break.

- Consider which teacher to ask for letters of recommendation.
- Explore summer program options.
- Take one or two SAT Subject Tests exams in June.
- Using my file/record/portfolio and information gathered from my MBTI and CISS, begin work on the College Profile provided in this handbook.

12TH GRADE—DECISIONS

- Talk openly with parents/guardian about my feelings, concerns, interests, and plans as I visit colleges and narrow the list of colleges to which I will apply.
- Continue to make academics my priority.
    - ☑ Continue to stretch and challenge myself.
    - ☑ Choose senior-year courses wisely.
    - ☑ Check my transcript for accuracy and credit toward graduation.
    - ☑ Continue to practice wise time management and good study habits.
    - ☑ Continue to always give my best effort.
- Continue involvement in school activities and community service.
- Continue to maintain good attendance and to practice good citizenship.
- Make wise social choices.
- Attend presentations by visiting college representatives.
- Develop a final list of colleges.
- Meet with my counselor to review progress in my college search and application process.
- Parents/guardian should attend parents' programs offered by my school.
- Take SAT (October) and SAT Subject Tests (November and/or December).

- Meet with my advisor.
- Participate in class and advisory activities.
- Attend presentations by visiting college representatives.
- Attend area or school college fairs and college nights.
- Research scholarship opportunities.
- Visit colleges on my final list for the second or third time.
- File electronic applications.
- Request paper applications.
- Be sensitive and responsive to application deadlines.
- Submit Secondary School Report and request transcripts from my Counseling Office at least three weeks prior to application deadlines. With parental help, complete the College Scholarship Service (CSS) Profile (only if it is required by colleges to which I will apply).
- Talk to my counselor about any feelings or issues that arise during senior year and the college application process.
- Notify my college counselor of admission decisions I receive.
- With my college counselor, make decisions about colleges that have placed me on their "wait list."
- Reply to the college I plan to attend by May 1, the official Candidate Reply Date.
- Notify other colleges to which I was admitted of my decision not to attend.
- Write "thank you" notes to teachers for their recommendations.
- Attend college orientation and other programs that will help me make a smooth transition from secondary school to college.

APPENDIX D
ADDITIONAL RESOURCES

OTHER BOOKS YOU MIGHT ENJOY

Brain, Marshall. *Teenager's Guide to the Real World*. Raleigh, NC: BYG Publishing, 1997.

Canfield, Jack, Mark Hansen, Kimberly Kirberger, and Mitch Claspy. *Chicken Soup for the Teenage Soul IV: More Stories of Life, Love and Learning*. Deerfield Beach, FL: Health Communications, Inc., 1997.

Canfield, Jack. Mark Hansen, Kimberly Kirberger, and Deborah Reber. *Chicken Soup for the Teenage Soul: The Real Deal Challenges: Stories about Disses, Losses, Messes, Stresses & More*. Deerfield Beach, FL: Health Communications, Inc., 2006.

Carlson, Richard. *Don't Sweat the Small Stuff for Teens*. New York: Hyperion, 2000.

Covey, Sean. *The 7 Habits of Highly Effective Teens*. New York: Fireside, 1998.

Covey, Sean. *The 6 Most Important Decisions You'll Ever Make: A Guide for Teens*. New York: Fireside, 2006.

Graham, Stedman. *Teens Can Make It Happen: Nine Steps for Success*. New York: Fireside, 2000.

Levine, Mel. *Ready or Not, Here Life Comes*. New York: Simon & Schuster, 2005.

McGraw, Jay. *Life Strategies for Teens*. New York: Fireside, 2000.

Packer, Alex J. *How Rude!: The Teenagers' Guide to Good Manners, Proper Behavior, and Not Grossing People Out*. Minneapolis, MN: Free Spirit Publishing, 1997.

Resource Contact Information

America's Promise: The Alliance for Youth. Call 703-684-4500 or visit AmericasPromise.org.

Big Brothers Big Sisters of America. Call 215-665-7749 or visit BBBSa.org.

Communities in Schools. Call 703-519-8999 or visit CISnet.org.

Gaining Early Awareness and Readiness for Undergraduate Programs (GEAR UP), U.S. Department of Education. Call 202-502-7675 or visit Ed.gov/programs/gearup/index.html.

Jobs for the Future. Call 617-728-4446 or visit JFF.org/jff.

MENTOR/National Mentoring Partnership. Call 703-224-2200 or visit Mentoring.org.

Public/Private Ventures (Funding Opportunities). Call 215-557-4400 or visit PPV.org.

"Teen as Community Builders" (More Programs for Teen Involvement). Call 212-620-5660 or visit Project for Public Spaces at PPS.org/tcb/tcblinks.htm.

BIBLIOGRAPHY

Abbey Road Studios, EMI Records Ltd. "Abbey Road Studios Home Page." 2006. www.abbeyroad.com.

About, Inc. "About: Job Searching: Teen Jobs." 2007. http://jobsearch.about.com/cs/justforstudents/a/teenjobs.htm.

-----. "About: Economics 'Definition of Nonprofit.'" 2007. http://economics.about.com/cs/economicsglossary/g/nonprofit.htm.

ACT, Inc. "ACT: A Student Site for ACT Test Takers." 2007. www.actstudent.org/index.html.

-----. "PLAN: Time to Plan Ahead." 2007. www.actstudent.org/plan.

American Library Association (ALA). "Recommended Reading." www.ala.org/ala/yalsa/teenreading/recreading/recommendedreading.htm.

The American Red Cross. "American Red Cross Home Page." 2006. www.redcross.org.

Amnesty International. "About." http://web.amnesty.org/pages.aboutai-index-eng.

Anderson, Mary Lou. "Leadership." Government Leaders. www.govleaders.org/quotes7.htm.

Angelou, Maya. Quotation. The Quotations Page. www.quotationspage.com/quote/34697.html.

Arrowhead Library System. "College Bound Reading List." System. http://als.lib.wi.us/Collegebound.html.

Artbarn. "High School Internships." www.artbarn.org/programs/intern.html.

Associated Male Choruses of America. "AMCA Music Scholarships." http://amcofa.net/scholar.shtml.

Austin City Connection. "About Totally Cool, Totally Art." 1995. www.ci.austin.tx.us/tcta/about.htm.

Baja California Language College. "Spanish Immersion Programs." 2007. www.bajacal.com.

The Bakken Library and Museum. "Earl Bakken Science Program." www.thebakken.org/education/ebsp/index.html.

Barron, Thomas A. "Gloria Barron Prize for Young Heroes." 2006. www.barronprize.org.

Bell, Alexander Graham. Quotation. Baylor College of Medicine. 2006. www.bcm.edu/solutions/v2i2/traber.html.

Big Time Sports 24/7. "Big Time Sports 24/7." www.bigtimesports247.org.

Blair, Julie. "Report Says JROTC Benefits Students; Calls for More Funding for Programs." www.jrotc.or/jrotc_befifits.htm.

Boggs, Wade. Information about Bradley N. Gallagher.

Boston University—College of Fine Arts. "Visual Summer Arts Institute." www.bu.edu/cfa/visual/summerarts/index.htm.

Brain, Marshall. *Teenager's Guide to the Real World*, 1st Edition. Raleigh, NC: BYG Publishing, 1997.

-----. "The Teenager's Guide to the Real World, Online: 20 Ways for Teens to Help Others by Volunteering." BYG Publishing, Inc. 1997. www.bygpub.com/books/tg2rw/volunteer.htm.

Bridgers, Bill. Quotation. VegUSA. www.vegtheusa.com/page.php?6.

Campbell, David. "CISS (Campbell Interest and Skills Survey)." Pearson Education, Inc. 2007. www.pearsonassessments.com/tests/ciss.htm.

Canfield, Jack, Mark Hansen, Kimberly Kirberger, and Mitch Claspy. Chicken Soup for the Teenage Soul IV. Deerfield Beach, FL: Health Communications, Inc., 1997.

Canfield, Jack, Mark Hansen, Kimberly Kirberger, and Deborah Reber. *Chicken Soup for the Teenage Soul: Real Deal Challenges*. Deerfield Beach, FL: Health Communications, Inc., 2006.

Career Explorations. "Summer Internships for High School Students: Boston and New York 2007." 2007. www.ceinternships.com/home.asp.

Carlson, Richard. *Don't Sweat the Small Stuff for Teens: Simple Ways to Keep Cool in Stressful Times*, 1st Edition. New York: Hyperion Books for Children, 2000.

Carroll, Lewis. *Alice's Adventures in Wonderland*. The Millennium Fulcrum Edition 3.0. Chapters 5–6. www.cs.cmu.edu/~rgs/alice-table.html.

CBS News. "7,500 Miles on $5 in Gas, Veggie Oil." August 18, 2006. www.cbsnews.com/stories/2006/08/18/earlyshow/main1910319.shtml?CMP=ILC-SearchStories.

Children's Scholarship Fund. "Children's Scholarship Fund." www.scholarshipfund.org/index.asp.

Churchill, Winston. Quotation. The Quotations Page. www.quotationspage.com/quotes/Sir_Winston_Churchill.

CIEE. "CIEE Scholarships." www.ciee.org/study/scholarships.aspx.

Close-Up.org. "Welcome to Close-Up.org." www.close-up.org.

The Coca-Cola Company. "Corporate Responsibility: Education." 2007. www2.coca-cola.com/citizenship/education.html.

-----. "Coca-Cola Scholarships." 2007. www.coca-colascholars.org/cokeWeb/jsp/scholars/Index.jsp.

The College Board. "About SAT Subject Tests." 2007. www.collegeboard.com/student/testing/sat/about/SATII.html.

-----. "About PSAT/NMSQT." www.collegeboard.com/student/testing/sat/about/.PSAT.html.

-----. "About SAT Tests." www.collegeboard.com/student/testing/sat/about..html.

-----. "Trends in Student Aid." Executive Summary, (6). www.collegeboard.com/prod_downloads/cost06/trends_aid_06.pdf.

-----. "Trends in College Pricing." Executive Summary. (5) www.collegeboard.com/prod_downloads/cost06/trends_college_pricing_06.pdf.

College Options Foundation. "Welcome." www.collegeoptionsfoundation.net.

College Scholarship Service. The College Cost and Financial Aid Handbook. New York: The College Board, 2000. (25-26).

The College of William & Mary. "W&M Mock Trial Team" 2005. www.wm.edu/so/mocktrial/faq.php.

Colorado College. "Summer Sessions High School Program." 2006. www.coloradocollege.edu/summerprograms/summersession/precollege.asp.

Columbia County Schools. "eLearning Academy." www.ccboe.net/elearning/home.html.

Comcast. "Leaders and Achievers." 2007. www.comcast.com/corporate/about/inthecommunity/scholarships/leadersandachievers.html.

Community Film Workshop of Chicago. "About CFW." 2005. www.cfwchicago.org/about.htm.

Connecticut Career Choices. "CT Career Choices." 2005.
http://ctcareerchoices.org.

Cooley, Charles Horton. *Human Nature and the Social Order*. New York:
Scribner's, 1902. 179–185.

Corporation for National and Community Service. "Presidential Freedom
Scholarship." www.learnandserve.gov/about/programs/pfs.asp.

-----. "The President's Volunteer Service Award." www.presidentialser
viceawards.org.

Council for International Exchange of Scholars. "Traditional Fulbright Scholars
Program." www.cies.org/us_scholars/us_awards.

Covey, Sean. *7 Habits of Highly Effective Teens: The Ultimate Teenage Success
Guide*. New York: Barnes and Noble Books, 2003.

-----. *The 6 Most Important Decisions You'll Ever Make*. New York: Simon and
Schuster Trade, 2006.

CPP, Inc. "Myers-Briggs Type Indicator (MBTI) Assessment."
www.cpp.com/products/mbti/index.asp.

Creative Change Center (C3). "Preparing a Portfolio; Showcasing Your
Strengths." www.c3va.org/html/resources/readable_articles/preparing-a-
portfolio-vis.shtml.

The Cum Laude Society. "The Cum Laude Society Home Page."
http://cumlaudesociety.org.

cummings, e. e. Quotation. The Quotations Page.
www.quotationspage.com/quotes/e_e_cummings/.

DECA Inc. "High School Division." DECA Inc. 1999–2007.
www.deca.org/hsd.html.

Delaware Governor's School for Excellence. "Governor's School for
Excellence." www.udel.edu/govschool.

Delta Cyber School. "Our Mission." www.dcs.k12.ak.us/about.html.

Devon Arts in Schools Initiative (DAISI). "Welcome to DAISI: Devon Arts in
Schools Initiative." www.daisi.org.uk/index.htm.

DeVries, Peter. Quotation. The Quotations Page.
www.quotationspage.com/quotes/Peter_De_Vries/.

Discover Financial Services, Discover Bank. "Philanthropy: Discover Card Tribute Award Scholarship—Recognizing Excellence in High School Juniors." 2006. www.discoverfinancial.com/data/philanthropy/tribute.shtml.

DMOZ Open Directory Project. http://dmoz.org/Kids_and_Teens/.

Do Something. "Brick Awards." www.dosomething.org/brick.

Dr. Seuss (Theodore Geisl). *Oh, The Places You'll Go.* www.unc.edu/~hidy/Dr.Seuss.html.

Dutch Proverb. Quotation. The Quotations Page. www.quotationspage.com/quote/1502.html.

Excel High School. "Welcome to Excel High School." 2007. www.excelhighschool.com.

Fairfax County (VA) Public Schools. "Office of High School Instruction: Online Campus." www.fcps.edu/DIS/onlinecampus/index.htm.

FairTest Examiner. "Study: SAT Coaching Raises Scores." Spring 2002. http://fairtest.org/examarts/Spring%2002/SAT%20Coaching.html.

Felder, Richard N. Linda K. Silverman, and Barbara A. Soloman. "Index of Learning Styles (ILS)." North Carolina State University. www.ncsu.edu/felder-public/ILSpage.html.

Ferber, Thaddeus, Karen Pittman, Alicia Wilson-Ahlstrom, and Nicole Yohalem. "High School After-School: What Is It? What Might It Be? Why Is It Important?" The Out-of-School Time Policy Commentary #2, January, 2003. www.forumfyi.org/files//ostpc2.pdf.

Fiske, Edward B. and Hammond, Bruce G. *The Fiske Guide to Getting into the Right College*, 2nd Edition. Naperville, IL: Sourcebooks, Inc., 2004. "Selectivity of Institutions in Fiske's Guide to Colleges." Cate School. www.cate.org/public/index.php?id=243.

Florida Virtual School. "Welcome to the Florida Virtual School." 2006. www.flvs.net.

Forum for Youth Investment. "About Us." 2001–2007. www.forumfyi.org/_catdisp_page.cfm?LID=124.

Fosdick, Harry Emerson. Quotation. Wikiquote. http://en.wikiquote.org/wiki/Dedication.

The Foundation Center. "Youth in Philanthropy." 1995–2007. http://youth.fdncenter.org/health/scholarships.html.

Friedman, Pamela. "Mentoring Programs for High School Age Youth." Welfare Information Network, Vol. 7, No. 13 (October 2003). www.financeproject.org/Publications/mentoringprogramsRN.htm.

Gelband, Scott, Catherine Kubale, and Eric Schorr. *Your College Application*. New York: College Board, 1992. 95.

General Mills. Explorer Post Program. www.generalmills.com/corporate/commitment/corpCit2006.pdf/.

Gibran, Kahlil. "On Teaching." *The Prophet*. Chapter 18. www.geocities.com/Athens/5484/Gib18.htm.

Gingrich, Newt. Quotation. www.pbs.org/wgbh/pages/frontline/newt/newtquotes.html _gingrich.html.

Girl Scouts of the United States of America. "For Adults." 1998–2006. www.girlscouts.org/for_adults/.

Governor's Honors Program, Georgia Department of Education. "What is the Governor's Honors Program?" http://services.valdosta.edu/ghp/info.htm#one.

Governor's Mentoring Partnership. "Become a Mentor." 2003. www.mentoring.ca.gov.

The Governor's Prevention Partnership. "Connecticut Mentoring Partnership: Welcome." 2006. www.preventionworksct.org/mentor.html.

Graham, Stedman. *Teens Can Make It Happen: A Nine Step Plan for Success*. New York: Simon & Schuster Free Press, 1998.

Green Mountain College. "Make A Difference Scholarship." www.greenmtn.edu/makeadifference/index.asp.

Gross, Jennifer, "Surviving Your College Search: The Adventure Begins." Luy, Joyce. Quotation. *Steps to College Newsletter*, September, 2000. National Association for College Admission Counseling. www.nacacnet.org/MemberPortal/News/StepsNewsletter/Surviving+Your+College+Search.htm.

Guest, Edgar A. "It Couldn't Be Done." The Poetry Foundation. www.poetryfoundation.org/archive/poem.html?id=173579.

Habitat for Humanity. "Learn the Basics." 2007. www.habitat.org.

Haulsey, Kuwana. *Angel of Harlem*. New York: Random House, 2004. 202.

The Heart of America Foundation. "Scholarships: The Christopher Reeve
    Award." 2006. www.heartofamerica.org/scholarships.htm.

Heider, John. "A Time for Reflection." *Tao of Leadership: Lao Tzu's Te Ching
    Adapted for a New Age.* Atlanta: Humanics New Age, 1985. 23.

Hispanic Heritage Foundation. "Youth Awards."
    www.hispanicheritage.org/youth.php.

Hugh O'Brien Youth Leadership (HOBY). "HOBY Leadership Seminars."
    www.hoby.org/Schools/index.shtml.

HyperDictionary. "Meaning of Character."
    www.hyperdictionary.com/search.aspx?define=character.

Idealist.org, Action Without Borders. "Take the Lead in Your Community."
    1995-2007. www.idealist.org/kt/activism.html#SEC2.

iD Gaming Academy, University of California—Berkeley. "Program Overview."
    www.idgamingacademy.com

Illinois Virtual High School. "Welcome." www.ivhs.org/index.learn?bhcp=1.

Indiana University Jacobs School of Music. "Pre-College & Special Programs."
    2007. www.music.indiana.edu/special_programs/summer.shtml.

INROADS, Inc. "About INROADS."
    2007.www.inroads.org/inroads/inroadsHome.jsp.

Interlochen Center for the Arts. "Welcome." 2006. www.interlochen.org.

International Sports Training Camps. "Welcome to International Sports Training
    Camps." 2005. www.international-sports.com.

Intrax Study Abroad. "High School Study Abroad Programs." 2005.
    www.intraxstudyabroad.com.

It'sAboutUs.org. "Get A Job!" 2001.
    www.itsaboutus.org/employment/Default.asp.

Jack Kent Cooke Foundation. "Young Scholars." 2003. www.jackkentcooke
    foundation.org/jkcf_web/content.aspx?page=YounSch.

Johannson, Charles B. "IDEAS (Interest Determination, Exploration and
    Assessment System)." Pearson Education, Inc.
    www.pearsonassessments.com/tests/ideas.htm.

Johns Hopkins University. "Summer Programs: Programs for High School
    Students." www.jhu.edu/summer/pre-college/index.html.

Jordan, Barbara. Quotation. The Barbara Jordan National Forum on Public Policy, LBJ School of Public Affairs, University of Texas. www.utexas.edu/lbj/barbarajordanforum/aboutbj_quotes.htm.

Junior Achievement, JA Worldwide. "About JA." 2007. www.ja.org/about/about.shtml.

Junior Achievement, JA Worldwide. "High School Programs Overview." 2007. www.ja.org/programs/programs_high_overview.shtml.

Junior Engineering Technical Society (JETS). "Features." 2007. www.jets.org/index.cfm.

Junior Reserve Officer Training Corps (JROTC). "JROTC ORG." 1999–2005. www.jrotc.org.

Kentucky Virtual High School. "KY Virtual High School." www.kvhs.org.

Key Club International, Kiwanis International. "Key Club International: Caring—Our Way of Life." 2007. www.keyclub.org.

Kids and Teens Open Directory Project. "Kids and Teens: People and Society: Volunteering and Service: Community Service." www.dmoz.org/Kids_and_Teens/People_and_Society/Volunteering_and_Service/Teens/.

Lamb, Annette. "The Topic: Journal Writing." 42eXplore. http://annettelamb.com/42explore/journl.htm.

Laughter Heals Foundation, Community Partners. "What Laughter Heals Does..." 2002–2003. http://laughterheals.org.

Levine, Mel. *Ready or Not, Here Life Comes*. New York: Simon & Schuster Trade, 2005.

Lord Byron. Quotation. Webster's Online Dictionary. www.websters-online-dictionary.org/definition/dew.

MacDonald, George. Quotation.Professor Richard Millsap's Website. http://faculty.tcu.edu/rmillsap/PowerWords/Contents.htm.

MacDonald Youth Services. "MacDonald Youth Services Online Media Centre." 1997–2007. www.mys.ca/media/.

Marx, Groucho. Quotation. The Quotations Page. www.quotationspage.com/quotes/Groucho_Marx/.

Math Forum at Drexel University. "Virtual Math Teams (VMT)." Math Forum at Drexel University. www.mathforum.org/vmt/researchers/orientation.html.

The Mathematical Association of America. "American Math Competitions (AMC)." 2006. www.unl.edu/amc/whatswhat.shtml.

McGraw, Jay, Philip C. McGraw, and Benjamin Vincent. *Life Strategies for Teens.* New York: Simon & Schuster Adult Publishing Group, 2000.

Mead, Margaret. Quotation. GIGA Quotes. www.giga-usa.com/quotes/authors/margaret_mead_a001.htm.

MENTOR. "Connect with the Power of Mentoring." 2006. www.mentoring.org.

Mentor Alabama. "Frequently Asked Questions." www.ago.state.al.us/mentor/faq.htm.

Merriam-Webster Online Dictionary. Definition of "volunteer." www.webster.com/dictionary/volunteer.

Michigan State University Libraries. "Grants for Individuals: Pre-College Scholarships." www.lib.msu.edu/harris23/grants/3precol.htm.

Michigan Virtual High School. "About Us." 2007. www.mivhs.org/content.cfm?ID=30.

Mountain Dreamer, Oriah. *Your Heart's Prayer: Following the Thread of Desire into Deeper Life* (CD), May, 2005. www.oriahmountaindreamer.com/hearts_prayer.html.

National Aeronautics and Space Administration (NASA). "Learning Resources: Summer High School Apprenticeship Research Program (SHARP)." www.nasa.gov/audience/forstudents/9-12/learning/NASA_SHARP.html.

National Association of Independent Schools. "Diversity and Multiculturalism." 1997–2006. www.nais.org/equity/index.cfm?Itemnumber=145868.

-----. "Student Voices." www.nais.org/equity/index.cfm?itemnumber=146095&sn.ItemNumber=147382.

-----. "Student Diversity Leadership Conference." 1997–2006. www.nais.org/equity/index.cfm?Itemnumber=147342&sn.ItemNumber=147355&tn.ItemNumber=147377.

The National Beta Club. "Welcome." www.betaclub.org.

National Collegiate Athletic Association. "NCAA Scholarships and Internships." www.ncaa.org/about/scholarships.html.

National Commission for Cooperative Education (NCCE). "National Competition Guidelines and Criteria." www.co-op.edu.

The National Conference of Governors' Schools. "The National Conference of Governers' Schools Home Page." www.ncogs.org.

National 4-H Council. "National 4-H Council Mission." www.fourhcouncil.edu/about.aspx.

National Foundation for Advancement in the Arts (NFAA). "Awards for Young Artists." 1996–2006. www.nfaa.org.

National Honor Society, National Association of Secondary School Principals. "NHS & NJHS." www.nhs.us.

The National Organization of the 100 Black Men of America, Inc. "Mentoring." 2006. www.100blackmen.org/index.php?option=com_content&task=view&id=40&Itemid=63.

National Security Agency. "Student Programs: High School Programs." www.nsa.gov/careers/students_3.cfm.

National Youth Employment Coalition. "Welcome to the National Youth Employment Coalition." 2005. http://nyec.modernsignal.net/page.cfm?pageID=131&categorySearch=0.

NetAid, Mercy Corps. "NetAid Global Action Awards." 1999–2007. www.netaid.org/global_action_awards/.

New Urban Arts. "The Basics." www.newurbanarts.org/basics_programs.html.

No.1 Camps. "No. 1 Camps Mission Statement." http://no1soccercamps.com/about5.lasso.

North Dakota State University. "North Dakota Governor's School" www.ndsu.nodak.edu/govschool/.

Northwestern University—School of Communication. "Pre-College Students (NHSI)." 2006. www.communication.northwestern.edu/programs/nhsi/.

Ohio Newspaper Association. "Welcome Students." www.ohionews.org/students.html.

Orphan Foundation of America. "Casey Family Scholarships for Foster Care Youth." 2006. www.orphan.org/casey_scholarship.html.

Overland Summers. "Introduction: American Challenge." www.overlandsummers.com/article/view/6145/1/765/.

Packer, Alex J. and Jeff Tolbert. *How Rude: The Teenage Guide to Good Manners, Proper Behavior, and Not Grossing People Out.* McHenry, IL: Rebound by Sagebrush, 1999.

PAVE, Vanderbilt University. "PAVE Pre-College Summer Program." 2003-2006.
www.vanderbilt.edu/pave.

Pearson Education, Inc. "Northampton Area Senior High School, Northampton,
PA." 2007.
www.pearsondigital.com/successes/novanet/northhampton.cfm.

Pearson Education, Inc. "NovaNET." 2007.
www.pearsondigital.com/novanet/.

Phi Sigma Iota. "International Foreign Language Honor Society." 2006.
www.phisigmaiota.org.

Presidential Scholars Foundation. "Presidential Scholars Foundation Home
Page." 2006. www.presidentialscholars.org.

Princeton University. "The Princeton Prize in Race Relations".
www.princeton.edu/pr/news/04/q2/0420-prize.htm.

Project for Public Spaces, Inc. (PPS). "Our Mission." 2006.
www.pps.org/info/aboutpps/about.

Prudential Financial, Inc. "The Prudential Spirit of Community Awards." 2007.
www.prudential.com/overview/0%2C1468%2CintPageID%25253D4141%
252526blnPrinterFriendly%25253D0%2C00.html?furl=%2Fcommunity%2Fs
pirit%2Fawards.

RoAne, Susan. "The Secrets of Savvy Networking." 1999–2005.
www.susanroane.com/books_secrets.html.

Ronald McDonald House Charities, Inc. "Ronald McDonald House Charities
Home Page." www.rmhc.org/rmhc/index.html.

Roosevelt, Franklin D. Quotation. The Quotations Page.
www.quotationspage.com/quotes/Franklin_D._Roosevelt/.

Rotary International. "Ambassadorial Scholarships." 2003–2005.
www.rotary.org/foundation/educational/amb_scho/.

Rudner, Lawrence. "Commentary on Test Preparation." Clearinghouse on
Assessment and Evaluation. 1999–2005.
http://ericae.net/faqs/testprep.htm#testprep.

Rustic Pathways, Inc. "Rustic Pathways: The Finest High School Travel Programs
in the World." 2006. www.rusticpathways.com.

Saginaw Valley State University. "Introduction."
www.svsu.edu/careers/ccg/OT%20Portfolio/Introduction.htm.

The San Diego Foundation. "The Kyoto Scholarships."
www.kyotoprize.org/scholarship.htm.

Sandburg, Carl. Quotation. The Quotations Page.
www.quotationspage.com/quotes/Carl_Sandburg/.

Scholes, Roberta J. and Margaret M. Lain. "The Effects of Test Preparation
Activities on ACT Assessment Scores." (A paper presented at the Annual
Meeting of the American Educational Research Association. Chicago, IL,
March 24–28, 1997). ERIC, #ED409341.
http://ericae.net/faqs/testprep.htm#testprep.

Schweitzer, Albert. Quotation. The Quotations Page.
www.quotationspage.com/quotes/Albert_Schweitzer/.

Seaton, Thomas. "The Effectiveness of Test Preparation Seminars on
Performance on Standardized Achievement Tests." 1992. 12.
http://ericae.net/faqs/testprep.htm#testprep.

Seltzer, Neill. *The 500 Best Ways for Teens to Spend the Summer*. New York:
The Princeton Review, 2004.

Siemens Foundation. "About." 2005. www.siemens-foundation.org/awards/.

Siemens Foundations. "2006–2007 Siemens Competition National Finals."
2005. www.siemens-foundation.org/competition/.

Snow Farm: The New England Craft Program. "High School Program." 2006.
www.snowfarm.org/summerhsprogram.html.

Southern Regional Education Board (SREB). "Report on State Virtual Schools."
June 2005. www.sreb.org/programs/EdTech/onlinelearning/docs/
ReportOnStateVirtualSchools.pdf.

Sterne, Laurence. Quotation. The Quotations Page.
www.quotationspage.com/quotes/Lawrence_Sterne/.

Strickland, Alison. "Reflect On Where You Are Going." Personal Journaling.
Writers Digest. February, 2002.
www.writersdigest.com/articles/pj_mag/stickland_reflect_where_going.asp.

Target Brands, Inc. "Start Something Scholarship." 2006.
http://sites.target.com/site/en/spot/page.jsp?title=startsomething.

Teens4Hire. "Resources: Teens and Employment." 2002–2007.
www.teens4hire.org/resources.asp.

Tisch School of the Arts, New York University. "Special Programs: High School
Studnets." http://specialprograms.tisch.nyu.edu/page/hsStudents.html.

Tylenol, McNeil Consumer Healthcare. "The Tylenol Scholarship." 1998–2007.
www.tylenol.com/page.jhtml?id=tylenol/news/subptyschol.inc.

The United States Junior Chamber (Jaycees). "About the Jaycees." 2006.
www.usjaycees.org/learn_more.htm.

The University of Chicago. "Office of the Reynolds Club and Student Activities
(ORSCA)." 2006. http://studentactivities.uchicago.edu/.

University of Wyoming. "UW Summer High School Institute." http://uwadmn-
web.uwyo.edu/PROVOST/hsi/.

Van Buren, Abigail. Quotation. The Quotations Page.
www.quotationspage.com/quotes/Abigail_van_Buren/.

Veteran of Foreign Wars of the United States. "VFW Scholarships Program."
2007. www.vfw.org/index.cfm?fa=cmty.levelc&cid=1836&tok=1.

Virtual High School. "Welcome to Virtual High School." 1996–2007.
www.govhs.org.

Wallerstein Collaborative for Urban Environmental Education, New York
University. "Our Mission." 2005. http://steinhardt.nyu.edu/wallerstein.

Webster's Online Dictionary. Definition of "values."
www.websters-online-dictionary.org/definition/values.

Webster's Revised Unabridged Dictionary. Definition of "character."
Springfield, Massachusetts: G&C. Merriam Company, 1913.
www.webster-dictionary.org/definition/character.

Webster's II: New Riverside Dictionary. Definition of "debate." New York:
Berkley Books, 1984.

-----. Definition of "forensics." New York: Berkley Books, 1984.

-----. Definition of "moot." New York: Berkley Books, 1984.

Wellesley Centers for Women. "Our Work: SEEDS Project Overview." 2006.
www.wcwonline.org/projects/title.php?id=36.

Wikipedia. "Color Guard." http://en.wikipedia.org/wiki/Color_guard.

Williamson, Marianne. "Brilliant, Talented, and Fabulous" A Return to Love.
Audiobook. New York: Harper Collins, 1992.

Winfrey, Oprah. Quotation. The Quotations Page.
http://quotationspage.com/quotes/Oprah_Winfrey/.

World Affairs Councils of America. "The World Affairs Council System." 2007.www.worldaffairscouncils.org/aboutus.

Wooden, John. Quotation. 1998-2001. www.utpb.edu/JBS/quotes2.htm.

Youth Athletic Advocacy of Central Texas. "YAACT Programs." 2005. www.yaact.org/programservices.htm.

Youth for Understanding USA. "YFU USA." 2002–2007. www.yfu-usa.org.

Young Judaea Program. "About Young Judaea." 1999–2006. www.youngjudaea.org/html/overview.html.

Youth Mentoring Connection. "What is Mentoring?" 2002. www.youthmentoring.org/03ment.html.

ABOUT THE AUTHOR

Joyce Suber is a retired Director of College Counseling and English teacher. She has served on boards and committees for numerous national and state professional organizations and is a former Vice President for Professional Development with The National Association for College Admission Counseling. A Chicago native and graduate of the University of Illinois, she now resides in Atlanta, Georgia, where she works as an educational consultant and speaker and serves as President of College Options Foundation.

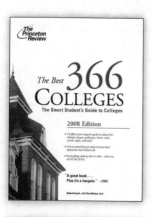

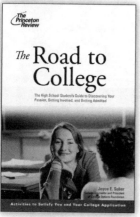